Labor Force and Employment in Egypt

Mostafa H. Nagi
foreword by
Edward G. Stockwell

The Praeger Special Studies program—utilizing the most modern and efficient book production techniques and a selective worldwide distribution network—makes available to the academic, government, and business communities significant, timely research in U.S. and international economic, social, and political development.

Labor Force and Employment in Egypt

A Demographic and Socioeconomic Analysis

PRAEGER SPECIAL STUDIES IN INTERNATIONAL ECONOMICS AND DEVELOPMENT

Praeger Publishers   New York   Washington   London

PRAEGER PUBLISHERS
111 Fourth Avenue, New York, N.Y. 10003, U.S.A.
5, Cromwell Place, London S.W.7, England

Published in the United States of America in 1971
by Praeger Publishers, Inc.

Printed in the United States of America

One of the major problems confronting most developing nations in their efforts toward modernization is rapid population growth. More often than not the very complex relationship between population growth and economic development is grossly oversimplified as being primarily a Malthusian race between population and food supplies. There are many other facets of this general problem that merit consideration, however. One of these is the impact of population trends, especially since the end of World War II, on the size and structure of the labor force and on the employment situation. This is the basic problem to which Dr. Nagi addresses himself in this book.

Egypt, or the United Arab Republic (U. A. R.), is one of those developing countries that is currently being overwhelmed by an unprecedented rapid rate of population growth that continues to pose a major obstacle to the country's program of economic development. Recent estimates indicate that the U. A. R. population is increasing at a rate of 2.8 percent annually, a rate that would double the 1970 population of nearly 34 million in 25 years. Further, since this rate of growth is the result of a persistently high birth rate in the face of declining mortality, it has created a very young age structure (it is estimated that over 40 percent of the population in 1970 was under age fifteen). In recent years the U. A. R. has also, along with many other developing societies, undergone a substantial "urban explosion" characterized by heavy migration out of rural areas into one or more major urban centers. The present systematic analysis of the complex interrelationship between trends in population size, composition, and distribution, on the one hand, and the size and structure of the U. A. R. labor force on the other hand, is thus very timely.

Methodologically, this study clearly demonstrates the inadequacy of using categories developed from the experience of more developed nations in analyzing how best to make fuller use of human resources in developing societies; and Dr. Nagi points to a number of inconsistencies and weaknesses in the kinds of statistics available for Egypt that complicate the measurement of various labor force categories, such as economically active women, child labor, family workers, and employment status. With regard to the latter, Dr. Nagi recommends some new approaches for measuring the extent of unemployment and especially underemployment in developing societies.

On the level of policy considerations, Dr. Nagi suggests a number of short-term programs to facilitate the modernization of

v

rapidly growing underdeveloped countries such as Egypt (e.g., redistribution of income through an expanded welfare state, encouragement of emigration of persons with nonessential skills, and creation of alternative productive activities among marginal groups unable to find employment in the modern sector). In the long run, however, the study emphasizes the need for serious efforts to reduce the rate of population growth by enhancing fertility control through the expansion of family planning services.

Dr. Nagi was a graduate student in sociology at the University of Connecticut when he began the study described here, and I had the pleasure of being closely associated with its development. Although one may not agree fully with all of his conclusions, he has written a book that must become required reading for all students of Egyptian society--and strongly recommended reading for students of social change and development in general.

Edward G. Stockwell

ACKNOWLEDGMENTS

Like many other undertakings of this kind, the final product represents the assistance of a great many people.

Professor Edward G. Stockwell, who kindly wrote the Preface, read early drafts of the book. His criticism and helpful suggestions were instrumental in getting this book to completion. I am extremely grateful for the encouragement I received from him.

I am also indebted to Professors Walter C. McKain and Jack L. Roach of the University of Connecticut, who read early drafts of the manuscript and who were kind enough to give me the benefit of their comments.

Particular thanks are due to Mr. Larry Snavley and Miss Cynthia Barnett, two of my graduate assistants at the Department of Sociology, Bowling Green State University, for their help in preparing the final draft of the manuscript. The assistance of Mrs. Sharon Hay in editing and Miss Lauretta Davidson in typing is most appreciated.

Finally, I am indebted to the Department of Rural Sociology, University of Connecticut, for all the support I received during my work on this study.

CONTENTS

LIST OF TABLES

xiii

xv

Labor Force and
Employment in Egypt

The descriptive analysis of demographic characteristics and trends is one of the most well-established approaches to the comparative study of human society. In part this is because such characteristics represent fundamental elements in the structure of all societies. It is also because demographic data, although subject to certain limitations, are more likely to be comparable from one cultural setting to another than are most other social-science data.

On a micro level, demographic characteristics have long been used by social scientists to explain various behavioral phenomena; in addition, numerous social, cultural, and economic factors have often been used to explain variations in rates of fertility, mortality, and migration as well as changes in other demographic variables.[1] On a macro level, demographic characteristics and changes have been associated with a number of major societal trends, such as economic growth, industrialization, urbanization, and rising education.[2]

This book is aimed at contributing to the growing body of descriptive and analytical literature dealing with the various demographic aspects of social change in different countries. The specific purpose of this study is to present a detailed analysis of recent trends and changes in the size and structure of the labor force of Egypt--the U.A.R.[3]--and to ascertain the relationship of other demographic and social variables to these changes.

DETERMINANTS OF LABOR SUPPLY AND EMPLOYMENT

Demographers are in general agreement that it would be impossible to discover a single statistical pattern which would both fit the past experience of all countries and have a reasonable chance of correctly forecasting the future in any single country. Nevertheless, certain basic demographic as well as nondemographic determinants of labor supply and employment are commonly recognized.

Demographic factors directly or indirectly affect the size, composition, and distribution of the labor force.[4] For example, long-term trends in fertility, mortality, and migration affect directly the supply of labor. Changes in rural-urban composition of a population, marital status, and life expectancy are factors with a direct bearing

3

on labor supply and employment. Demographic factors also have an indirect influence on labor and employment: their impact on educational development, housing, and other urban problems, as well as on such factors of economic growth as saving, investment, technological development, and industrialization, have a far-reaching effect on the qualitative as well as the quantitative aspect of the labor force. It is important to note that demographic trends could also be an outcome of changes in the size, the composition, and the distribution of the labor force. For example, increasing female participation in economic activities could have a depressing effect on the general level of fertility.[5] Also, increasing employment opportunities in urban centers would definitely affect the rural-urban composition of a given population.[6]

The relationship between the size of the labor supply and the size of the total population is also determined by many social, economic, and political variables. Among the social aspects of manpower and labor supply are a variety of structural and cultural features. Prominent among these features would be the status of women in the community as homemakers or professional breadwinners;[7] the level of education of the population as well as laws governing the age for compulsory education;[8] the general health status of the population (which determines the number of physically able workers within various age and sex groups); the stratification system and the general institutional structure insofar as they favor or disfavor education, mobility, and employment of certain segments of the society;[9] and labor policy and legislation insofar as they standardize such things as conditions under which women and children are permitted to work, retirement age, and pensions as well as other work provisions.[10]

The economic theory of labor supply has an evident bearing on the analysis of factors associated with the trends of the labor force.[11] Although an examination of economic theory is not among the major purposes of this study, some of the statistical analyses presented here are pertinent to the effects of economic factors, and they are discussed from a practical point of view. Among the most relevant economic variables that affect the labor force are the level of income as it affects the supply of labor and its distribution in different sectors;[12] changes in the level and patterns of saving and investment as they affect increasing employment opportunities;[13] the size of the market and the development of economics of scales insofar as they shape the development and expansion of industry;[14] foreign trade and the international prices of principal commodities as they affect the pattern of manpower participation by forcing the population into certain types of activities and impeding any move towards a reallocation of the country's resources;[15] and land and agrarian reforms insofar as income redistribution and agricultural mechanization affect underemployment of the rural population.[16]

Political factors also play an important role in shaping the setting for labor force growth and development. The most prominent of these factors are the degree and direction of state control over the economy;[17] the concern which some regimes express with regard to maintaining popularity and avoiding social unrest;[18] and the degree of influence that trade unions possess in the society.[19]

Another point that needs to be emphasized at the outset is that manpower problems resulting from demographic changes are different in developing countries and industrialized countries. In the developing countries, constantly high birth rates and rapidly declining mortality rates result in a phenomenal growth of population. In the industrial countries the relatively low birth rate in connection with the low mortality rate result in population increases mainly among the older age groups. Population growth in industrialized countries, therefore, does not necessarily mean an increase in the labor force. In developing countries, however, population increases soon result in a corresponding increase in the population of working age. As a result, the developing countries, more so than the industrialized countries, are faced with the problems of dealing with underemployment and providing employment for the growing labor force.[20]

THE NATURE AND BACKGROUND OF THE PROBLEM

In their efforts toward modernization, developing areas are grappling with serious socioeconomic and demographic problems. Rapid population growth is one such problem. The complex relationship between population growth and economic progress is often grossly oversimplified as primarily a race between population and food supply. Much less attention has been paid to the effects of rapid population growth on the labor force and employment. However, now that the population explosion of the 1950's is swelling the labor force of the developing countries, the latter are starting to receive more attention.

Egypt is one of the developing countries currently being overwhelmed by a rate of population growth that continues to pose a serious problem to the country's program of economic development. Population growth rate continues to outstrip production increase from existing agricultural land, the latter even now being cultivated almost to its maximum possible intensity. The country's recent commitment to industrialization was a result of an awareness of both her limitations in land resources and the unlikelihood of any substantial increases in land productivity. Industrialization was believed to be the cure-all for old ills. More recently, however, Egyptian scholars and policymakers have come to realize that in spite of the fact that Egypt has an abundance of human resources for any conceivable program of economic development, these resources are largely underdeveloped.[21] Hence, the present course of industrialization by itself will not be a magical solution to the problems of providing employment for the growing labor force.[22]

Although a great deal of attention has been given to studying the effects of rapid population growth on the food supply, the systematic analysis of the complex relationship between trends in population size, composition, and distribution on the one hand, and the size and structure of the labor force on the other, has been neglected by social scientists in Egypt. This study tries to place the impact of population growth on labor force and employment in better perspective.

Social and economic conditions in Egypt before 1952 have been discussed in some detail by a number of authors.[23] Egypt's demographic position has also received attention.[24] Since the 1952 revolution, Egypt has put forth a strenuous effort to accelerate social and economic development. The results, while not impressive, have nevertheless been noticeable. The problems which face this country are many; but most observers would agree that the path of Egyptian development is relatively slow because it has been necessary not only to raise the standard of living of the existing population but also to provide for an extremely rapid increase in population.[25]

Egypt's social and economic conditions since 1952 have been analyzed and a great deal of insight on the changes which the country has experienced toward industrialization,[26] urbanization,[27] mass education,[28] and other thrusts for modernization[29] have been discussed in detail. The changes which occurred in Egypt's economic system,[30] capital resources,[31] foreign trade,[32] land and agrarian reforms,[33] and other structural changes[34] have also been investigated. A much neglected aspect of the Egyptian setting, however, is the country's present and potential use of human resources.

Most of what has been written on Egypt's manpower and labor force represents an auxiliary treatment of other general research on socioeconomic and demographic trends. As early as the 1930's, Wendell Cleland clearly recognized how population posed a serious problem in Egypt: according to him, the potential expansion of the country's crop area was limited by the desert, and its industrial potential was limited by lack of fuel and mineral resources.[35]

In the early 1940's, Clyde Kiser projected a population of between 18 and 21 million by 1970. In spite of the fact that his projections proved to be gross underestimates, he did anticipate the serious demographic situation then emerging in Egypt.[36] Similarly, Charles Issawi presented population growth as one of the most powerful factors depressing the standard of living in Egypt. He even went further to affirm that "if ever the word overpopulated could be applied to a country, that country is Egypt."[37]

One of the earlier dissenters of the view expressed by the preceding authors is E. L. Nassif.[38] Writing in 1950, Nassif expressed the view that Egypt's population was substantially less than its economic carrying capacity. He argued that the type of agriculture practiced in Egypt required a somewhat higher population density. However, he considered the extension of the area under cultivation to be an important factor for economic progress.

More systematic research on the subject during the 1950's indicated a close relationship between the pressure of population and a number of social and economic problems pertinent in Egypt. Several observers looked at population pressure as both a cause and a consequence of most of Egypt's ills--namely, low average income, low productivity, unemployment, high illiteracy, poverty, and malnutrition.[39]

Still more recent considerations of Egypt's population problems have been given in the official publications of a number of governmental agencies, such as the Permanent Council of Public Service, the Central Statistical Committee, and the Central Agency for Public Mobilization and Statistics.[40] In these publications, the slow rate of economic growth prior to and during the first planning period was attributed largely to the pressure of population increase. As in most official publications, the analytical observations revealed by these reports lack impartiality. However, they contain valuable statistical information.

Since it is highly impractical to attempt to review all the expressed ideas on the adverse effects of rapid population growth on the growth of the Egyptian economy, it is hoped that the authors cited illustrate how the growth of population has come to be considered responsible for a large number of Egypt's social and economic problems. However important it is, the rate of population growth is not the only demographic characteristic which is relevant as a determinant of the supply of labor, and emphasis on the problems of size and growth should not lead to a neglect of these other problems. Other demographic characteristics of the Egyptian population which have been cited as important include the following: very high population density, especially in the Nile Valley;[41] a young but relatively stable age structure, especially during the period between 1927 and 1947;[42] a low but rapidly rising life expectancy at birth, especially since the late 1940's;[43] a persistently high level of fertility, with some recent signs of the emergency of fertility differentials;[44] an increasing trend toward a younger age structure since 1947 and, subsequently, a larger load of economic dependency;[45] and a negligible in- or out-migration from the country, which means that the Egyptian population is virtually closed.[46]

A more recent but somewhat analytical approach to the demographic study of the labor force and employment can be seen in a number of memorandums that have appeared under the auspices of the Institute of National Planning. This new interest developed particularly in connection with the ten-year development plan begun in 1960. An early concern of the institute was an investigation of the supply and demand sides of the different technical and professional groups during the planning period.[47] In the work of the Institute of National Planning, employment problems have received special attention and number of research papers have been written on the subject.[48] The controversy which the findings of this research instigated concerning the existence and the extent of rural unemployment led the institute to ask for the technical assistance of the International Labor Organization in investigating this problem further.

Determinants of the qualitative aspects of manpower and labor force such as vocational training,[49] health,[50] and nutrition[51] have been examined in a number of research papers and monographs. The low standards of health, nutrition, and vocational training of manpower in Egypt in relationship to developed nations are considered major factors influencing the low productivity of labor.[52]

Nondemographic determinants of labor supply received early attention from observers of the Egyptian economy, more so than did the demographic determinants. The attention which was given to them, however, did not settle a number of questions. Most of these questions concern the problem of underutilization of labor in rural Egypt. To begin with, there is no agreement, for example, as to the existence and nature of underemployment in rural Egypt.[53] The question of whether or not agricultural production should be mechanized under the present circumstances of land scarcity and labor abundance is still unsettled.[54] Further, the net effects of land reforms on the employment aspects of the rural labor force are not fully ascertained;[55] nor are the best future alternative methods of cultivating the newly reclaimed land.[56] The choice between state farms or privately owned ones, for example, will have important effects on the capacity of the agricultural sector to absorb more labor.

The failure of the industrial sector to ease the employment problem at a time when industry's share of the national economy is rising rapidly has been questioned.[57] The rapid expansion of the service sector in terms of employment and its share of the national economy has been cited as the major structural transformation which has taken place in the Egyptian society since the prewar years. The determinants and the consequences of this trend have also been a subject of discussion and speculation.[58]

The history of the labor movement in Egypt has been recorded, with an assessment of the weaknesses and the strengths of the movements.[59] Labor legislation has received attention from a large number of observers with varied backgrounds: [60] lawyers, legislators, economists, sociologists, and administrators have shown some interest in this issue. The Egyptian labor code is relatively advanced and complicated; in addition, a continuous effort is made to keep it up to date with the standards of the international labor agreements. The role of labor legislation in effecting changes in the Egyptian society has also been discussed; and three major trends in labor legislation have been observed. These trends are toward industrial democracy, increased use of labor legislation as a means of realizing the economic policies of the country, and uniformity in all labor legislation.[61]

THE STUDY OBJECTIVES

So far a number of studies on the socioeconomic and demographic determinants of the labor supply in Egypt have been cited in the belief that they fairly represent the present state of the existing literature. However, it can be noted that most of these studies are either very limited in scope or lacking in historical perspective. The most serious shortcoming, in our opinion, is a neglect of the demographic factors, at least until recently, in discussions of the determinants of the labor supply. Further, the recent considerations of demographic factors generally neglect nondemographic factors. To our knowledge, there is no single comprehensive study which integrates both demographic and nondemographic determinants of labor supply in an overall view of the economy. The need for such a study has been expressed in the existing literature. As early as 1954, one author wrote, "An urgent matter which has not yet received sufficient attention is the use to which Egypt's enormous resources of unemployed labor can be put. Labor is the only commodity which is abundant in Egypt, and is the only one which is most wasted."[62] And as recently as 1966, another author pointed out that

> proper research into the current and potential utilization
> of manpower in Egypt began, in fact, after the inauguration
> of the five-year plan. Information on and interest in the
> employment problem is definitely scant. Labor is the
> country's most abundant resource; with a worsening prob-
> lem of underemployment in the countryside coupled with
> growing urban unemployment, more attention and resources
> should be devoted towards utilizing labor.[63]

The present study seeks to remedy this long-standing deficit and to examine the labor force situation in Egypt in relation to both demographic and nondemographic determinants in order to provide a basis

for assessing more accurately the present and future manpower
potential in that country.

The main objective of this study is to gain perspective on the
demographic trends that occurred in the Egyptian manpower supply
and to identify some of the significant socioeconomic factors associated with these trends. Stated more specifically, the purposes of
this study are to provide an analysis of the general demographic
characteristics of the population which have a direct bearing upon
the size, composition, and distribution of Egypt's labor supply; to
analyze changes in the size, composition, and distribution of her
economically active population; to identify the various factors and
trends that are associated with the demographic aspects of manpower
and labor force (such as industrialization, education, vocational
training, participation of women and children in economic activities,
and other relevant structural features and changes in the Egyptian
setting); and to derive and analyze projections of the economically
active population in Egypt through the year 1985 on the basis of projections of the total population that have been made by the Central
Agency for Public Mobilization and Statistics.

METHODOLOGY AND SOURCE OF DATA

Knowledge of the various determinants of labor supply and
employment was substantially advanced during the 1950's and 1960's
as a result of several factors. The more significant of these developments may be summarized briefly as follows: the development and
application of more statistically sophisticated methods of data collection
and analysis have been improved, and related improvements have
been produced in the quality of labor force estimates and projections;[64]
all concerned have recognized the interdisciplinary nature of the
problem, and the contribution of numerous scholars from such different
fields as demography, sociology, economics, education, and public
administration is mounting;[65] efforts by several international organizations to standardize concepts, procedures of data collections, and
compilations have to some extent facilitated comparative studies;[66]
and the growing need for manpower and labor force analysis of trends
and projections by governments and economic planners has given the
field a practical utility which enhances research and the development
of a growing literature.[67]

However, it remains true that analytical studies in this field
are still hampered by the complete absence of basic data in some
cases, and by inadequate historical or international comparability of
statistics in others.

Patterns and trends in the three demographic variables--

population size, composition, and distribution--as well as changes in the demographic processes, fertility, mortality, migration, marital status, and household characteristics affect the supply of labor in a number of ways. Specialists of manpower and labor force usually determine the impact of these demographic factors according to the following six topics: trends and patterns of economic dependency; trends and patterns in the level of economic activity; changes in length of working life and its implications for the labor force; demographic aspects of employment and unemployment; changes in the occupational structure of the labor force, and socioeconomic correlates of the supply of labor.

In this study, standard techniques of demographic analysis are used to assess the trends in population and labor force supply. These include the computation of rates, ratios, and percentages in addition to the adaptation of a set of population and labor force projections. The analysis of the structure of the labor force and the economic activities of the Egyptian population follow the conventional methods adopted by the International Labor Organization. This includes consideration of such specific topics as rates of economic activity, occupational distribution of the labor force, sectoral distribution of economic activities, employment status of the population, and so forth.

A macrodemographic framework is adopted, incorporating a descriptive, comparative, and analytical approach in the investigation of the nature of the relationships among population growth, labor force and employment trends, and structural changes in Egyptian society.

The data used consist of both official government statistics (published and unpublished) and secondary sources based on these official statistics. The official statistics used were vital statistics; labor force surveys; family budgets surveys; and, most important, the national censuses of population, industrial production, business establishments, and agriculture. In addition to official reports published by the Egyptian government, such data were contained in the Demographic Yearbooks and Statistical Yearbooks of the United Nations, the Yearbook of Labor Statistics, the International Labor Review, other publications of the International Labor Organization, and various reports on the labor force in the U.A.R. published by the U.S. Department of Labor. Finally, use was made of the growing literature dealing with Egypt's socioeconomic and demographic problems. Due to the diversity of data sources, much of the preliminary work involved a review of these sources to ascertain their relative accuracy and especially their comparability.

A brief description of data and data sources as well as a discussion of the adequacy of the data could be helpful for the reader who plans to carry on future research on the Egyptian society.

In modern Egypt, census-taking originated with the 1882 census. This was followed by a second census in 1897, and by a third in 1907. [68] From 1897 to 1947, censuses were taken every ten years. The census scheduled for 1957 was postponed because of the Suez War; instead, there was only a general population count. [69] The most recent decennial census was taken in 1960. In 1966, Egyptian authorities for the first time experimented with census by sampling to collect information on a few items. The decennial census scheduled for 1970 was also post-poned because of the June, 1967, war in the Middle East. The Israeli occupation of the Sinai Peninsula, the war mobilization of manpower, as well as the refugee problems from the Suez Canal cities made it impossible to conduct the scheduled census. Registration of all births and deaths has been compulsory in Egypt, at least officially, in rural as well as urban areas, since 1921; and there has been gradual improvement in coverage since then. [70]

During this century, the principal agencies responsible for the collection of statistical data on population and manpower have under-gone a number of changes. The Department of Statistics and Census was established as the principal statistical agency in 1904 in the Ministry of Commerce, and was charged with taking the decennial census. A new statistical policy was set up in 1957 to meet the need for solving the practical problems of national development planning as well as to coordinate the various data-gathering agencies. Accordingly, the Central Statistical Committee was founded at this time as an independent advisory institution and was eventually attached to the National Planning Commission. In addition, the Department of Statistics and Census was placed directly under the president of the republic. The Department of Statistics and Census was reinforced and reorganized again in 1963, when it was combined with the General Mobilization Department under the new name of the Central Agency for Public Mobilization and Statistics.

Labor force statistics in Egypt have been collected only in census years, starting in 1897. Their utility has been somewhat limited, consequently, because of the delay in their release and because they have been so far apart. [71] The recognition of the significance and, indeed, the imperativeness of probing more and more into the population and manpower dimensions of development led the former permanent Council for Public Services to recommend taking a sample of the labor force. The matter was taken up again in 1957, with the creation of the Central Statistical Committee, and in July of that year the committee authorized the carrying out of a periodic labor force sample survey. [72] The objectives of the survey as specified by the committee were to measure the volume of manpower and the labor force; to ascertain the geographical, age, sex, and

industrial distribution of persons in the labor force; to measure
seasonal fluctuations in the variables stated above; and to measure
the percentage of employment.[73]

In addition to the population census and labor force surveys,
statistical information about employment in industry and its development
is available from censuses of production and establishment. From the
employment point of view, censuses of industrial and commercial
establishments cover all establishments in Egypt belonging to both
public and private sectors. Censuses of industrial production embrace
all the industrial establishments employing ten or more persons in
both the public and private sectors.[74]

Several national surveys provide additional information on the
question of manpower and labor in Egypt. Among these are the agricultural censuses, the last of which was taken in 1961; the 1958-59
family budget sample survey; the labor record survey on the extent
of unemployment and underemployment in rural areas, taken by the
Institute of National Planning in 1964-65; and the five-year plan for
statistical development during the period 1961-65. The last sought
to determine employment with reference to agricultural labor annually
from 1961-62, employment and wages in smaller establishments every
six months from 1961, and quarterly index numbers for employment
and wages in the organized sector for 1962 to use in updating the
sampling frame of establishments.

In addition, several statistical units in special organizations
and a number of administrative agencies collect periodical information
on manpower and labor force. The Ministry of Agriculture publishes
annual estimates of farm labor based on the findings of the most recent
censuses. Such estimates are brought up to date by the application of
technical coefficients computed from observations of the organization
of labor in special farms administered by the authorities. The Department of Statistics collects information on government employment
directly from the reporting units, and it collects and compiles annual
statistics on employment, payrolls, and hours of work in establishments with at least ten workers; and the Ministry of Education presents
annual reports of educational activities, including the number of yearly
enrollments at the vocational training centers and other professional
institutions responsible to it.

The yearly and other periodical publications of the United Nations
and its affiliated offices and organizations constitute other official
sources of statistical information on manpower and employment in
Egypt. Data compilation by the United Nations follows an international
standard which permits some comparison. The published data, however, are useful only for the purpose of ascertaining very broad trends.
Detailed and specialized data on specific countries or problems are
mostly lacking.

Other statistical information on the qualitative aspects of manpower and labor force in Egypt, such as productivity, level of training, and health conditions, can be gleaned from a number of reports and studies conducted by the United Nations Department of Social and Economic Affairs, as well as by the U.S. Department of Labor.[75]

The third major source of statistical information on labor and employment in Egypt is the growing number of books, monographs, and journal articles published in the 1960's dealing with Egypt's socio-economic and demographic problems.[76]

In comparison to other Middle Eastern countries, Egypt is recognized as very advanced in census taking and collecting vital statistics.[77] However, it is believed that the early censuses were not very accurate because of considerable differences in the content of schedules and variations in the degree of coverage.[78] Also, age data in the Egyptian census is believed to suffer from heaping and misrepresentation, especially among the female population.[79] Like population censuses, vital statistics compilations also suffer from a number of inadequacies: perhaps the most serious weaknesses have been the underreporting of infant mortality and the incomplete coverage of birth and death in rural areas without health bureaus.[80]

In order to serve the purpose of historical perspective it is necessary that all labor force statistics be based on essentially similar concepts.[81] In this regard, it is comforting to note that the definitions in the Egyptian census of what constitutes the labor force did not change from one census to another; however, the inclusion or exclusion of certain groups in the labor force does constitute a real problem. Fortunately, the Department of Statistics and Census has applied a number of adjustments to enhance the historical comparability of census data on the economically active population.[82]

Another problem of labor force statistics relates to the frequently changing methods of enumeration and classification adopted in taking the industrial censuses and the censuses of establishments. These two sources of industrial employment are defective insofar as they do not include persons employed outside recorded establishments, and in Egypt unrecorded establishments are of great importance from the point of view of employment. Furthermore, owing to changes in definition, all figures about employment in small establishments are useless.[83] In the agricultural sector, the estimates of farm labor published annually by the Ministry of Agriculture also suffer from incompleteness since they do not cover farm owners, other self-employed persons, and unpaid family workers. Further, the employment figures of the agricultural census suffer from the fact that they include only permanent laborers and exclude seasonal and occasional workers.[84] The very low rates of female participation in economic

activities is believed to reflect not only a traditional ban against the
employment of women, but also a tendency not to acknowledge their
participation in economic activities. [85]

Sample surveys also suffer, as their returns are not comparable
with census returns because of an initial downward bias in the frame
of the survey. This bias resulted from the fact that it was based on
the households recorded in the 1957 population count. Another problem
of these surveys of the labor force is that although the same definition
of labor force was maintained throughout the surveys, in later rounds
the exclusion of unpaid females giving incidental help only in agricultural
field work caused an apparent deflation in the size of the labor force. [86]
Finally, one of the most serious deficiencies of labor force statistics
in Egypt is the fact that neither the returns of the census nor those of
the labor force sample surveys give direct measurements of the extent
and the nature of underemployment in rural Egypt.

The statistical data obtained from secondary sources are based
on government returns; therefore, they are subject to the same limitations cited above. However, in some cases secondary sources may
be more consistent due to the fact that researchers have attempted to
correct and/or adjust specific data for their particular purposes. A
word of caution is warranted in this regard against comparing different
figures from these secondary sources without a careful appraisal of
the adjustment procedures undertaken by the different researchers;
otherwise, erroneous conclusions could be reached. Where relevant,
these limitations will be brought up for further discussion when particular topics are considered.

In general, many labor force statistics are collected in Egypt,
but most suffer from a variety of limitations. Their limitations stem
from a number of factors: most statistics are of a very recent origin
and thus lack the historical perspective; the lack of coordination among
the number of organizations which collect this information causes some
conflicting reports on labor and employment situations; some reports
are hardly comparable, due to the use of different concepts and methods;
most of the statistical information is incomplete, especially when it
comes to the problem of rural employment and unemployment; most
of the employment figures cover a very short period (for example,
the day of reference or the week of reference) and thus miss the
seasonal fluctuations in employment; the employment figures do not
depict the extent of underutilization of labor; and the recent merger
of the Department of Statistics and Census with the General Mobilization
Department led to a higher degree of secrecy for most of the statistical
data.

As one observer commented, ''The analyst working on this
question is blessed or cursed with a large diversity of sources,

varying widely in coverage, in classification, and in concept of employment used.''87 However, despite all their limitations, manpower and labor force statistics can provide an indication of the general trends in labor force growth and of the relationship between the characteristics of the population and these trends. The data are sufficient to establish the outlines of major trends and relationships but not to measure them precisely.

MAIN FINDINGS

The general finding of this study is that the population of Egypt has increased rapidly in recent years due to a rise in the rate of natural increase, but that socioeconomic factors have limited the size of the supply of labor. However, the analysis suggests that a distinction between short-term and long-term effects of socioeconomic determinants of the labor supply is warranted. At this early stage of Egypt's economic transformation from a rural-agrarian to an urban-industrial economy, the overall impact of modernization trends is a reduction in the size of the labor force. The long-term impact of the same trends might actually be the reverse, however, and these modernization trends could ultimately enhance the employment prospects, especially outside the agricultural sector.

The findings reported in this study are relevant for a number of theoretical and methodological issues as well as for a number of policy considerations. Throughout this study the Malthusian and the transitional models (demographic) as well as Clark's and Lewis' models (economic) were tested. In line with the findings, these theoretical models appear to be less than comprehensive explanatory devices for the development experiences of Egypt, which, in turn, renders them less useful as general theory. A number of specific weaknesses characteristic of these various models are noted. The applicability of a number of theoretical labor force and employment concepts and measurements are questioned and the gap between concepts and their demographic-economic indicators are outlined. New approaches for measuring the extent of underemployment are recommended.

On the level of policy considerations, this study reveals three alternatives open to underdeveloped areas with a rapidly growing population such as Egypt. As a long-term solution, the study emphasizes the need for serious efforts to reduce population growth through the control of fertility by providing family planning services. The encouragement of migration should also be considered, although the chances of losing scarce skilled manpower are real.

It is hoped that this case study of Egypt will, at the very least, result in an increase in our understanding of the grave obstacles that this country faces in providing gainful employment to its rapidly growing supply of labor; a better understanding of the dynamics of change within that country; progress toward a broader comparative analysis of man-power trends and problems in other developing countries; and a compre-hensive analysis of the problems of manpower and the labor force that could be of interest and value to policy-makers and economic planners in Egypt.

NOTES

1. A selective list of recent studies of the interrelationship between demographic and socioeconomic variables on a microsocial level can be found in Edward G. Stockwell and Mostafa H. Nagi, The Social Areas of Metropolitan Connecticut, Bulletin 404 (Storrs, Conn.: Agricultural Experiment Station, March, 1968), pp. 3-4.

2. For a general discussion of this topic, see United Nations, The Determinants and Consequences of Population Trends (ST/SAO/ Series A/17; New York: U.N. Publication, 1953).

3. For simplicity, the name " Egypt " will be used by itself throughout the remainder of this study.

4. United Nations, The Determinants and Consequences of Population Trends, Chapter 11. For a recent summary of such labor force determinants, see United Nations, Proceedings of the World Population Conference, 1965 (New York: U.N. Publication, 1967), I, 219-43, and IV, 251-338.

5. United Nations, "Conditions and Trends of Fertility in the World," Population Bulletin, No. 7 (New York: U.N. Publication; Sales No. 64XII. 2).

6. D. G. Bogue and K. C. Zachariah, "Urbanization and Mi-gration in India" in R. Turner, ed., India's Urban Future (Berkeley: University of California Press, 1962), p. 45.

7. International Labour Conference Report, I: 1, Women Workers in a Changing World (Geneva: International Labour Office, 1963).

8. An excellent discussion of the relationship between education, manpower, and economic development can be found in Frederick Harbison and Charles A. Myers, Education, Manpower and Economic Growth (New York: McGraw-Hill Book Co., 1964). See also J. Vaizey, The Economics of Education (London: Macmillan Co., 1966).

9. Wilbert E. Moore and Arnold F. Feldman, eds., Labor

Commitment and Social Change in Developing Areas (New York: Social Science Research Council, 1960); and Morroe Berger, Bureaucracy and Society in Modern Egypt (Princeton, N.J.: Princeton University Press, 1957).

10. Arthur M. Ross, ed., Industrial Relations and Economic Development, International Institute for Labour Studies (London: Macmillan Co., 1966).

11. W. A. Lewis, Economic Development With Unlimited Supplies of Labor: Readings in Economic Development (Belmont, Calif., 1963).

12. Clarance D. Long, The Labor Force Under Changing Income and Employment, a study by the National Bureau of Economic Research (Princeton, N.J.: Princeton University Press, 1958).

13. See International Labour Organization, Employment Objectives in Economic Development (Geneva; 1962), New Series No. 62, Chapters IV and V; and the special supplement to the Journal of Political Economy, LXX (October, 1962).

14. See United Nations, Progress and Problems of Industriali-zation in Underdeveloped Countries (New York, 1955); and Bert F. Hoselitz and Wilbert E. Moore, eds., Industrialization and Society (Mouton: UNESCO, 1963).

15. See International Labour Office, "Repercussions of Com-modity Price Fluctuations on Primary Producing Countries," International Labour Review, LXXIX, 6 (June, 1959), 567.

16. Gabriel S. Saab, The Egyptian Agrarian Reform, 1952-62 (London: Oxford University Press, 1967), pp. 143-48, 157-58, and 194ff. See also the following publications of the United Nations: Progress in Land Reform, Second Report (New York, 1956; Sales No. 11.B.3, 1956), pp. 13-25; and Economic and Social Council, 34th session, Progress in Land Reform, Third Report (Mimeographed Document E3603, April 5, 1962), pp. 43-105.

17. For an account of the factors ensuring full employment in the Soviet economy, see P. P. Litvyakov, "Economic and Social Factors Ensuring Full Employment (Experience of the Soviet Union)," Proceedings of the World Population Conference, 1965, pp. 307-12.

18. A comprehensive treatment of this subject is to be found in James S. Coleman, Education and Political Development (Princeton; N.J.: Princeton University Press, 1965).

19. See E.M. Kassalow, National Labor Movements in the Post-War World (Evanston: Northwestern University Press, 1963); and E.V. Berg, "The External Impact of Trade Unions in Developing Countries: The Record in Africa," in Industrial Relations Research Association, Proceedings of the Sixteenth Annual Meeting (Boston, 1963), pp. 89-101.

20. International Labour Organization, Report of the Meeting of Experts on Measurement of Underdevelopment (Geneva: October 21-November 1, 1963).

21. Alan B. Mountjoy, Industrialization and Underdeveloped Countries (Chicago: Aldine Publishing Company, 1963), Chapters 4 and 9.

22. Frederick Harbison and Ibrahim Abdel Kader Ibrahim, Human Resources for Egyptian Enterprise (New York: McGraw-Hill Book Co., 1958).

23. An example of these studies can be found in Charles Issawi, Egypt at Mid-Century (New York: Oxford University Press, 1956), and A. E. Croucheley, The Economic Development of Modern Egypt, 1800-1850 (New York: Oxford University Press, 1962).

24. See Wendell Cleland, The Population Problem in Egypt (Lancaster, Pa.: Pennsylvania Printing Corp., 1936). See also his Demographic Studies for Selected Areas of Rapid Growth. (New York: Milbank Memorial Fund, 1944), p. 98. Also in the same source is Clyde V. Kiser, "The Demographic Position of Egypt," 383-408.

25. To cite a few of the authors who stressed this point of view in their analysis, the following are immediately significant: Ali A. El-Gritly, Population and Economic Pressures in Egypt (Cairo: Misr Press, 1962); and Magdi El-Kamash, Economic Development and Planning in Egypt (New York: Frederick A. Praeger, Publishers, 1968).

26. See for example Ali A. El-Gritly, "The Structure of Modern Industry in Egypt," L'Egypte Contemporaine, Nos. 241-42 (November-December, 1947), 534-54; United Nations, The Development of Manufacturing Industry in Egypt, Israel and Turkey (New York: U.N. Publication, 1958); and Kurt Grunwald and Joachim Ranall, Industrialization in the Middle East (New York: Council for Middle Eastern Affairs Press, 1960).

27. An example of the literature on this subject can be found in Janet L. Abu-Lughad, "Urbanization in Egypt: Present State and Future Prospects," Economic Development and Cultural Change, XIII,

3 (April, 1965), 313-43; and Ali Badri Abdu-Rahman, "Internal Migration in the U.A.R.," L'Egypte Contemporaine, No. 319 (January, 1965), 31-44.

28. Numerous books, articles, and reports have been written on the progress of education in Egypt, such as Fahim I. Qubain, Education and Science in the Arab World (Baltimore: Johns Hopkins Press, 1966).

29. Daniel Lerner, The Passing of Traditional Society: Modernizing the Middle East (Glencoe, Ill.: Free Press, 1958).

30. The most comprehensive treatment of this subject is Patrick O'Brien, The Revolution in Egypt's Economic System (New York: Oxford University Press, 1966).

31. George K. Kardouche, "Monetary Development and Policy in the U.A.R. (Egypt) 1952-1962." (unpublished Ph.D. dissertation, Brown University, June, 1965); and S. El-Naggar, "Foreign Aid and the Economic Development of the U.A.R." (preliminary research paper No. 1964, B; Princeton Program in Near Eastern Studies, Princeton University Press, 1965).

32. S. H. Abdel-Rahman, "A Survey of the Foreign Trade of Egypt in the Post-War Period, With Special Reference to Its Impact on the National Economy" (unpublished Ph.D. dissertation, Faculty of Commerce, Cairo University, 1959).

33. Sayed Marei, Agrarian Reform in Egypt (Cairo: S.O.P. Press, 1957); and M. A. W. Ezzat, "The Land Tenure System in Egypt," in K. H. Parson, et al., eds., Land Tenure (Madison: University of Wisconsin Press, 1956).

34. See J. Lacouture and S. Lacouture, Egypt in Transition (London: Macmillan Co., 1958); K. Wheelock, Nasser's New Egypt (New York: Frederick A. Praeger, Publishers, 1960); and P. Mansfield, Nasser's Egypt (Baltimore: Penguin Books, 1965).

35. Cleland, op. cit., p. 101.

36. Kiser, op. cit., p. 98.

37. Charles Issawi, "Population and Wealth in Egypt," The Milbank Memorial Fund Quarterly, XXVII (January, 1949), 98-113.

38. E. L. Nassif, "L'Egypte Est-Elle Surpuplée?" Population, V, 3 (July-September, 1950), 513-32.

39. Eva Garzouzi, Old Ills and New Remedies in Egypt (Cairo: Dar El-Maaref, 1958); and Hanna Rizk, "Population Growth and Its Affects on Economic and Social Goals in the U.A.R.," in S. Mudd, ed., Population Crisis and Use of World Resources (Bloomington: Indiana University Press, 1964), p. 169.

40. Republic of Egypt, Permanent Council of Public Services, The Population Problem of Egypt (Cairo, 1955); United Arab Republic, Central Statistical Committee, Population Trends in the U.A.R. (Cairo, 1955); and Central Agency for Public Mobilization and Statistics, Population Increase in the U.A.R. and Its Deterrents to Development (Cairo, 1966).

41. Robert C. Cook, "Egypt's Population Explodes," Population Bulletin, XII (July, 1956), 57.

42. M. A. El-Badry, "Some Demographic Measurement for Egypt Based on the Stability of Census Age Distribution," The Milbank Memorial Fund Quarterly, XXXIII, 3 (July, 1955), 268-305.

43. S. H. Abdel-Aty, "Life Table Functions for Egypt Based on Model Life Tables and Quasi-Stable Population Theory," The Milbank Memorial Fund Quarterly, XXXIX, 2 (April, 1961), 350-77; R. Makar, The Egyptian National Life Table No. 3 for 1947 (Cairo: Government Press, 1957); and Central Statistical Committee, Population Trends in the U.A.R. (Cairo, 1962).

44. H. Rizk, "Fertility Patterns in Selected Areas in Egypt" (unpublished Ph.D. dissertation, Princeton University, 1959); and Girgis Abdu Marzouk, "Fertility of the Urban and Rural Population in Egypt," L'Egypte Contemporaine, Vol. XLVIII (January, 1957), 27-34.

45. M. A. El-Badry, "Trends in the Components of Population Growth in the Arab Countries of the Middle East: A Survey of Present Information," Demography, II (1965), 140-85.

46. Ibid., p. 158.

47. I. H. Abdel-Rahman, "Manpower Planning in the U.A.R.," Etude Mensuelle sur la vie Economique at financiere de la R.A.S. et pays Arabes, No. 66 (January, 1963), 34-47.

48. Institute of National Planning, "Marginal Productivity Wage Theory and Subsistence Wage Theory in Egyptian Agriculture," Memo. No. 547 (Cairo, March, 1965); and M. El-Tomy and B. Hansen, "The Seasonal Employment Profile in Egyptian Agriculture," Memo. No. 501 (Cairo, October, 1964).

49. M. Al-Arabi, "Experience of Apprentice Training in the United Arab Republic," International Labour Review, XCII, 6 (December, 1965), 490-505; also his "A Modern Apprenticeship School in the U.A.R.," International Labour Review, LXXXIV (December, 1961), 478-98; and Majid Lliyya, "Upgrading Training of Skilled Workers in the U.A.R.," International Labour Review, XC (July, 1964), 35-44.

50. M. H. Abdel-Razi, "Expenditure on Social Reform," Majaliat al Iqtisad wal Muhasabah, No. 53 (May 15, 1953), 18-19; and J. M. Weir and associates, "An Evaluation of Health and Sanitation in Egyptian Villages," Journal of the Egyptian Public Health Association, XXVII, 3 (1952), 55-122.

51. Sami Mutawalli, "Nutrition Standard in the U.A.R.," Majallat Ghurfat H Al-Qahirah, Nos. 7 and 8 (1965), 10-14; and Shehata S. Shehata, "Cooperative Efforts and Food Consumption in the U.A.R.," L'Egypte Contemporaine, LV (January, 1964), 67-70.

52. United Nations, The Development of Manufacturing Industry in Egypt, Israel and Turkey, pp. 9-11.

53. This disagreement can be seen in the recent work of Donald C. Mead, Growth and Structural Change in the Egyptian Economy (Homewood, Ill.: Richard D. Irwin, Inc., 1967); and B. Hansen and G. Marzouk, Development and Economic Policy in the U.A.R. (Amsterdam: North Holland Publishing Co., 1965).

54. National Planning Committee, "Report of the Committee on the Mechanization of Agriculture," Memo. No. 253 (Cairo, 1959; in Arabic).

55. Saad Gadalla, Land Reform in Relation to Social Development in Egypt (Columbia: University of Missouri Press, 1962).

56. Al-Ahram (Cairo), January 8, March 7, 8 and 11, and May 6, 7, 8 and 11, 1965.

57. Patrick O'Brien, "Industrial Development and the Employ- ment Problem in Egypt, 1945-1965," Middle East Economic Papers (1962), 90-120.

58. Mead, op. cit., Chapters 6 and 11.

59. Frederick Harbison and Ibrahim A. Ibrahim, "Some Labor Problems of Industrialization in Egypt," Annals of American Academy of Political Review, CCCV (May, 1956), 114-24; F. Harbison, Chapter on Egypt in W. Galensen, ed., Labor and Economic Development (New York: John Wiley and Sons, 1959); and U.S. Department of of Labor, Survey of the Labor Situation in Egypt, 1955 (Washington, D.C.: Government Printing Office, 1955).

60. See Muhammed Hilmy Murad, "Modern Trends in the U.A.R. Labor Legislation," L'Egypte Contemporaine, LIII (October, 1962), 5-18; and U.S. Department of Labor, Bureau of Labor Statisitics, Labor, Law and Practice in the U.A.R. (Washington, D.C.: Govern-ment Printing Office, 1965).

61. Murad, op. cit., pp. 5-18.

62. Issawi, Egypt at Mid-Century, pp. 251 - 52.

63. O'Brien, The Revolution in Egypt's Economic Society (New York: Oxford University Press, 1966), pp. 278-323.

64. See the United Nations, "Economic Characteristics of the Population," in Handbook of Population Census Methods, XI, 1959; and "Meeting B-11, Definition and Measurement of Economically Active Population Employment, Unemployment and Underemployment," Proceedings of the World Population Conference, 1965 (New York: U.N. Publication, 1966), IV 339-95.

65. The reader can find a number of recent bibliographies on the subject, such as "Human Resources and Economic Growth, an International Annotated Bibliography," (Menlo Park, Cal.: Stanford Research Institute, 1963).

66. The efforts of the International Labour Organization in this regard are numerous in a number of publications such as International Standards of Labour Statistics, Geneva, 1959, Report of the Meeting of Experts on the Measure of Underemployment (document M.EMU/Br, Geneva, 1963), and others. Also, a number of publications in this regard appeared under the sponsorship of the OECD (Organization for European Cultural Development). The UNESCO's efforts in this area of educational statistics and school enrollment projections need no elaboration.

67. United Nations, Determinants and Consequences of Population Trends, p. 265.

68. For an excellent survey of the development of census techniques during the twentieth century, see Abdelmegid Mostafa Farrag, "Demographic Developments in Egypt During the Present Century" (unpublished Ph.D. dissertation, London School of Economics and Political Science, 1957).

69. One writer commented that the postponement of the scheduled census for 1957 to 1969 was intended to facilitate international compat-ibility; see Magdi El-Kamash, Economic Development and Planning in Egypt, p. 67.

70. For a discussion of the reporting of births and deaths, see United Arab Republic, Department of Statisitcs and Census, Introduction Vital Statistics, I (Cairo, annual).

71. National Bank of Egypt, "Statistics of Labor Force in the Southern Region," Economic Bulletin, XIII (Cairo, 1960), 86.

72. See Abdel-Moneim El-Shafei, "The Current Labor Force Sample Survey in Egypt," International Labour Review, LXIII, 6 (June, 1957), 432-49.

73. United Arab Republic, Central Statistical Committee, The Labor Force Sample Survey in the Egyptian Region of the U.A.R. (Cairo, 1959).

74. For an example of the published returns of these censuses, see Central Bank of Egypt, "Industrial Census for 1962," Economic Review, VII, 1 and 2 (Cairo, 1967), 10-22; and National Bank of Egypt, "The Census of Establishment," Economic Bulletin, XXI, 3 (Cairo, 1968), 239-47.

75. United Nations, Department of Economic and Social Affairs, Economic Development in the Middle East (published three times a year); United Nations, Economic Commission in Africa, Industrial Growth in Africa: A Survey and Outlook (U.N. Document E/CN.14/-INR/1; New York; October 15, 1962).

76. Theodore K. Ruprecht, "The Demographic Factors in Egyptian Economic Progress" (unpublished Ph.D. dissertation, Berkeley: University of California, 1965); Patrick O'Brien "Industrial Development and the Employment Problem in Egypt, 1945-1965,"; M. Sekelani, "Population, Active et Structure Economique de L'Egypte," Population, No. 3 (July-September, 1962), 465-90; and Robert Mabro, "Industrial Growth, Agricultural Underemployment and the Lewis Model: The Egyptian Case, 1937-1965," The Journal of Development Studies, III, 4 (July, 1967), 322-51.

77. See Robert C. Cook, "Egypt's Population Explodes," Population Bulletin, XII (July, 1956), 59; and Clyde V. Kiser, "The Demographic Position of Egypt," Milbank Memorial Fund Quarterly, XXII, 4 (October, 1944), 383-404.

78. Issawi, Egypt at Mid-Century, op. cit., pp. 54-55, 61, and 79-80.

79. M. A. El-Badry, "Some Demographic Measurement for Egypt Based on the Stability of Census Age Distribution," the Milbank

Memorial Fund Quarterly, XXXIII, 3 (July, 1955), 268-305.

80. For a discussion of this difference in the vital rates between rural and urban areas, see M. A. El-Badry, "Trends in the Components of Population Growth in the Arab Countries of the Middle East: A Survey of Present Information," Demography, II (1965), 140-85.

81. For a general discussion of the applicability of the concepts of labor force, manpower, and employment developed in the industrialized countries to underdeveloped areas, see Wilbert E. Moore, "The Exportability of the Labor Force Concept," American Sociological Review, XVIII, 1 (February, 1953), 68-72.

82. For a discussion of these adjustments, see U.A.R. Department of Statistics and Census, Population Census, 1960, II (Cairo, 1963), Introduction.

83. Hansen and Marzouk, op. cit., p. 124.

84. Mead, op. cit., pp. 87-91.

85. A. M. El-Shafei, op. cit., pp. 432-49; also Institute of National Planning, Final Reports on Employment Problems in Rural Areas U.A.R., (Cairo, 1968), p. 37.

86. National Bank of Egypt, "Population and Manpower," Economic Bulletin, XVI, 1-2 (Cairo, 1963), 11.

87. Mead, op, cit., p. 31.

1

**POPULATION AND
LABOR FORCE:
GENERAL GROWTH
TRENDS**

Like most underdeveloped nations of the non-Western world, Egypt is contributing heavily to the modern population explosion. According to the official census data, the population of Egypt rose from 11.3 million in 1907 to 26.1 million in 1960. This represents more than a doubling of numbers during the 53-year intercensal period.[1] According to the official estimate of the Central Agency for Public Mobilization and Statistics, the population of Egypt rose from 26.1 million in 1960 to 34 million in 1970. This represents an increase of approximately one-third during the 1960's.[2]

GENERAL POPULATION GROWTH TRENDS

The history of population growth in Egypt during this century can be divided into two periods: the period before World War II, during which annual growth rates were only about 1 percent, and the postwar period, during which annual growth rates have soared to nearly 2.5 percent. The reason for this change in annual growth rates lies in a basic change in the balance between birth and death rates. During the pre-World War II period, the slower rates of increase were due to a relatively stable balance between high crude death rates (26 to 28 per 1,000, on the average) and even higher crude birth rates (generally between 40 and 45 per 1,000).[3] Since the end of World War II, however, the Egyptian death rate, following a pattern that has been observed in many underdeveloped parts of the world, has undergone substantial reductions.[4] These mortality declines have come about as a result of the introduction of antibiotics, insecticides, and public health measures. These measures have been so successful that the crude death rate had by 1960 reached a level of less than 17 per 1,000. During this same period, however, the crude birth rate remained at its prewar level of more than 40 per 1,000. The obvious result of this situation has been a marked acceleration in the crude rate of natural increase (from an average of about 15 per 1, 000 prior to 1946 to a level of 26 per 1, 000 by 1960).

Since the changing pattern of birth and death has exerted such a profound impact on Egyptian population growth trends, it is desirable to examine the specific trends of these two demographic processes more closely before moving on to a discussion of labor force trends.

The registration of births and deaths did not become compulsory in Egypt until 1912. Vital statistics were not very comprehensive at first, but coverage has improved somewhat over the years, especially in urban centers. There are still some fairly notable differences in the completeness of coverage between rural and urban areas; registration generally is less complete in the rural areas.[5] It is extremely important that such limitations be kept in mind when interpreting the vital statistics data of such underdeveloped countries as Egypt.

Table 1 compares general fertility rates of the last three censuses with the corresponding crude birth rates. The slight fall in crude birth rates shown in Table 1, at a time when the general fertility rates increased, may be ascribed to changes in the age structure of the population.

Cumulative fertility rates are generally considered to be a better indicator of long-term trends in reproductive behavior. In Table 2, for example, it would appear that there has been a rise in the average

TABLE 1

Fertility and Crude Birth Rates, 1937, 1947, and 1960

Year	Crude Birth Rate[a]	General Fertility Rate[b]
1937	43. 9	181. 4
1947	43. 6	171. 9
1960	42. 9	190. 0

[a]Births per 1, 000 population.

[b]Births per 1, 000 women between the ages of fifteen and forty-nine.

Source: U. A. R. Central Statistical Committee, Population Trends in the U. A. R. (Cairo, 1962), p. 53.

number of children per married women from 3. 80 in 1947 to 4. 17 in 1960. Hansen and Marzouk believe, however, that this rise does not necessarily reflect long-term trends; rather, they explain it as an outcome of a speed-up of births during and after World War II, a speed-up which resulted from an increase in the marriage rate and a fall in the average marriage age at that time. [6]

Demographers studying Egyptian fertility have been impressed primarily by the constancy and uniformity of the birth patterns. For more than two generations the crude birth rate has fluctuated narrowly around an average of 43 per 1, 000 per year, and only minor fertility differences have been identified between urban and rural populations, between occupational classes, and between religious groups. [7] Comparing the regional fertility differences in 1947, Mohamad El-Badry

TABLE 2

Cumulative Fertility Rates--Average
Number of Children Born to
Married Women[a]--During Specific Marriage Duration
Periods, 1947 and 1960

Marriage Duration	All Egypt		Cairo and Alexandria		Other Parts of Egypt	
	1947	1960	1947	1960	1947	1960
Less than 5 years	0. 78	0. 75	0. 93	0. 85	0. 75	0. 73
5-9	1. 46	1. 81	1. 45	1. 95	1. 46	1.7 7
10-19	2. 06	2. 24	2. 16	2. 32	2. 04	2. 23
20-29	1. 65	1. 65	1. 59	1. 64	1. 68	1. 66
30 and over	0. 69	0. 44	0. 30	0. 38	0. 74	0. 46
All women	3. 80	4. 17	3. 69	4. 35	3. 82	4. 14

[a]Excluding married women who did not state number of children born.

Source: B. Hansen and G. Marzouk, Development and Economic Policy in the U. A. R. (Egypt) (Amsterdam: North Holland Publishing Co., 1956), pp. 44-45, Tables 2. 17 and 2. 20.

concluded that parity averages were lowest in Aswan, the southernmost governorate, and rose gradually as proximity to Cairo increased, with a slight drop in the neighboring governorates of middle-upper Egypt. He also found the governorates closer to Cairo to have the highest parity averages in upper Egypt. Variation in parity in the nonurban governorates of lower Egypt was not random, but had a general upward trend from west to east and from south to north. Regional fertility differences in 1960 were strikingly similar to those of 1947. [8]

A recent study suggests that educational and income variables are becoming significant determinants of differential fertility, whereas another recent study documents the emergence of significant fertility differentials by 1960 in Egypt's largest city, Cairo. [9] According to the evidence reported, education of the husband appears to be the most significant of the variables affecting the fertility of urban Egyptian women.

It is not the intention of this study to present an extensive analysis of fertility data. However, a comparison of fertility trends for both Egypt and the United States shows the much higher level of fertility characteristic of Egypt. Table 3 compares birth rates by age groups

TABLE 3

Age-Specific Fertility Rates for Egypt in 1947 and 1960,
and for the United States in 1950 and 1960

Age Group	Egypt		United States	
	1947	1960	1950	1960
15-19	47. 8	34. 0	70. 0	80. 0
20-24	256. 7	218. 6	190. 0	250. 0
25-29	338. 0	343. 4	165. 0	196. 0
30-34	270. 0	366. 1	103. 0	112. 0
35-39	163. 1	195. 8	51. 0	59. 5
40-44	40. 8	58. 0	16. 0	16. 0
45+	16. 8	18. 2	4. 5	2. 3

Source: U.A.R. Central Agency for Public Mobilization and Statistics, Population Increase in the U.A.R. and Its Deterrents for Development (Cairo: November, 1966), p. 81, Table 33.

for both Egypt and the United States at approximately comparable census years. The comparative figures show the highest fertility ever reached was for Egyptian women between the ages of twenty-five and twenty-nine in 1947. With the exception of the youngest age group, the birth rates of Egyptian women were consistently higher than those of their American counterparts. Between 1947 and 1960, the highest rate of fertility recorded for Egyptian females moved to the age group comprising women between the ages of thirty and thirty-four.

According to a report from the Central Agency for Public Mobilization and Statistics, the noticeable increase in fertility rates between 1947 and 1960 for ages twenty-five and over is believed to be a result of an increase in medical care available to women during their childbearing and delivery periods. This improved care resulted in a noticeable decline in infant mortality, and may also have reduced the incidence of miscarriage and/or stillbirth. Fertility increases between the last two censuses were also attributed to a decrease in the proportion of married women who did not have children, and to an increase in marriage duration due largely to improvements in health and medical facilities that have lowered the incidence of maternal mortality. [10]

An examination of the data that are available on fertility in Egypt may lead the researcher to different conclusions. The constancy of the high level of fertility for the last two decades, as well as the absence of major differences of fertility between urban and rural areas, contradicts the recent findings of the emergence of fertility differential in Cairo as well as fertility differentials according to education and income. Demographers have speculated on the reasons responsible for the inconsistency of these data. A generally accepted interpretation is that the recent rise in the standard of living, especially in urban areas, has brought some increases in fertility, at least temporarily. The Malthusian theory, with its predication of an increase in fertility with the rise in per-capita income, is suggested as applicable to Egypt at the present stage of the country's economic and social development. However, there are also changes which support the expected trends of the demographic transition. These would include the fall in the fertility of the youngest women between 1947 and 1960, the inverse relationship between fertility and social class positions, and the emergence of fertility differentials in urban Egypt. It may very well be that the immediate effects of improving the standard of living in Egypt have been consistent with Malthusian theory. [11] In the long run, however, it is hoped that industrialization, urbanization, and rising levels of education will gradually depress fertility, as asserted by transition theory, to a level more in balance with the lower death rates. [12]

As indicated earlier, changes in mortality have largely been responsible for the rapid population growth which Egypt experienced during this century. An examination of the age-sex specific death rates presented in Table 4 shows a noticeable reduction for all age and sex groups. However, the figures also show that there is still a long way to go if Egypt is to reach the mortality level of such industrialized countries as the United States. The mortality level is still quite high compared to Western standards, despite the big decrease that has taken place since the end of World War II. A main cause of this overall high level is infant mortality: roughly 60 infant deaths per 1,000 births in 1960. It is certainly possible for Egypt, in the light of the experience of other countries, to lower substantially its present infant mortality rate, and consequently to bring the death rate to the level which other developing countries have already reached. [13] In any case, Egypt is presently faced with a dilemma. On the one hand, the prospects seem to be gloomy if the goal of a lower death rate is achieved while fertility is kept at its presently high level. Such a development would lead to even faster rates of population growth·and this in turn would compound the already serious

TABLE 4

Death Rates for Different Age Groups, 1937, 1947, and 1960

Age Group	1937		1947		1960	
	Male	Female	Male	Female	Male	Female
0-4	120.0	108.6	83.6	73.5	61.1	62.1
5-9	8.4	6.5	5.9	4.5	2.5	1.9
10-14	5.5	3.5	5.1	3.2	2.2	1.5
15-19	6.5	4.2	5.4	3.3	2.5	1.8
20-29	3.2	5.2	7.5	5.0	3.0	2.1
30-39	10.1	7.1	11.3	8.1	4.4	3.3
40-49	14.1	8.8	15.5	9.6	7.8	4.5
50-59	21.7	13.2	21.7	13.1	16.5	8.4
60-69	34.1	21.8	31.3	20.7	32.0	19.1
70+	134.7	155.5	150.7	113.2	102.4	109.5
Average crude death rate (total)	29.4	24.9	23.4	19.3	17.7	16.2

Source: U.A.R. Central Agency for Public Mobilization and Statistics, Population Increase in the U.A.R. and Its Deterrents for Development (Cairo: November, 1966), p. 106, Table 42 and p. 110, Table 43.

demographic obstacle to economic development. On the other hand, the presently high level of infant and early childhood mortality costs the government a substantial annual financial loss. A sizable number of the country's human resources are wasted before reaching the age of work and productivity. To illustrate, the annual investment in children who die before reaching their fifteenth birthday was estimated at $22 million in 1960. [14]

Another way to evaluate mortality conditions for a given country is to examine the country's life tables. A number of life tables have

TABLE 5

Life Expectation in U. A. R. by Age Groups, 1937, 1947, and 1960

Age	1937 Males	1937 Females	1947 Males	1947 Females	1960 Males	1960 Females
0	35.6	42.1	41.4	47.0	51.6	53.8
1	42.1	48.8	47.1	53.2	56.2	59.9
2	47.0	54.4	50.7	57.5	59.7	64.4
3	49.6	57.4	52.3	59.6	61.0	66.3
4	50.4	58.3	52.6	60.0	60.9	66.4
5	50.4	58.3	52.3	59.9	60.5	66.0
10	47.4	54.5	49.3	56.8	56.6	62.0
15	43.5	50.1	45.4	52.8	62.2	57.5
20	39.8	46.1	41.5	58.6	47.7	52.9
25	36.3	42.7	37.4	44.5	43.3	48.4
30	33.0	38.2	34.1	40.4	39.0	43.9
35	29.5	34.5	30.5	36.3	34.7	39.4
40	26.1	30.8	27.0	32.3	30.5	35.0
45	22.7	27.1	23.5	28.2	26.4	30.6
50	19.4	23.4	20.1	24.2	22.4	26.3
55	16.3	19.8	16.7	20.3	18.6	22.1
60	13.3	16.2	13.5	16.4	15.1	18.0
65	10.5	12.7	10.5	12.8	11.8	14.1
70	7.9	9.5	7.9	9.6	9.1	10.7
75	5.8	6.9	5.8	6.9	6.7	7.8
80	4.1	4.7	4.1	4.8	4.9	5.3
85	2.8	3.1	2.8	3.2	3.5	3.7
90	1.9	2.0	1.9	2.0	2.4	2.4
95	1.3	1.3	1.3	1.3	1.4	1.3

Source: U. A. R. Central Agency for Public Mobilization and Statistics, Basic Statistics, 1964 (Cairo, 1964), p. 39.

been constructed for Egypt by using a variety of techniques. [15] The
official age-sex specific expectance of life values in Egypt at successive
census dates from 1937 to 1960 are those of the Central Agency for
Public Mobilization and Statistics.   They are presented in Table 5.
Because of the noticeable drop in mortality rates, the expectancy of
life at birth in 1960 exceeded that of 1937 by 16 years for males and
by nearly 12 years for females.   Increases in life expectancy at the
older ages was smaller.   Two reasons account for this relatively
slight improvement in the life expectancy of older people: first, most
of the drop in the death rate was due to a pronounced decline in infant
mortality; and second, previous life tables gave high estimates for
the survival rates and life expectancies of the older age groups.

Another important aspect of the study of mortality is the analysis

TABLE 6

Proportionate Distribution of Leading Causes of Death in
Localities in Egypt Having Health Offices in 1951 and
During the Four-Year Period, 1957-60

Causes of Death	Proportionate 1951	Distribution 1957-1960
Diseases of gastro-intestinal tract	37. 8	39. 4
Diseases of respiratory system	14. 1	13. 8
Diseases of early infancy	12. 1	10. 2
Infections and parasitic	4. 5	3. 7
Heart and circulatory diseases	3. 8	7. 5
Accidents	2. 6	3. 3
Ill-defined causes	15. 2	13. 5
All other causes	25. 1	22. 1
Total	100. 0	100. 0

Source: A. E. Sarhan, "Mortality Trends in the United Arab
Republic," Proceedings of The World Population Conference, 1965,
4 vols.   (New York: United Nations, 1967), II, 360, Table 2.

of mortality by cause of death in order to show the varying impact of particular causes of death and especially to determine the changes which occur in this respect over a period of time. Table 6 shows the percent of deaths attributed to broad cause groups for the years 1951 and 1957-60, inclusive. The three leading causes of death are those which are common to infants and young children (diseases of the gastrointestinal tract, of the respiratory system, and of early infancy). Together they account for nearly two-thirds of the total mortality. While the first two causes can be regarded as preventable, prematurity is the most important ingredient in the third group (diseases of early infancy), and these deaths are much more difficult to control. However, a substantial decrease in the share of the first two leading causes of death--which account for over half of all the deaths--can be achieved with an improvement in health sanitation and preventive medicine.

It is of interest to note that heart and circulatory diseases, which were the fifth leading cause in 1951, took fourth position during 1957-60, while infectious and parasitic diseases, which occupied fourth position in 1951, ranked fifth. This may be explained by the increasing control over communicable diseases and by the trend of increased life expectancy of the population.

In summary, although mortality figures in Egypt have improved substantially during the postwar years, they are still substantially higher than those of the more developed nations of the Western world. The dilemma that this creates for Egypt has already been noted: high mortality, especially infant mortality, puts a heavy financial strain on the economy, but further declines in mortality (unless accompanied by some radical reduction of fertility) will serve only to aggravate the problems posed by an increasingly rapid rate of population growth.

It is necessary to mention the third basic process of demographic change--human migration. As far as overall population change in Egypt is concerned, this is the least important process. In fact, for most purposes, Egypt's population could be considered a closed population. Egypt has not experienced any sizable migration into or out of the country in recent history. Census data show that the number of foreigners in Egypt increased from 112, 000 in 1897 to about 250, 000 in 1927, and then decreased to 186, 000 in 1937 and to only 143, 000 in 1960. The number of Egyptians residing abroad has also been very small. It was estimated at 25, 000 in 1937 and at less than 100, 000 in 1960. [16] This increase, which involves very few people relative to the size of the total population, is due mainly to the employment of teachers and professionals in other Arab countries.

LABOR FORCE GROWTH TRENDS

The first point to make here is that the labor force and employment data available in recent Egyptian censuses are not completely comparable, a fact that makes their interpretation somewhat more difficult. For one thing, in both 1937 and 1947 the labor-force figures included persons five years old and over. In 1960, however, the census recorded the employment of persons six years old and over. This is a very small problem, however, and for most purposes the population censuses provide comprehensive and reasonably consistent figures.

A more serious weakness of these census figures concerns the treatment of female workers. Although the dividing line between the employed, the unemployed, and those outside the labor force has remained the same over the last three censuses, the inclusion or exclusion of certain groups in these categories has changed from one year to another. In 1947, for example, the inclusion of 3.3 million farm wives as being engaged in home duties significantly inflated the employment figures of that census.

Before beginning a more detailed examination of trends in the labor force and in employment, it should be noted that the various sources of data available give slightly different figures; therefore, the data should be considered, at best, an approximation of the trends rather than a precise measurement. Table 7 shows the employment figures as reported in the three latest censuses, together with the adjusted figures of the Department of Statistics and Census. [17] According to the adjusted figures, the economically active population expanded by 1.1 million between 1937 and 1947 and by 800,000 between 1947 and 1960. This represents a total increase of 1.9 million, or 32.5 percent, between 1937 and 1960. Population increase during this

TABLE 7

Population and Labor Force, 1937, 1947, and 1960

	Labor Force	Population
1937		
Census	7, 275	15, 933
Adjusted	5, 838	- - - -
1947		
Census	8, 218	19, 022
Adjusted	6, 995	- - - -
1960		
Census	7, 666	26, 085
Adjusted	7, 734	- - - -

Source: U.A.R. Department of Statistics and Census, Population Cenus, 1960 (Cairo, 1963), II, xiv.

same period was about 10.2 million, or 64 percent. In other words, population increase far outstripped growth in the size of the labor force. The relationship between population trends and changes in the labor force perhaps could be better ascertained when the employment of male adults (fifteen and older) is considered, since this group represents the real backbone of the labor force. Table 8 presents adjusted figures for population and employment of males age fifteen and over at the last three censuses. During the decade 1937-47, Egypt's population rose by approximately 20 percent, while the number of people employed increased at nearly the same rate. During this period the participation ratio remained virtually unchanged. In the following intercensal period, however, while the participation rate for adult males stayed nearly unchanged, the participation rate for the whole economy fell quite sharply. [18] The ratio of not employed to employed in the whole population rose from 1.88 in 1947 to 2.33

TABLE 8

Population and Employment, 1937, 1947, and 1960
(in Thousands)

	1937	1947	1960
Total population	15,933	19,022	26,085
Total employment	5,783	6,590	7,833
Ratio of not employed	1.76	1.88	2.33
Argiculture	4,020	4,075	4,406
Industry	337	589	771
Services	1,386	1,927	2,656
Total adults/males[a]	4,806	5,761	7,333
Employment, adults/males[a]	4,457	5,246	6,594
Ratio of not employed to employed	.08	.10	.11
Agriculture	2,976	3,139	3,560
Industry	330	514	715
Services	1,151	1,593	2,318

[a]Males ages fifteen and over.

Source: Donald C. Mead, Growth and Structural Change in the Egyptian Economy (Homewood, Illinois: Richard D. Irwin, Inc., 1967), p. 33, Table 2.9.

in 1960. In terms of dependents--of adult male workers only--the
rise was only about 13 percent. One result of this is that the average
employed worker had nearly 25 percent more dependents in 1960 than
in 1947.

Another way of looking at the manpower and labor-force situation
in Egypt is to compare the 1960 census returns with the results of
the sample surveys of the labor force. [19] Between 1957 and 1960 the
Department of Statistics and Census carried on thirteen rounds of a
nationwide sample survey. In these surveys, manpower was defined
as the proportion of the population whose energy could be used in
economic activity. This excluded the very young (under six, and from
1961 those under twelve) as well as disabled persons and those over
sixty-five. Manpower was divided into two groups: the labor force,
which includes both employed and unemployed persons, and those
outside the labor force (i. e., persons who are able to work but are
neither working nor looking for paid work). This last group included
housewives engaged in household work, full-time students, and persons
not looking for work either because they had private means of support
or because they received subsidies.

In 1960, according to the national sample survey, the labor
force amounted to 6 million persons. This compares with 7. 7 million
recorded in the population census (see Table 7). The difference of
1. 7 million is due to several factors. For one thing, the sample

TABLE 9

Labor Force and Manpower, 1957-58, 1959, and 1960

	Labor force		Manpower		Total
	Number in Millions	% to Total Population	Number in Millions	% to Total Population	Population in Millions
Average of first four surveys (1957-58)	7. 0	29. 7	18. 1	76. 6	23. 6
Round 5 (1959)	6. 8	28. 6	18. 3	76. 6	23. 8
Round 13 (1960)	6. 0	25. 0	18. 8	77. 7	24. 2

Source: B. Hansen and G. Marzouk, Development and Economic
Policy in the U. A. R. (Egypt) (Amsterdam: North Holland Publishing
Co., 1965), p. 35, Table 2. 9.

surveys estimated the total population at 24 million, or 9 percent lower than the total recorded in the population census. This is because the sample surveys used as their frame the population count of 1957, which was an underestimate. The figures in Table 9 also indicate that while total manpower increased by 600,000 during the period covered by the surveys, thus remaining stable in relation to total population, the labor force fell by about 1 million between the 1957-58 surveys and the 1960 surveys. This drop can be explained by two major factors. The first is the decrease in the number of employed children under twelve from 248,000 in the first four surveys to only 39,000 in survey number 13. Second, it seems that in the more recent surveys the interviewers excluded unpaid females working mainly in agricultural field work. As a result, the number of female workers fell from 718,000 in the first four surveys to 253,000 in the last survey.[20] The fact that these differences seriously impaired comparison of the returns of sample surveys over time led demographers to prefer working with the adjusted figures of the first four rounds. Marzouk and Hansen raised the average returns of the first four rounds by 11 percent to take into account the downward bias in the frame (9 percent) as well as the rise in employment during the two years after they were made. The resulting adjusted figures were in much closer agreement with the 1960 census results, not only for the total labor force, but also for distribution by sector.

TABLE 10

Employment According to Labor Force Surveys and
Population Census, 1957-58 and 1960
(in Thousands)

	Labor Force Surveys		1960 Population Census (Adjusted)
	Average 1957-58	1957-58 Adjusted Upwards by 11 Percent	
Agriculture	3,929	4,322	4,406
Industry and construction	764	840	930
Services	2,199	2,418	2,398
Unidentifiable, not reported	138	152	--
Total	7,029	7,732	7,734

Source: B. Hansen and G. Marzouk, Development and Economic Policy in the U.A.R. (Egypt) (Amsterdam: North Holland Publishing Co., 1965), p. 36, Table 2.10.

For industrial employment, the 1957-58 figures, after adjustment, are still lower than the 1960 figures by 11 percent, while for agriculture and services, the agreement is good. The apparent difference between labor force sample surveys and the census returns must be borne in mind in subsequent discussions of industrial employment.

NOTES

1. U.A.R. Central Statistical Committee, Population Trends in the U.A.R. (Cairo, 1962), p. 3.

2. Al-Ahram (Cairo, November 27, 1970).

3. A. E. Sarhan, "Mortality Trends in the United Arab Republic," Proceedings of the World Population Conference (4 vols.; New York: United Nations, 1967), II, 358-60, Table 1.

4. For a discussion of the "miraculous" decline in the death rate in the underdeveloped areas during the postwar period, see George J. Stolwitz, "A Century of International Mortality Trends," Population Studies, IX, 1 (July, 1955), 24-55, and X, 1 (July, 1956), 17-42.

5. For a discussion of the reporting of births and deaths, see U.A.R. Department of Statistics and Census, Vital Statistics (Cairo, annual), Introduction to vol. 1.

6. U.A.R. Central Agency for Public Mobilization and Statistics, Population Increase in the U.A.R. and Its Deterrents to Development (Cairo; 1966), p. 85.

7. Clyde V. Kiser, "The Demographic Position of Egypt," Milbank Memorial Fund Quarterly, XXII, 4 (October, 1944), 97; M. A. El-Badry "Some Aspects of Fertility in Egypt," Milbank Memorial Fund Quarterly, XXIV (January, 1956), 34, 22-43; and Janet Abu-Lughod, "Urban-Rural Differences as a Function of the Demographic Transition," American Journal of Sociology, LXIX (March, 1964), 476-90. Dissenting from this view is Girgis Marzouk, "Fertility of the Urban and Rural Population in Egypt," L'Egypte Contemporaine, XLVIII (1957), 27-34.

8. M. A. El-Badry, "Trends in the Components of Population Growth in the Arab Countries of the Middle East: A Survey of Present Information," Demography, II (1965), 149-51.

9. Hanna Rizk, "Fertility Patterns in Selected Areas in Egypt" (unpublished Ph.D. dissertation, Princeton University, 1959); his

"Social and Psychological Factors Affecting Fertility in the U.A.R.,"
Marriage and Family Living, XXV (February, 1963), 69-73; and
Janet Abu-Lughod, "The Emergence of Differential Fertility in
Urban Egypt," Milbank Memorial Fund Quarterly, XLIII, 2 (April,
1965), 235-53.

10. U.A.R. Central Agency for Public Mobilization and Statistics, op. cit., p. 85.

11. W. Peterson, "The Demographic Transition in the Nether-
lands," American Sociological Review, XXV, 3 (June, 1960), 341.

12. For a fairly extensive discussion of the relation between
economic development and fertility that contrasts Malthusian theory
with transition theory, see D. Heer, "Economic Development and
Fertility," Demography, III, 2 (1966), 423-44.

13. El-Badry, "Trends in the Components of Population Growth
in the Arab Countries of the Middle East: A Survey of Present Information," p. 156.

14. U.A.R., Central Agency for Public Mobilization and Statistics, op. cit., p. 107.

15. M. R. El-Shanawany, "The First National Life Table of
Egypt," L'Egypte Contemporaine, 62 (1956), 209-69; Kiser, op. cit.,
pp. 383-408; M.A. El-Badry, "Some Demographic Measurements for
Egypt Based on the Stability of Census Age Distribution," The Milbank
Memorial Fund Quarterly, XXXIII, 3 (July, 1955), 268-305; S. H.
Abdel-Aty, "Life Table Functions for Egypt Based on Model Life
Tables and Quasi-Stable Population Theory," The Milbank Memorial
Fund Quarterly, XXXIX, 2 (April, 1961), 350-77; A. G. Abdel Rahman,
The Egyptian National Life Tables No. 2 (Cairo: Government Press,
1948); R. Makar, The Egyptian National Life Table No. 3 for 1947
(Cairo: Government Press, 1957); and U.A.R. Central Statistical
Committee, Population Trends in the United Arab Republic (Cairo,
1961).

16. El-Badry, "Trends in the Components of Population
Growth in the Arab Countries of the Middle East: A Survey of Present
Information," p. 158

17. For a discussion of the adjustment procedures, see: U.A.R.
Department of Statistics and Census, Population Census, 1960 (Cairo,
1963), Introduction to vol. XI.

18. For more elaborate description of trends, see: Donald
C. Mead, Growth and Structural Change in the Egyptian Economy,

(Homewood, Ill.: Richard D. Irwin, Inc., 1967), pp. 32-35.

19. For a good description of the survey and an analysis of the early rounds in 1957, see: A. M. N. El-Shafei, '' The Current Labor Force Sample Survey in Egypt (U. A. R.), '' International Labour Review, LXXXII, 5 (November, 1960), 432-49.

20. Bent Hansen and Girgis Marzouk, Development and Economic Policy in U. A. R. (Egypt) (Amsterdam: North Holland Publishing Co., 1965), p. 36.

2

The relationship between the number of economically active persons and the size of the total population in Egypt is influenced by a number of social and economic variables. Among the most important are the status of women, the extent of child labor, the general levels of health and nutrition of the population, and labor legislation. The changes in the size of the economically active population are not equivalent to variations in the supply of labor, because a number of additional factors determine the relationship between these two variables. These factors include the following: education, vocational training and apprenticeship; amount of working time and labor movement; and the effects of the activities of trade unions.

THE SUPPLY OF WORKERS

The Status of Women

Like other developing societies, Egypt has inherited a tradition of male domination. Among other things, this tradition has emphasized the seclusion of women and the restriction of their life to the home. The emancipation of Egyptian women has come gradually and does not show such sharp breaking points as in some other Islamic countries.[1] In Egypt today the traditional complex of male domination and female restriction is opposed by two strong trends toward improving the status of women.[2] The first of these is the long-time trend toward increasing the educational status of women.

The second trend is of a more recent origin: after a decade of declining emphasis on female subjugation, the revolutionary government came out openly in the national charter of 1962 and explicitly supported

42

equality of the sexes.[3] The government preceded this official position
with a number of measures designed to improve women's status in the
society. Among these measures were the right to vote and the right
to membership in the cabinet and the national assembly.

Despite these two trends, Egyptian society is still largely a
traditional one as far as male dominance is concerned. The low status
of adult women is indicated by an illiteracy rate of 84 percent, and the
small proportion of women who are employed outside the home (4 percent, according to the 1960 census). Comparable figures for men are
57 percent illiterate and 55 percent employed outside the home. Further progress toward real emancipation will depend on the continued
expansion in girls' education, legislation regarding marriage and
divorce, and the availability of employment opportunities for women
outside the home.

The most impressive gains for the movement towards women's
emancipation in Egypt were achieved through the channel of education.
The statistics are clear and indicate a very rapid increase in girls'
enrollment at the different levels of education. In 1960, approximately
50 percent of the girls of elementary school age were in school. In the
preparatory school age group (thirteen to fifteen), about 10 percent
were in school; in the secondary school age group (sixteen to eighteen),
about 6 percent were enrolled. By 1965-66 these proportions had been
increased to 58 percent for the elementary school age groups and to 9
percent for the secondary age group. The number of girls enrolled in
the university between the years 1953-54 and 1965-66 increased from
4,729 to 28,640, approximately a six-fold increase. By comparison,
male university enrollment increased from 49,360 in 1953-54 to
140,143 in 1965-66, only a three-fold increase.[4] While these figures
show that female enrollment continues to lag behind that of males at
all levels of education, they also reveal that the gap between them is
narrowing rapidly. The quantitative advancements in girls' education
are believed to be matched by qualitative ones. All observers agree
that the work of the schoolgirls compares very favorably with that of
the schoolboys at every level of education.[5]

However, the main question to be considered in connection with
the education of women and with the level and character of their training is this: What have women to offer as workers? To a very large
extent the answer depends on their preparation for work, and in Egypt,
unfortunately, this side of a girl's life is not yet taken seriously. The
problem lies mainly in the nonvocational nature of the training generally
received by women. Outside of agriculture, the employment problem
of women centers around two cases. First, girls and young women
are entering the work force without any kind of vocational qualification
and often with only a fragmentary general education. Second, women

with a high standard of academic education are seeking employment unrelated to the present needs of national development.

The training of women in rural areas for gainful activity constitutes the key problem of female participation in the economic life in most parts of Egypt. One reason for this may be the general labor situation. In a country where manpower is abundant and underutilized, and the major single factor which hinders women's emancipation, as one writer commented, "is the widespread unemployment and under-employment of men, "6 it would be unrealistic to prepare girls and women to compete with boys and men in their world of work.

Education has done much to raise the status of Egyptian women, but changes in the divorce laws and contemplated alterations in marriage laws would probably achieve more, provided they could be effectively enforced. A number of proposals have been under consideration to update the marriage and divorce laws in order to grant more rights to women. Among these proposals were raising the legal age of marriage, making polygamy illegal except in cases of necessity (i.e., where the wife is sterile or suffers from an incurable disease), making divorce more difficult by requiring any husband who wishes to divorce his wife to obtain court permission, and abolishing what is called Bait Eitah or the House of Obedience Law, whereby a husband can summon the police to force a wife who has left him to return. The incorporation of some of these proposals in laws will undoubtedly affect the superior authority which men formerly retained over women, especially in matters of divorce. Any effects of these measures are expected to be long range, since the enforcement of such laws will depend on many factors in the Egyptian society. Prominent among these factors is the desire and the ability of women themselves to appeal to the law to guard their rights. Their severe economic dependency on their husbands and/or their fathers or brothers would always give them a limited voice even in such very intimate affairs of their personal life. However, these measures would no doubt help immensely to improve the position of women in Egyptian society.

As things now stand, two facts stand out with regard to female employment in Egypt. First, comparative census data show that Egypt has one of the lowest female labor force participation rates in the world. The crude female activity rates are reported to be 4.8 in 1960 in comparison to 24.6 in the United States and 27.9 in India. [7] Second, among women who are actively engaged in some kind of economic activity, the vast majority are engaged in agriculture and personal services. To illustrate, 1960 census data put the percentage of females working in agriculture at 47 percent of the total female labor force and those working in services at 42 percent. The remaining 11 percent were distributed in all other branches of employment.

TABLE 11

Sectoral Distribution of Female Labor Force, 1960

Sector	Total Labor Force	Female Labor Force	Percent	Percent of Female Labor Force in Sector to Total Female Labor Force
Agriculture	4,405,227	270,602	6.14	47.0
Commerce	630,260	27,644	5.97	6.5
Industry	704,279	34,526	3.48	4.3
Transportation	256,676	2,474	0.96	0.043
Construction	157,652	585	0.37	0.001
Electricity and gas	36,349	277	0.76	0.0001
Mining and quarrying	20,880	112	0.54	---
Services	1,348,766	240,049	17.80	41.7

Source: U.A.R. Department of Statistics and Census, Population Census, 1960, 11 (Cairo, 1962), Table 30.

Several factors account for the concentration of working women in agriculture, the most relevant of which are the following: (1) most agricultural operations are simple and do not require any training or skills; (2) a great part of the female agricultural labor force is composed of young girls whose low skills fit the requirements of farm labor; (3) the wages paid for female labor in agriculture are far less than the wages paid for male labor; (4) female employment in agriculture is of a seasonal nature and does not require separation from the home for long periods; and (5) legislative restrictions on the amount of hours worked are not enforced in agriculture, especially for females and children, which frequently results in their working extra hours, often without pay.

The employment of women in the industrial sector dates back as far as the early 1920's, when they were first employed in the textile industry. Their early employment was motivated mainly by the desire for cheap labor which could be easily exploited. Employment in industry remained closed for women with a university education for a number of reasons. First, under the British occupation, industrial establishments generally refused to employ Egyptian women with higher education, preferring to employ foreign personnel instead. Second, the wages offered to them were incredibly low and the opportunities for promotion were limited. Third, opportunities were available for nonindustrial employment, such as teaching and social services, where they could receive the same wages as men. Fourth, the laws which regulated the employment of Egyptians in mixed capital industrial establishments, while stipulating that 75 percent of the total employment be allotted to Egyptians, did not specify any portion of this percentage to be reserved for university graduates.

Women's employment has entered a new phase since the 1952 revolution and serious efforts are now geared to encourage their entry into the world of work. Perhaps one of the most important steps in this direction which has recently received some attention is the development of cottage industry. The allocation of 5.5 million Egyptian pounds to promote the cottage industry in rural areas in the first five-year plan was no doubt a step creating work for women in the rural areas. At the present, several ministries and institutes proliferate a number of programs geared to promote rural industry. The eventual success or failure of these schemes is yet to be judged.

Outside of agriculture and cottage industries, employment for females will be greatly affected by a perceptible rise in their skills which, in turn, depends upon the government vocational policy. Expansion in wage-earning employment for women, and especially for married women, entails some enlargement of part-time employment as well as development of child care facilities. The government efforts on these three fronts--vocational policy, part-time employment, and child care facilities--seem to be encouraging.

In conclusion, Egyptian women have entered the world of work, yet still represent a marginal type in that world. Apart from agriculture, the sharp competition between men and women often tends to deprive the latter of work opportunities in modernized industry at a time when the gradual mechanization of small industries tends to lead to the replacement of women workers by men. Moreover, while the service sector and seasonal activities continue to provide employment opportunities for women, these are frequently unstable, subject to underemployment and to temporary unemployment. As far as equality of wages is concerned, men are paid twice as much as women in virtually every branch of economic activity, despite soaring wages during the 1960's.

In spite of serious disadvantages as far as employment opportunities and types of work to be performed, women are gradually assuming a growing role in the economic life of Egypt. Yet, in the final analysis, it remains true that many aspects of the Egyptian social, economic, and demographic structure have to be changed before women achieve a significant place in the employment structure. Cultural and personality factors are equally important. A high degree of opposition, especially from older generations, toward women's emancipation-- in particular, toward their work outside the home--is expected in a society which prescribed male domination for centuries. As one observer stated, "There is much in the near eastern tradition and in the psychology of men that stands in the way of this trend."[8]

Child Labor

The exceptionally low cut-off age of five and six in the definition of the labor force in the Egyptian census stems from the simple fact that child labor has long been an integral and numerically important part of the Egyptian labor force. Children and young persons are, as a general rule, employed in fairly large numbers. This is an entirely normal situation in a country with a relatively unmechanized economy and in which many children never go to school at all.

In absolute terms, the number of young people under fifteen who are listed as employed has continued to rise slowly. This has occurred in spite of laws passed in 1959 forbidding the employment of children under the age of twelve. In relative terms, however, there is a declining trend, especially in male child labor. For instance, the percentage of the labor force made up of males under fifteen decreased from 22 percent in 1937 to only 12 percent in 1960.[9]

As is the case with women, the bulk of the child labor in Egypt is employed in agriculture and services. The demand for young people to work in agriculture is highly seasonal, reaching a peak in June for planting rice and combatting cotton worms. There is a second reason in September, when cotton is picked.

The second major sector where child labor is prevalent is the service sector. Most young people working in this sector are employed in personal services. Between 1937 and 1947, the number of employed males under fifteen rose from 25,155 to 48,741; between 1947 and 1960, it declined to 29,333.[10]

The extent of child participation in economic activities differs in Egypt from rural to urban localities. Child labor in rural areas is much higher than in urban areas. However, in urban areas, child labor seems to be spread in large urban centers more so than in towns. A substantial decrease in the labor force participation of young people has taken place since 1957, especially in rural areas and small towns. Increased school enrollment is no doubt a major cause of this trend.[11]

Rural-urban differences of young persons' participation in the labor market reflect the type of economic activities prevalent in both the city and the village. However, in the major metropolitan areas, opportunities exist for work in the services and crafts industry more so than in small cities and towns.

The sex differential is the second major characteristic of child labor in Egypt. Table 12 presents percentages of the economically active population under the age of fifteen and between fifteen and nineteen by sex in the censuses of 1937, 1947, and 1960. What these figures first reveal is a slight decline in boys' participation in economic activities at both ages. Such a decline should be expected in the face of universal school enrollment in secondary and technical education.

As far as girls are concerned, however, there has been a substantial rise in the percentage of economically active girls, especially those under fifteen. If these figures are correct, it certainly indicates a pronounced increase in child labor among girls. Part of this rise is no doubt due to demographic factors (i.e., the increase in the proportion of the age group under fifteen to the total age structure of the population). But since no similar increase was noticed for boys (in fact the reverse trend was the case), the most probable explanation is that there was an actual trend to put more girls to work at these earlier ages. The fact that girls' enrollment in compulsory education lags considerably behind boys' partially explains this phenomenon. The noticeable expansion in personal services, where young girls are very much preferred as house servants, is another point to account for this rise. It is also very probable that girls were put to work by their families in agricultural activities on their farm or as paid labor to substitute for boys who went to schools. Further, the timing of the census-taking could have some bearing. The 1960 census data were

TABLE 12

Percentage of Young Workers in the Economically
Active Population, 1937, 1947, and 1960

Year	Boys		Girls	
	Under 15	15–19	Under 15	15–19
1937	11.6	12.5	11.9	11.5
1947	10.1	13.1	19.6	16.8
1960	9.6	10.6	36.5	14.4

Source: Computed by the author. 1937: International Labour Office, Yearbook of Labour Statistics, 1956 (Geneva, 1956), p. 9, Table 3; 1947: Yearbook of Labour Statistics, 1960 (Geneva, 1960), p. 12, Table 3; and 1960: Yearbook of Labour Statistics, 1962 (Geneva, 1962), p. 12, Table 3.

collected in September, a month of peak employment of girls in picking cotton. However, the figures for 1937 and 1947, which are more comparable, indicate that the increases in the percentage of young girls in the economically active female population started earlier.

The employment of children and young persons in Egyptian industry was regulated by law as early as 1933. The minimum age of admission to employment has been fixed at twelve. However, such regulations have not been enforced; they do not even apply in principle to agricultural workers nor to persons in workshops where only members of the employer's family work. Thus, a great proportion of child labor in industry was actually those boys or girls working to help their families and to learn their family trade.[12] The rationale of the laws in this regard was not to intefere with parents to safeguard the rights of their children.

Age of admission to employment in industry has been subject to certain other exceptions. Prior to the adoption of the Labor Code of 1959, the employment of children between the ages of nine and twelve was authorized in some industries (e.g., spinning, weaving, and knitting establishments). The 1959 act does not authorize any exceptions to the rule fixing the minimum employable age at twelve, but it does state that the minister of labor may specify the industries in which the employment of juveniles under fifteen or seventeen is prohibited. Some 20 operations were mentioned, including underground work in mines and quarries, the extraction of stones, the manufacturing and handling of explosives, and the manufacturing of alcoholic drinks.

Although child employment has diminished, children constitute an important--although not officially recognized--segment of the industrial labor force;[13] however, the amount of child labor in industry constitutes a very small proportion of the total child labor. The 1960 census return showed only 4 percent of males under fifteen in the labor force were in industry, as compared to 6 percent in services and 90 percent in agriculture. Since all the pressure of the society at the present is to reduce the employment of young people, it is expected that child labor in the labor force will continue to decline.

Health Conditions

Health conditions affect the relative numbers of workers and dependents, as well as the capabilities of the workers. Poor health, not only among the older workers but also within younger age groups, is well documented as a major cause of low productivity of the labor force in Egypt. As one writer has observed, "Poor health, more, perhaps, than any other single factor, is responsible for the wretchedness of the Egyptian peasants."[14]

The most salient characteristic of Egypt's health situation is the widespread prevalence of debilitating diseases. Major epidemic diseases such as malaria and typhoid fever are not as much of a threat to the country's health conditions as are the enervating parasites which infect the vast majority of the people. The most serious of these is bilharzia, a parasitic disease which reduces the productivity of the victim by 25 to 50 percent.[15] The second of these parasitic diseases is anklostoma, which as of the late 1950's was estimated to infect 30 percent of the population.[16] These diseases, which are brought about mainly by perennial irrigation problems and inadequate drainage, affect mainly rural villagers.

Medical reports indicate that bilharzia victims can be cured but must undergo a series of painful injections and a period of complete inactivity, neither of which seems within reach for most rural Egyptians.[17] The rate of reinfection is also quite high. Since the early 1950's, the government has carried on a widespread campaign to clean irrigation canals and drains. The magnitude of the task may be judged by the fact that in 1960, no less than 17,000 kilometers of irrigation canals and drains were treated against bilharzia. Another important step toward the eradication of bilharzia was the recent enlargement of the program for providing pure drinking water. In 1936 it was estimated that pure drinking water from government or municipal installations was available to 3.5 million city dwellers but not to any rural dwellers; by 1952 these figures had risen to 5 million and 2 million, respectively. By the end of the first five-year plan, in 1965, pure drinking water was available to the entire population.[18]

Although parasitic diseases are the most serious as far as labor productivity is concerned, this should not detract from the problem of infectious diseases. By far the most significant diseases in this class are typhoid and measles. The incidence of tuberculosis would appear to be very low, but it is suspected to be far more common than the figures indicate.[19]

The number of hospital beds and medical personnel convey only a very partial idea of the extent of medical facilities available. Nevertheless, they may serve a useful comparative purpose. In 1951 there were 5,200 doctors, or roughly one for every 4,000 inhabitants, and in 1964 there were 13,000, or one for every 2,000 inhabitants. In 1966 there were more than 67,000 beds in all the treatment establishments in the country, or one for every 447 inhabitants. This compares with one for every 600 inhabitants in 1952.[20]

Certain reservations, however, should be kept in mind when considering these changes. The first is that hospitals, and most medical facilities and personnel as well, are concentrated largely in

the towns, and in practice are not accessible to a considerable proportion of the population in the rural areas. Second, the presence of an
adequate medical staff and auxiliary health workers such as medical
assistants, sanitary personnel, dispensers, nurses, and midwives,
is not sufficient to deal with public health problems. Further, the
level of training of the existing staff is low. The efforts of the present
regime to improve health conditions and to enlarge medical facilities
in Egypt can be seen from the growth in the budgetary allocation for
public health. In 1951-52 the Egyptian public health budget was 10.1
million Egyptian pounds; in 1964-65 it was 44.3 million. Also, although
a start had been made before the revolution in establishing health services in rural areas, a comprehensive six-year plan was launched in
May, 1962, to establish 2,500 rural health centers, each serving
5,000 inhabitants, at a cost of about 13.5 million Egyptian pounds.[21]
By 1964 about 800 of these centers had been opened, in addition to
168 comprehensive treatment units for endemic diseases and 275
combined units which include all health sections.[22] In general,
improving standards of health are indicated by decreases in the death
and infant mortality rates, but the health problem, complicated as it
is by ignorance, widespread undernutrition or malnutrition, and lack
of medical facilities and personnel, particularly in the rural areas,
remains formidable.

Food Consumption and Nutrition

Food costs constitute an important part of total expenditures on
consumption, especially in low-income countries.[23] The effects of
changes in population size and composition on the levels and patterns
of consumption are not of immediate relevance at this point; rather,
our major concern is a description of the nature of the diet and level
of nutrition of the Egyptian people, insofar as diet and level of nutri-
tional status influence general health and levels of productivity.

Per-capita food consumption, calories per day, and the changes
which occurred in them between the years 1957-58 and 1960-61 are
shown in Table 13. The figures indicate first of all that total caloric
consumption has remained fairly constant over the years. Second, and
more significant, they reveal that a substantial proportion (roughly
70 percent) of total caloric consumption is derived from cereal, whereas there is an extremely low consumption of meat, eggs, and other
animal protein products (7 percent in 1960). According to one recent
author, this level of food consumption that has prevailed in Egypt in
the postwar years has been neither adequate, in terms of total caloric
intake, nor nutritionally balanced.[24]

TABLE 13

Per-Capita Calorie Consumption
(Calories per Day)

	1957-58	1960-61	1963-64
Total calories	2,530	2,530	2,931
Percent from cereal product	70.7	69.9	68.8
Percent from animal protein products	7.1	6.9	6.5

Source: Percents computed by author. Donald C. Mead, Growth and Structural Change in the Egyptian Economy, (Homewood, Illinois: Richard D. Irvin, Inc., 1967), p. 303, Table II-A-10; and U.A.R. Central Agency for Public Mobilization and Statistics, Population Increase in the U.A.R. and Its Deterrents to Development (Cairo, 1966), p. 209, Table 91.

The lack of adequate sources of animal protein is a serious economic problem as well as dietary problem in Egypt. In the mid-1960's, it was estimated that in order to raise daily per-capita consumption of animal protein from roughly 12 to 30 grams, an annual increase in livestock value of 240 million Egyptian pounds would be needed (an increase equal to about one-third of the annual animal production).[25] Such estimates show the magnitude of the problem, especially in the face of rapid population increase. Obviously, the importation of meat and other similar animal protein products would place a heavy strain on the economy and would reduce the importation of capital goods badly needed for development.

It has been suggested that the shortage of animal protein could be lessened by two main methods: by developing valuable vegetable protein mixtures, and by enriching certain vegetables and cereals with the badly needed amino acids.[26] Other experts have emphasized the need for numerous production and marketing measures to improve the patterns of food consumption. In the meantime, however, the diet of the average Egyptian suffers from serious protein deficiency. Among the poorer elements of the population, the inadequate diet is due not only to the unavailability of many foodstuffs, but also to the low purchasing power of these people. Thus, such commodities as milk, meat, and

eggs are not consumed because they are too expensive. Finally, diet
is also the result of prejudice and faulty food habits which education
has not yet succeeded in eradicating.

Labor Legislation

Working conditions were regulated by legislation as early as 1890
in Egypt. With the advance of modern industry during the 1930's and
1940's, a number of legislative acts laid down provisions concerning
such things as minimum conditions of work (regulating individual con-
tractors of employment, allowing for the organization of trade unions
and governing labor-employer relations, etc.). In spite of the existence of an extensive body of labor legislation in Egypt, at midcentury
only a very small proportion of the Egyptian labor force actually benefited from the rights and protections envisioned by the law. This was
in large part due to the fact that agricultural laborers and workers in
the public sector were not covered by such legislation.

Since 1952 the government has extended other forms of protection
to the workers. In April, 1959, a comprehensive, unified labor code
repealed most of the labor laws that were introduced between 1933
and 1953. The most remarkable feature of this code is its extension
of coverage to all workers, including agricultural workers. The code
includes provisions for the formation of trade unions, consultation,
arbitration and collective bargaining procedures, hours of work,
wage fixing and inspection, placement of workers and dismissal
procedures, apprenticeship and vocational rehabilitation, and provisions for the employment of women and juveniles.

A detailed and comprehensive account of the Labor Code of
1959 and its amendments exists elsewhere. [27] Our purpose here is
to point out some of the provisions which are directly related to the
employment policy of the government. One important aspect is the
restriction which the code imposed on the freedom of management to
seek labor for industrial establishment. The establishment of official
placement offices was a primary step toward organizing the labor
market and toward preventing of nepotism, exploitation, and subjective
selection. Methods of dismissal also came under scrutiny and revi-
sions.

An important amendment to the 1959 law established a minimum
wage for workers in government and nationalized industry. An important provision of this amendment regulated working hours and restricted
the employment of industrial workers to one enterprise only. [28]

The organization of the labor market and employment procedures were enhanced further by a number of provisions which dealt with labor administration, industrial manpower, labor and management, conditions of employment, civil service, alien workers, and wages and supplemental payments.

The labor code also embodied a number of provisions which aimed at improving the qualitative aspect of the labor force. The law specifies in detail the responsibility of government in instituting a pattern whereby its own power, control, and direction are clearly felt in all fields of labor training;[29] the regulations concerning safety at work, workmen's compensation, and social security ought to be considered in this regard. Despite the extension of the body of social-welfare legislation in scope and coverage, the government had not found it feasible to extend this legislation to agricultural laborers and to many in the services sector.[30] By the government's own estimate, only 21 percent of the total labor force benefited from social-welfare legislation at the end of 1962.[31] In 1963, about 775,000 workers in industry and services participated in social insurance, in addition to 429,000 civil servants already covered, which meant a total of approximately 1.2 million workers out of a total labor force of nearly 6.6 million covered by the government's provisions for social security.[32]

A comprehensive social insurance legislation was passed in March, 1964. It extended previous legislation to include health and unemployment insurance, in addition to the existing system of old-age, disability, survivor's, and work-injuries insurance. The total number of workers covered by all types of insurance under the 1964 laws was estimated at 1.25 million workers under the provisions of the social insurance law, 600,000 under the government insurance system, and 3 million under health insurance plans for workers in nationalized companies, self-employed persons, government workers, and their families.[33] As late as 1966, the government was contemplating a plan to provide insurance for agricultural workers through the agricultural cooperatives, and by implementing the provisions of the 1964 legislation to agricultural workers. Eligible workers would be tenant farmers with holdings of less than 3 feddans, which would mean that another 3.5 million workers would be covered.

One might conclude that the Egyptian worker's basic rights are at present very well protected by legislation. However, it remains to be seen how the laws will be applied now that the government has become the nation's major employer. Although labor inspection services have increased substantially in Egypt, it is necessary to keep in mind that, in practice, most of the labor laws represent targets to be achieved gradually rather than required standards to be enforced. The government did not press hard to enforce the provisions to regulate agricultural wages because of its fear that an increase in wages might cause a rise in agricultural prices in the international market. Such a price increase would reduce Egypt's competitiveness and subsequently the value of exports. The weakness of trade unions in the agricultural sectors, as a result of the difficulty of organizing a mass of illiterate workers, left this unfortunate group, which constituted about 40 percent of the rural population, without real gains.

Some observers believed that a few of the protective measures of the labor code could have had a harmful effect on productivity,[34] such as the curtailment of the right of management to fire unproductive or redundant labor. Government intervention in the labor market has also been criticized on several points.[35] For one thing, some of the labor law restrictions are believed to have hampered labor mobility; for example, no employee can be transferred from one firm to another without the agreement of his original employer. Labor mobility has been further hampered by the introduction of an elaborate system of jobs and wage classifications, and by government control of the employment of certain categories of skilled manpower (such as engineers and doctors) and the directing of these graduates to work in specific places. Even government intervention in the labor market to minimize differences in the wage structure may limit the movement of labor from one firm to the other.

The enforcement of the labor laws affected the employment structure in two different directions. No doubt, some provisions have expanded employment figures very noticeably (especially the 1961 laws covering industrial employment). Other provisions, especially those geared toward controlling the employment of women and children, have definitely contributed toward a reduction in the rate of increase in the size of the total labor force, a trend that is likely to continue. In other words, some legislative measures which are aimed at proving the qualitative aspects of the labor force tend to reduce its size.

One important aspect of labor legislation which deserves separate attention because of its great impact on the volume of employment is the regulation concerning hours of work. It is only in the industrial sector that the consideration of the changes which occurred in work time becomes actually relevant, although transportation and construction also come under this discussion. Hours of work in agriculture and personal services have not been subject in practice in any legislative restrictions. The nature of work, the existence of substantial underemployment in these sectors, as well as the large proportion of women and children working them make it impossible as well as analytically irrelevant to talk about reductions in work time in agriculture and personal services.

The Labor Code of 1959 set up a 48-hour work week--a six-day week of eight hours a day. A government decree of July, 1961, further reduced the work week to 42 hours in nationalized industry, and in May, 1964, the minister of labor passed a decree fixing the minimum working hours for all workers at 42 hours a week.[36] As the nationalization of industry progressed, nearly all workers in that sector have come to be covered by the above limitation of work time.

These regulations are strictly enforced in industry. The law stipulates that part-time employment as well as authorization of overtime requires permission from the Ministry of Industry. Workers are allowed a maximum of 12 hours overtime a week.

The 1961 legislation which fixed the maximum working day in industry at seven hours was received with great apprehension from management. A fear of a decrease in productivity was voiced in opposition to the law. However, the minister of industry asserted that productivity actually increased "because productivity of a worker working nine hours is much less the last two hours of his working day than of the seven hours he is now working."[37] The objective of the 1961 law fixing the maximum working day at seven hours was to increase employment rapidly. After one year of the law, the minister of labor stated that this measure had resulted in the employment of an additional 35,000 workers.[38]

Labor Organizations

Labor organizations were introduced in Egypt at the beginning of this century.[39] The labor movement has always been regarded with suspicion and hostility by the authorities, who have viewed it as a potential threat to national security.[40] It was only during World War II that the movement received qualified legal recognition. Between 1942 and 1952 the labor movement struggled to achieve a greater role as the workers' representative and bargaining agent. In 1952, the Republican Government granted agricultural workers the right to organize. This revision was in line with the new regime's desire to widen the base of support for its policies and to weaken the control of the landed aristocracy as a complementary move to land redistribution. Employees in the public sector, however, were still prohibited from organizing a trade union.

The labor code introduced in 1959 restructured the organization of trade unions and permitted any general union to set branch unions at the level of each governate and union committees at the establishment level.[41] Such a policy has strengthened and unified the movement and done away with small separate units. In March, 1964, Presidential

Decree No. 62 extended the right of unionism to government workers--workers who were denied that right under earlier laws. There were two crucial periods in the enlargement of union movements: the period which immediately followed World War II, and the early 1960's.

The distribution of trade union organizations and membership, according to economic sectors, is presented in Table 14. These figures indicate the relative strength of the union movement in industry, especially in contrast to agriculture, where the labor movement is still very retarded.

Students of the labor movement in Egypt differ in their assessment of the strength and independence of the movement. Some observers believe that the Egyptian labor unions are completely government controlled, and that Egypt has no real foundation for an independent labor movement. To support their argument, they cite the facts that the movement has been always nonpolitical and that it has never enjoyed the right either to bargain collectively or to strike, except with permission from the government. [42] Still other students have asserted that Egyptian unionism has not always developed according to plan, and has proved to be a strong agency for mobilizing and

TABLE 14

Number of Trade Union Organizations and Membership
by Economic Sector (As of October 31, 1963)

Economic Sector	General Union	Branch Unions	Trade Union Committees	Membership
Agriculture	1	7	4	2,897
Industry	30	142	591	289,582
Commerce	5	21	53	17,408
Service (including transportation)	23	119	237	98,679
Total	59	288	885	408,566

Source: U.A.R., Ministry of Labor, Trade Unions in the U.A.R. (Cairo, 1964), p. 17, Table 3.

managing worker protest. [43] In point of fact, union-employer relationships are limited by the authority of the state as a third party. Neither
unions nor employers are free to negotiate as they please. With the
growth of labor organizations, especially in recent years, the pater-
nalistic relationship by which management has always attempted to
recognize but to appease union activity has changed to a situation of
mutual accommodation on an equal footing. [44]

Most observers agree that the labor movement is gaining some
strength in Egypt; nevertheless, they see that most of the improvements
in the status and conditions of workers do not emanate from trade union
activity but come about from state enforcement of the comprehensive
labor legislation. [45] Some observers point to the limitations imposed
on the workers' right to strike as a real loss to the movement. [46]
Others believe that the system has worked reasonably well so far.
As one observer commented, "There is no ground swell of industrial
discontent, and loss of productivity from worker-coddling has to be
set against what might have been lost through go-slow strikes and
walk-outs." [47]

The nationalization movement in industry and in most commercial and business enterprises has increased the state's responsibility
toward the labor movement. The fact that the state is today the major
employer has not altered the encouragement the working classes
received from the government to organize. The government still
retains the overall responsibility for most of the matters pertaining
to workers' welfare. Workers appear to have benefited from direct
government intervention in the form of labor laws and legislation
more than from any union activity. [48] Yet unions perform the important task of ensuring the enforcement of these laws. Thus, growth
of the labor movement in size and strength no doubt exerts an indirect
pressure on the government policies.

Education and Vocational Training

During the twentieth century, Egypt has made substantial progress in reducing its illiteracy rate, especially among males, although
in absolute terms the number of people who cannot read or write has
continued to increase. [49] Further evidence of the decline of illiteracy
is presented in Table 15, which contains data on illiteracy rates by
age groups. The declining rate of illiteracy among the youngest age
groups between 1947 and 1960 reflects the extensive literacy campaign
which the government has pursued since 1952. By contrast, there
were no major changes in the level of illiteracy for the groups age
fifteen and over. The fight against illiteracy has been slow because
of the fact that although the number of pupils and students rose by

almost 120 percent from 1947 to 1960, their share of the age group comprising pupils between the ages of five and nineteen remained almost constant at 35 percent.

Government efforts since 1952 to decrease illiteracy are clear from the figures on enrollment trends at the compulsory attendance ages (six to twelve). In Table 16, for example, it is seen that the level of enrollment at the ages rose from 57 percent in 1953-54 to 83 percent in 1965-66 for boys, and from 35 to 56 percent for girls. Although the position of the latter has improved substantially, female school enroll-ment still lags considerably behind male enrollment. According to official statements, it is hoped that full enrollment for all children in the ages of compulsory education will be attained by the mid-1970's.

The changes that have occurred in the different levels of

TABLE 15

Percentage of Illiteracy by Age Group, 1947 and 1960

Year of Census or Survey	Age Group	Percentage of Illiteracy:		
		Total	Male	Female
1947	10-14	64.2	57.5	71.5
	15-19	72.6	65.3	80.6
	20-24	75.5	64.8	86.0
	25-34	70.6	66.3	91.6
	35-44	82.0	60.7	94.7
	45-54	83.4	70.8	96.2
	55-64	85.9	73.8	97.1
	65+	89.2	79.2	97.8
1960	10-14	59.6	50.2	69.6
	15-19	72.9	63.6	81.9
	20-24	77.3	66.5	86.8
	25-34	78.2	63.3	90.1
	35-44	80.8	67.6	93.4
	45-54	84.8	73.5	96.0
	55-64	86.3	74.0	97.5
	65+	90.5	80.6	98.8

Source: U. N. UNESCO Statistical Yearbook, 1965 (Paris, 1965), p. 50, Table 5.

TABLE 16

Percentage of Enrollment in Compulsory Education, Selected Years From 1953 to 1966
(Numbers in Thousands)

	Estimates of Population	Boys			Girls			Total		
		In Age of Compulsory Education	Number Enrolled	Percentage	In Age of Compulsory Education	Number Enrolled	Percentage	In Age of Compulsory Education	Number Enrolled	Percentage
1953-54	22,003	1,660	949.2	57.0	1,593	553.2	34.7	3,253	1,502.4	46.0
1960-61	25,952	2,164	1,612.9	74.5	2,136	997.3	46.7	4,300	2,610.2	60.7
1961-62	26,557	2,215	1,700.1	76.8	2,187	1,054.5	48.2	4,402	2,754.6	62.6
1962-63	27,362	2,295	1,791.7	78.0	2,243	1,118.3	49.8	4,538	2,910.0	63.8
1963-64	28,290	2,381	1,918.2	80.6	2,287	1,211.5	53.0	4,668	3,129.7	67.0
1964-65	29,006	2,441	2,009.8	82.3	2,345	1,285.0	54.8	4,786	3,294.8	68.8
1965-66	29,740	2,503	2,077.9	83.0	2,404	1,339.9	55.7	4,907	3,417.8	69.7

Source: U.A.R. Central Agency for Public Mobilization and Statistics, Population Increase in the U.A.R. and Its Deterents to Development (Cairo, November, 1966), p. 196, Table 84.

education since the revolution are illustrated by the data presented in Table 17. These data leave no question that since the Republican Government came to power in 1952, one of its chief efforts in the field of education has been directed toward the expansion of technical training at all levels. This is in line with its general program for the economic development and industrialization of the country. The policy of expansion is motivated by the desire to diversify education after the elementary cycle, to reduce the pressure on general academic education, to provide other training avenues for those who cannot be absorbed in general schools, to equip boys and girls with special skills that will increase their employability and raise their income potential, and to create the needed manpower for industry, agriculture, commerce, and other services. The emphasis on the expansion of vocational training is reflected in the five-year plan of general education, where the largest allocation (about 22 million Egyptian pounds),

TABLE 17

Student Enrollment in Different Educational
Levels, 1953-54 and 1965-66

Level of Education	Enrollment (Thousands) 1953-54	1965-66	Percentage of Average Increase
Primary	1,393	3,418	145
General preparatory	349	574	64
Vocational preparatory	3	27	800
General secondary	92	209	127
Vocational secondary	19	101	432
Teachers institutes	24	49	104
Universities	54	124	130
Total	1,934	4,502	132

Source: U.A.R. Central Agency for Public Mobilization and Statistics, Population Increase in the U.A.R. and Its Deterrents to Development (Cairo, November, 1966), p. 190.

representing 35 percent of total expenditures, is devoted to vocational education.[50]

Vocational education in Egypt includes several types of schools. The most common are industrial, agricultural, and commercial schools. In addition, there are technical schools for girls (usually preparatory only) and domestic science schools (usually on the secondary level).

Industrial education experienced the most rapid expansion of any type of vocational training; and industrial training, which hardly existed in 1953-54, despite an acute need,[51] is now beginning to make some headway. Nevertheless, industrialization is now proceeding at a fairly rapid rate, and the production of the industrial technicians, both in qualitative and quantitative terms, continues to lag far behind the increasing demand.

Commercial education registered the greatest expansion after industrial training. Probably one of the most important aspects of vocational commercial training has been the increasing participation by girls. Their rising percentage and number in the secondary cycle year by year, from 495 in 1953-54 to 19,856 in 1962-63, represents a real social revolution in Egyptian society.[52] The trend seems to be a start toward bringing girls out of the seclusion of the home into the labor market and providing them with a measure of economic independence.

Agricultural education also experienced some marked gains between 1953-54 and 1962-63; enrollment in agricultural schools increased more than seven-fold, while the number of graduates increased more than twelve-fold.[53]

Another aspect of the vocational training in Egypt which should be mentioned is the apprenticeship programs carried on by the Ministry of Industry, with the cooperation of the International Labor Organization.[54] During the period from 1956 to 1960, enrollment in these programs expanded rapidly because of a great demand for their graduates to fill the needs of the first five-year plan. Since then, however, there has been a gradual decrease in enrollment resulting from a reorganization of the centers as many of them became attached to several industrial, agricultural, and commercial establishments, in order to give their students more on-the-job training.

Although the rate of expansion of general secondary education has been slow since the 1952 revolution, especially as compared with elementary education, in absolute terms it has developed fairly rapidly to absorb the ever-increasing flow of students who complete the

elementary level. This expansion in general secondary education
has caused a serious unemployment problem. This is because the
number of secondary school graduates who have not been admitted to
the universities has risen sharply in recent years. These high school
graduates are without any special skills and, therefore, are difficult
to absorb in a limited labor market. Their problem is further compounded by a number of social and economic difficulties. First, the
sociocultural climate of Egyptian society is such that once a student
receives a secondary school certificate he becomes an "urban"
person who tends to seek and accept only white-collar employment.
Second, students who come from rural communities cannot return to
work on the farms because this would be socially unacceptable, as
well as economically undesirable. Third, government departments
and business establishments are grossly overstaffed and can absorb
very few additional clerks. In an already limited labor market which
stigmatizes manual and blue-collar work, the plight of high school
graduates, ill-equipped to handle blue-collar tasks even if they existed,
is serious indeed.

There were four state universities and some 40 independent
state colleges and higher institutes in Egypt in the mid-1960's. In
addition, there was the old Al-Azhar University, and the American
University of Cairo. A significant feature of higher education in
Egypt was the maldistribution of facilities; most of the universities
were concentrated in Cairo and Alexandria. It was only in 1957 that
Asyut University was established to serve upper Egypt, while the
Delta, where the population is most heavily concentrated, is still
without a university.

The most impressive facet of the expansion of higher education
in Egypt has been in the student enrollment, which rose from 56,966
in 1953-54 to 135,462 in 1963-64. Another important aspect of the
growth in higher education is the great increase in female enrollment,
both in absolute and relative terms. Between the 1953-54 and 1961-62
academic years, the number of girls enrolled in Egyptian colleges and
universities increased more than three times, rising from 6,121 to
19,762.[55]

The rapid expansion of higher education, particularly since the
revolution, has been due to several factors. First, there has emerged
an obsessive desire of young people in every class of Egyptian society
for higher education. A second factor related to government policy,
which, in response to public pressure, enhanced the expansion in arts,
law, and commerce. Further, in order to meet the needs of the country
for trained specialists, the government promoted increased enrollment
in science, engineering, agriculture, and medicine. The need for
trained technical persons has become progressively greater in recent

years as a result of the increasing trend toward industrialization.
And third, the rapid expansion in university enrollment has been
influenced by the democratization of education in the sense that financial barriers no longer represent a serious obstacle to those who are
seriously interested in obtaining a university education. After gradually reducing tuition fees and granting extensive exemptions and gener-
ous financial aid, a presidential decree in July, 1962, made all higher
education entirely free. Financial assistance is also provided to needy
students as well as to the superior students as a recognition of excel-
lence.

In the following discussion, attention turns more directly to a
consideration of the supply and demand of professional and technical
manpower. Egypt today is a Socialistic state whose economy is moving
rapidly toward state control. The government has nationalized, or is
in the process of nationalizing, all industrial enterprises, banks,
insurance operations, the press, and all other major business establishments. The private sector, while still economically viable, has
nonetheless declined and will continue to decline in importance. The
greater part of this private sector consists of agriculture, housing
and real estate, small business, and a few other enterprises that
have a small effect on the employment market of professional and
technical manpower. For all practical purposes, the government
has become virtually the only employer of professional manpower.

The scientific community of Egypt in the early 1960's was estimated at about 3,500 persons holding graduate degrees in science,
engineering, medicine, agriculture, and other fields; the majority
(about 2,600) held doctorates. The great majority of the top scientists
were employed by the state and the universities. Less than 7 percent
were in industry or private practice.[56] In addition, there were about
35,000 Egyptians with Bachelor of Science degrees. No official statistics are yet available on the distribution by employer of holders of
Bachelor of Science degrees; however, it is generally known that the
vast majority of these specialists are employed by the government or
industry.

Nor are data available on the attrition rate among Egyptian
scientists; however, two indicators provide some evidence. First,
they are encouraged to retire at age 60, especially since the recent
adoption of social security legislation. Second is the fact, noted
above, that the great majority of scientists have been employed by
the government or by state-controlled institutions. It has been estimated that about 20 percent of the some 40,000 scientists of various
levels in Egypt in 1961 were fifty years old or over, which means
that some 8,000 new scientists will be needed over the next ten years
to replace those who will be retiring.[57]

Despite the fact that the state employs the majority of scientists, there is no official restriction in principle on the mobility of scientists between different departments, or between government and industry.[58] The only commanding position the state has is the assignment of scientists to locations and positions. In this respect, the government experiences considerable difficulty in recruiting university graduates for employment in the provinces and particularly in rural areas.

It is generally believed that Egypt is experiencing an acute shortage of scientists at all levels and of all kinds because of the programs of rapid industrialization, agricultural development, the expansion of education and university training, and the expanding need for research and defense establishments. However, this shortage is believed to be most acute in four specific areas.[59] First, there is a shortage of scientists with advanced graduate degrees to fill present and future vacancies in the colleges, universities, and research organizations. Second, a severe shortage of engineers at all levels and branches of engineering has been reported. In 1962 the shortage was estimated to be on the order of 4,000 engineers as against the 900 per year which the engineering colleges are able to produce.[60] Some of these positions can be filled even more effectively with technicians trained specifically for the job.[61] There are several indications that the severe shortage of engineers was eased somewhat in the late 1960's. This is indicated by the growing numbers of engineers who were permitted to emigrate to Canada, the United States, and other countries. Third, there is a need for teachers for industrial vocational schools. The manpower secretariat has estimated that 2,700 additional teachers will be needed in the immediate future to provide for the anticipated expansion in the industrial training program.[62] Finally, there is a shortage of science teachers on the Bachelor of Science level for general secondary schools. No statistical data are available concerning the exact magnitude of this shortage, but it is believed to be pressing.[63]

Industrialization in Egypt is also reported to suffer from a serious shortage of technicians. It is estimated that technicians could be employed at the rate of at least three technicians for one engineer.[64] According to the Manpower Secretariat, a total of 30,000 technicians were needed by 1970 to meet the needs of industry alone. If other fields are included, a figure in the magnitude of 50,000 would probably be a conservative estimate.[65] An attempt was made in 1962-63 to introduce a program for the training of technicians at the higher industrial institutes, but the proposal was rejected due to social and political pressures. Thus, despite this obvious massive need for technicians, no formal training program for such personnel exists today, aside from sporadic attempts by the Ministry of Industry and other organizations.

The adverse impact of education on employment centers chiefly on the large number of high school and university graduates being produced. So far, the educational system has produced limited numbers of the skilled workers and foremen so urgently needed for industrialization programs. Instead, it has created a surplus of high school and university graduates in such economically unproductive fields as law, liberal arts, and commercial accounting. Malcolm Kerr has pointed out two main reasons for this. First, there are the traditional attitudes which for a long time placed a high premium on membership in the genteel professions, even if such membership was economically unrewarding. Second is the lag of the educational system behind the job market.[66] The turnover of thousands of high school and university graduates every year constitutes a growing force of unusable manpower whose social and economic expectations have been raised to unrealistic levels.

The economic and social prospects of these groups have always been linked with the state, whose massive and immobile bureaucracy has operated as a national employment agency since the nineteenth century,[67] but the rapid growth of population since the turn of the century has made the bureaucracy a shrinking employment outlet. The rapid construction since 1957 of a state-owned industrial and commercial enterprise and the nationalization of all the larger businesses since 1961 have somewhat broadened job opportunities, but the rapid growth of the university-attending population has been proportionately far greater.

In terms of human resource development, Egypt seems to have two paradoxes. First, Egypt is a country which appears to be overproducing high-level manpower in terms of its stage of economic growth. In this regard, Egypt is really a semiadvanced country.[68] Second, Egypt is a country with a high level of illiteracy as compared to other countries. The appropriate education and manpower policy, therefore, should be quite different from what it has been in recent years.[69] University enrollment should be dictated by the actual demands of the job market; and the curtailment of enrollment in such programs as liberal arts, law, and commerce should go side by side with an expansion and improvement of technical education at all levels.

Egypt has been proceeding rapidly toward universal and compulsory primary education. The present government expects to reach this target in the near future. Adult education is strongly needed to stamp out illiteracy among those past primary-school age. Measures recently taken mark a start,[70] but they will have to be greatly accelerated if worthwhile results are to be obtained. Egypt's massive need for technicians can be partially filled by placing special emphasis upon in-service training in both public and private establishments.

Service in the military can be used as a training period for producing both skilled technicians and higher administrative personnel. Finally, Egypt can and should expand the use of its high-level human resources for technical-assistance activities in less-developed nations. Although the strategy of the present government is to press forward on all these fronts, the pressures which it receives from different directions make this course of action politically difficult. Therefore, Egypt's strategy of economic development would be more realistic if it ultimately evolved around an intensive use of high-level manpower.

So far in this chapter we have been concerned with the actual supply of labor, and a number of socioeconomic determinants of labor supply have been discussed. This, however, is only one aspect of the problem. In order to appreciate the labor situation fully we need also to look at the efficiency of labor. In the following section, then, labor efficiency and general productivity in the different sectors of the Egyptian economy are discussed.

LABOR EFFICIENCY AND GENERAL PRODUCTIVITY

The Industrial Sector

Most observers would agree that labor productivity in Egyptian industry, while rising rather rapidly, is still very low compared to that of advanced countries.[71] Studies of productivity per worker reveal some changes in the productivity of the industrial worker since 1944.[72]

It must be stressed here that comparison of Egyptian labor productivity with other countries is risky. Apart from the technical difficulties of measurement to be encountered in industrial comparisons, there are technological and organizational differences in the economy of each country. Nonetheless, it is accurate to say that Egypt was greatly inferior to most highly industrialized countries at midcentury.

The low efficiency of labor in Egyptian industry may be accounted for by the prevalence of low standards of health, bad housing and transportation, and illiteracy; by the fact that industry is less mechanized in Egypt than in other industrially advanced countries; by overstaffing of some Egyptian industries;[73] by a lack of technical ability and knowledge;by the high rate of absenteeism and labor turnover;[74] by industrial fatigue, and by the instability of seasonal labor.

Further, several features of the wage structure were and continue to be responsible for low productivity:[75] (1) the level of wages in industry is low in comparison to the irreduceable minimum required for maintaining efficiency; (2) wage differentials between town and country are much less marked due to the high cost of living in towns; (3) workers are paid according to the amount of time they work rather than on the basis of the amount of work they perform; (4) the existence of unemployment, total and disguised, and the inequality of bargaining power leads labor to accept any price offered for their labor power; and (5) prior to state control of most industry, the prevalence of monopoly and trade associations and the spirit of group solidarity among enterpreneurs enable them, in the absence of trade union pressure, to maintain low wages and to resist any upward trend.

There are still more factors outside of the control of the worker which tend to lower productivity of labor as compared with that of industrially advanced countries. Among them is the fact that industrial production in Egypt is handicapped by the desire to economize in the use of capital in some industries, which leads to heavy reliance on large numbers of unskilled workers in lieu of modern machinery.

The absence of control over labor, a result of the shortage of foremen, and the high number of laborers engaged in services continue to be important reasons for the low net output per worker. Viewing the problem of industrial efficiency in a more economic perspective, Hansen and Marzouk emphasized that the heart of the problem in today's Egypt is not the quality of managers or even the institutional arrangements for production in the public sector; rather, it is the question of prices.[76] Distorted prices are considered to be a more potent cause of inefficiency than are all the inadequacies of managerial and labor qualities. The analysis made by Hansen and Marzouk, which focuses primarily on the question of consumer's efficiency, shows that the government's fair-price policy encourages preferences and leads to shortages and black markets.

There are, at present, two conflicting views on the productivity of Egyptian workers. A United Nations report indicates that the low productivity of Egyptian workers is not entirely a reflection of a low capital-labor ratio; Egyptian workers are also less efficient when compared with their counterparts abroad employed in the same tasks and utilizing similar productive equipment.[77] On the other hand, an earlier report of the British Goodwill Trade Mission to Egypt held that Egyptian workers show a capacity to master mechanical operations quickly. The report stated that "under close supervision and continued instructions there appears no reason why output per man hour should not reach a more competitive level."[78] The conflicting views on labor productivity in Egypt are even pertinent in describing the character and adaptability of the Egyptian worker himself. Thus, Charles

Issawi believes that "the Egyptian worker has shown himself to be intelligent and adaptable and given better leadership and training, as well as more favorable living conditions, there is no reason why he should not equal those of other countries."[79] On the other hand, Patrick O'Brien cites "the rural character of the industrial labor force, antipathy among the educated to work at the bench, the nepotism of managers, among others, as constituting a complex of cultural and sociological obstacles to raise industrial efficiency."[80]

The Service Sector

Any attempt to evaluate the actual trends of labor productivity in this composite sector requires a closer look at its major components. With the exception of a few government activities, such as health and educational services, where specific services are rendered and can be evaluated, it is very difficult to evaluate productivity changes in the government sector. However, the fact that over 40 percent of all new jobs in the economy between 1947 and 1960 were in the government sector alone leads one to suspect that this large an increase in government employment was actually an excessive overstaffing of the government departments. Many observers have, in fact, commented on the practice of overhiring and the resulting underemployment of workers in the government sector.[81]

Productivity of labor in commerce suffered a noticeable decline between 1937 and 1947. Some estimates put this decline at 14 percent.[82] The 1947-60 period, however, showed a noticeable rise in labor productivity in this sector. Output per worker was estimated to have risen by more than 50 percent during this latter period.[83] Three factors were considered responsible for this rise: first, an increasing utilization of the underemployed labor in this sector since 1947, following a period of rapid expansion during the 1937-47 decade; a decline in the proportion of those who were self-employed between 1947 and 1960, which implies a shift of workers from small family stores to larger enterprises; and the decline of less-productive groups (e.g., women and young people) from 14.9 to 8.5 percent of total employment in trade. Labor productivity in the commercial sector was estimated to have decreased by 13 percent during the 1937-47 period, and to have increased an estimated 30 percent between 1947 and 1960.[84] In the case of transportation, the 1947-60 rise was largely attributed to the substantial capital investment in this sector and a noticeable updating of the traditional means of transportation to modern ones. It is important to note that the 1937-47 decade was also a period of rapid expansion in employment in the sector.

During the first five-year plan, 1960-65, productivity per worker in the total service sector increased by 19.5 percent, while average

wages per worker increased by 26.4 percent. This compares to
increases in industry of 9 percent in output per worker and 23 percent
in average wages per worker. Only in the transportation sector was
the percentage increase in average output per worker (34.4 percent)
greater than the percentage increase in wages per worker (21.6 percent). Employment increases coupled with wage increases were
mainly responsible for declining productivity per worker in the service
sector during the five-year plan.

It is customary to break construction into house building, other
building (government offices, factories, etc.) and all other construction
work (transport facilities, dams and irrigation work, etc.). In terms
of employment, the great majority of the workers in the construction
sector--over 80 percent in 1960 and close to 70 percent in earlier
censuses--were engaged in the construction of buildings, a great part
of which was house building.[85] The growth of the construction sector
in general, especially after World War II, continued to be impressive,
even after several government interventions to limit rent in order to
redirect investment in industry.[86] There are no precise estimates
of the actual rise in labor productivity in the period under study.
Nevertheless, the increase in output between 1947 and 1960 was substantially higher than the 45 percent increase in employment during

TABLE 18

Average Output and Wages per Worker in the Service
Sector During the First Five-Year Plan,
1959-60 and 1964-65
(in Egyptian Pounds at Current Prices)

Sector		1959-60	1964-65	Total Increase	Percent Increase for Base Year
Total services	A[a]	350.0	418.4	68.4	19.5
	B[b]	149.9	189.5	39.6	26.4
Total industry	A	1,805.7	1,968.0	162.3	9.0
	B	147.6	181.3	33.7	22.8

[a]A-Average output per worker
[b]B-Average wages per worker
Source: U.A.R. Central Agency for Public Mobilization and
Statistics, Population Increase in the U.A.R. and Its Deterrents to
Development (Cairo, 1966), pp. 186 and 187, Table 82

the same period, and this indicates a rise in labor productivity in
this sector during the postwar period. [87]

The marked expansion of employment in personal and other
services between 1947 and 1960 does not seem to have been accompanied by any substantial rise in the real value of the services performed
in the country during this time. The fact that a great portion of the
increase in this sector was of the less-skilled workers, and that a
large proportion of young girls and boys were working in personal
and other service jobs, make it difficult to assess precisely the extent
of changes in labor productivity in this sector. The general belief is
that substantial underemployment developed in this sector during the
years 1947-60 as a result of the increase in population pressure,
which indicates underutilization of labor capacity.

The Agricultural Sector

Egyptian agriculture is characterized by several features which
ought to be stated from the beginning in order to make the discussion
of labor efficiency and productivity in the agriculture sector more
meaningful. These characteristics include a high man/land ratio,
labor-intensive methods of production, high yield per acre, the high
cost of labor, low output per worker, and a limited area for expansion.

Since most of these characteristics hinge on the first one (the
high man/land ratio), this characteristic will be subjected to a detailed
examination, whereas the other features will be discussed only briefly.
Throughout the following analysis, concern will be given to the implications of these features for labor productivity.

In spite of noticeable progress in other branches of the economy
since the turn of the century, agriculture still contributed one-third
of the Egyptian national income in 1960, 72 percent of the total exports,
and, most important, employment for 58 percent of the labor force.
The cultivated area constituted almost one-thirtieth of the total area
of the republic. However, the richness of the soil permitted its cultivation with two or more crops every year so that every 60 feddans of
cultivated areas were estimated to equal 100 feddans of crop areas.

The effects of population increase since 1897 on the limited
areas are shown in Table 19. Population increased from 9.7 million
in 1897 to roughly 30 million in 1966 (an increase of 210 percent),
while the cropped area increased from 6.8 million to 10.3 million
feddans, or by only 52 percent during the same period. The disproportionate increase of population in relation to land reduced the cropped
area per capita by more than half and resulted in a decline in the

TABLE 19

Population and Cropped Areas, Census Years from
1897 to 1966

Year	Population in Millions	Cropped Area	
		Feddans (million)	Per Capita
1897	9.7	6.8	.71
1907	11.2	7.6	.67
1917	12.8	7.7	.60
1927	14.2	8.7	.61
1937	15.9	8.4	.53
1947	19.0	9.2	.48
1960	26.0	10.2	.39
1966	30.0	10.4	.34

Source: U.A.R. Central Agency for Public Mobilization and Statistics, Population Increase in the U.A.R. and Its Deterrents to Development (Cairo, 1966), pp. 62 and 143.

amount of work days per worker from 230 per year in 1907 to only 144 per year in 1966.

Since there is good reason to have some reservations on the consistency of the data on female and child labor in agriculture from one census to another,[88] the consideration of the changes in man/land ratio in terms of adult males only would be desirable. Comparative figures indicate a greater relative rise in the man/land ratio between 1917 and 1960. They also indicate the break of the 1930's to be a reduction in the rate of increase rather than a change in the direction of movement toward an increasing man/land ratio.[89] A comparative analysis of the man/land ratio problem in Egyptian agriculture reveals that Egypt stands substantially higher than a number of Asian countries that are generally considered to be heavily populated, such as India and Pakistan. Only Korea and Japan had comparable ratios.[90]

Almost all observers agree that Egyptian agriculture is wasteful in its use of labor.[91] They see the tendency toward technical stagnation in agriculture as due partly to absentee landlordism (mitigated to a large extent by the land reforms of 1952 and 1961), small individual holdings (mitigated by recent land consolidation schemes), overworking of the soil (mitigated by an increase in the use of chemical fertilizers), and the traditionalism of the fellahin. Other factors include the abject poverty of the fellahin, which contributes to their continued use of the tools of their ancestors, although this poverty also has recently been somewhat alleviated by the funds available in the cooperative units. The fact that Egypt's major crops (cotton, rice, and onions) need much more labor input than cereals is also an important factor in explaining why Egyptian agriculture was and continues to be organized around labor-intensive methods of cultivation. It is not quite clear, however, whether Egyptian agriculture did not lend itself easily to mechanization because of these features or if it is wasteful in the use of labor because of the low level of agriculture technology and the existence of available labor. No doubt mechanization is and probably will continue to be stimulated as a result of the different steps taken to overcome some of these obstacles.[92]

In spite of the high man/land ratio and the intensive use of labor, Egyptian agriculture is considered relatively advanced insofar as yield per acre is concerned.[93] This high per-acre yield in Egyptian agriculture is considered by some economists a natural result of the law of diminishing returns, where heavy application of fertilizers and labor intensive methods of production should show a high yield.[94] Others point to the fact that there are a number of countries with a high man/land ratio that have very low per-acre yield.[95] They believe that Egyptian agriculture is not primitive or backward, awaiting the application of modern machinery to yield massive production. Rather, it is their opinion that the scope of improvement in per-acre yields is limited and, therefore, rural poverty is primarily a result of the unfortunate factor proportion between people and land; hence, it will be very difficult to eliminate.

Under Egyptian farming conditions, labor costs occupy the second position after rent as the most important single item among total farm costs.[96] Labor costs accounted for approximately one-fifth of the total farm costs in 1955-56, and they were put at a high percentage of total farm costs in 1961.

It is important to note that the share of labor costs in total farm costs declines with an increase in the size of the farms (see Table 20). Greater utilization of the productive capacity of agricultural labor seems to be a function of working in large farms.[97] The underutilization of labor capacity in Egyptian agriculture in general, and in small farms in particular, becomes more apparent when labor inputs required per crop and for different farm sizes are compared to actual labor input.[98]

Labor costs continued to increase during the 1960's and have shown a phenomenal rise since 1964. Between 1960 and 1966, labor

TABLE 20

Total Labor Cost as a Percentage of Total Farm Cost
for Different Crops and for Different Farm Size, 1966

Farm Size	Less than 1Feddan	1-2 Feddans	2-3 Feddans	3-5 Feddans	5-10 Feddans	10+ Feddans	Average
COTTON:							
Labor cost (L. E.)	20.10	18.64	18.41	17.42	17.23	16.61	17.84
Percent to total farm cost	33	33	32	32	31	31	32
WHEAT:							
Labor cost (L. E.)	8.94	7.67	7.44	6.21	4.80	5.03	6.68
Percent to total farm cost	22	20	20	17	14	16	18
CORN:							
Labor cost (L. E.)	6.92	5.84	5.84	4.28	4.99	5.37	5.23
Percent to total farm cost	24	21	20	17	18	20	19

Source: Abed Hamied Fawazi El-Atar and El-Disoki A. El-Malatti, "Analytical Study for the Problems of the Use of Labor Resources in a Combined Center Area," L'Egypte Contemporaine, 333 (July, 1968), p. 618, Table 7.

costs as a percentage of total farm costs (excluding rent) reached about 30 percent for most of the crops and about 50 percent for cotton. The rise which occurred in agricultural wages, especially since 1964, was mainly responsible for that trend.[99] The increases in the wages of agricultural labor since 1964 have been a surprise, especially to those observers of the Egyptian economy who believe in the existence of widespread disguised and seasonal unemployment in the agricultural sector. This rise will be considered in more detail in a later discussion of employment and unemployment. Suffice it to say at present that wage increases seem to have been an outcome of direct government efforts to improve agricultural wages and to ensure minimum income for poorer segments of the population, as well as of indirect programs as the land reform laws which transferred a number of agricultural laborers to land owners, a rise in labor demand for land-reclamation schemes, and the construction of the High Dam at Aswan and associated projects.

It is important to note, however, that the rise in the wages of agricultural labor was also matched by an increase in output per worker. However, wages increased more, thus widening the gap between average wages and output. Average output and wage per worker during the first five-year plan (1960-65) are shown in Table 21. While the percentage increase in average wages per worker from the base year (1959-60) was 46.7 percent, the corresponding figure for average output per worker was only 9.7 percent. In addition to employment increases in the agricultural sector during the first five-year plan, wage increases no doubt increased the gap between developments in the level of productivity and the wages of agricultural labor.

TABLE 21

Average Output and Wages per Worker for the First
Five-Year Plan, 1960-65, Agriculture

	Average Output per Worker	Average Wages per Worker
1959-60	179.2	30.2
1960-61	161.9	27.5
1961-62	156.9	32.5
1962-63	172.3	34.8
1963-64	184.3	37.9
1964-65	196.5	44.1
Increase total	17.3	14.1
Increase percentage	9.7	46.7

Source: U.A.R. Central Agency for Public Mobilization and Statistics, Population Increase in the U.A.R. and Its Deterrents to Development (Cairo, November, 1966), p. 186, Table 82.

The disproportionate increase of wages and productivity in agriculture during the 1960's resulted in a greater expenditure in consumption, a corresponding decline in the rate of saving and, subsequently, a sizable deficit in the balance of payments. Economists are divided in their appraisal of the best way to achieve saving in labor costs of agriculture production in Egypt.[100] The advocates of extensive use of machinery build their case on the actual trends in agricultural wages in comparison to productivity.[101] Mechanization, in their opinion, is the only way to lower the cost of plowing, irrigation, pest control, transportation, and other agricultural operations; mechanization of agriculture, in addition, will help to reduce loss of time and crops, and could be a reasonable substitute for the use of animal power, thus making it possible to raise better breeds of livestock. The trend toward the mechanization of agriculture is already one of the basic policies of the development schemes of the government.

In spite of the noticeable trend in this direction, widespread application of agricultural machinery requires a substantial capital stock in addition to a large supply of skilled workers and technicians, which may require several years to create. Accordingly, a number of economists recently expressed the opinion that the improvement of Egyptian agriculture does not require intensive mechanization.[102] They consider the present policy of pushing mechanization as not based upon a proper analysis of the cost and benefits involved; further, they hold that this policy may aggrevate the underemployment problem. However, most observers agree that reducing the labor bill is not the ideal way to economize in the use of labor under present-day conditions,[103] because the number of options which are open to reduce labor costs are neither quite acceptable nor even practically feasible. First, a general objective is to increase work and employment, rather than to limit it, so no reduction in the size of the agricultural labor force is recommended. Second, the majority of farms are family farms and the labor force on the farm is generally determined by the size of the family rather than by the labor requirement. Third, reducing the wage rates will be contrary to the general principles of income redistribution. In fact, all government pressure, whether in the form of legislation or otherwise, is geared toward an increase in agricultural wages. The trend, as we have already seen, is upward, and the likelihood is that it will continue to rise. Fourth, the substitution of lower-paid categories of workers--women and children-- for higher-paid categories is contrary to the prohibition of child labor. Indeed, increasing school enrollment works to make such an alternative in practice an impossibility. Finally, the encouraging of casual workers to replace regular workers stands in contrast to current employment objectives of providing stable income and secure employment for a large part of the labor force. Unless alternative employment in other sectors of the economy is accessible, the best way to

economize labor is not to save labor, but rather to increase the
efficiency with which labor is utilized.

In considering labor efficiency, it is necessary to distinguish
between the efficiency of individual workers themselves and the efficiency with which workers are organized. Efficiency of laborers
implies their acquaintance with the farm tasks, their level of skill,
and the technical capacity with which they perform their daily work.
This centers on the question of recruitment and training. The efficiency
of labor organization, on the other hand, includes the combined use of
labor with machines and other forms of inputs. This centers on problems of management and factor proportion of production. While these
are analytically two separate dimensions, empirically they are difficult
to measure separately. Most observers agree that although Egyptian
farm workers have an adequate understanding of agriculture techniques,
they tend to lack managerial skill.[104] The development of cooperatives,
which is enhanced by the land reform laws, seems to have changed the
picture somewhat.[105] Farm management before the reform was
largely shared between tenants and the landowner or his agent. In
the new setup, the cooperatives step in to bridge the gap in management. Cooperatives seem to have contributed noticeably to the efficiency in the use of labor by improving the quality of work through
certain joint operations (e.g., the use of the new advancing agricultural
technology and the creation of opportunities for the cooperatives to
exercise a beneficial influence on the managerial side of farming as
well as investment activities).

Most of Egypt's 1 million square miles is actually a desert.
The cultivated part which stands now at approximately 6 million
feddans constitutes only 5 percent of the country's total area. The
extension of the cultivated land is limited mainly by the availability
of water. While the country has one of the most effective and most-
regulated irrigation systems in the world, it does not alter the fact
that most of the Nile water used to go to waste, especially at the
time of the flood. The building of the High Dam at Aswan will make
it possible to regulate the flow of the water over the course of the
year. One of the goals of building the dam is to bring 1.3 million
new feddans under cultivation, as well as the conversion of about
700,000 feddans in upper Egypt from basin to perennial irrigation.[106]
Even if such estimates prove to be high in terms of availability of land
that can be economically brought under cultivation, nonetheless, the
construction of the dam is expected to increase the total area already
under cultivation by from 10 to 20 percent.[107]

Two different opinions are expressed concerning the future use
of the newly reclaimed land. First, the advocates of state-operated
farms see the formation of state companies to grow fruit, vegetables,

and other crops mainly for export.[108] They consider such large
state farms desirable in order to provide foreign exchange and employment for thousands of laborers who would not have access to land distribution in small plots. This type of farm will also take advantage
of the economies of scale and mechanized techniques open to large,
centrally directed farms. The exponents of state-operated farms
build their case on the need to circumvent the inefficiency of small
holders who are bound to old institutions and traditional farming
methods. However, some experts object to state farms on the grounds
that they were not overly successful in the Soviet Union, and because
earlier experiences with state farms in Egypt proved to be no more
efficient than privately owned concerns.[109] They recommend the
exploitation of the new land by the kind of cooperatives which had
developed under the agrarian reform laws of 1952 and 1961; and they
dismiss the idea that Egyptian agriculture requires highly mechanized
production because the country suffers from a surplus--not a shortage--
of labor.

No doubt the outcome of these different opinions will prove to
be highly significant, not merely for the new lands but probably for
the whole of agriculture. Nevertheless, the ultimate question which
will decide the future agriculture policy in regard to this land will
not be the question of private ownership and individual enterprise
versus state ownership and official control; the question will be whether
Egypt will continue to grow her traditional crops of cotton, wheat, rice,
and so forth, in the new reclaimed areas or decide to concentrate her
new land and water in producing such new crops as fruit, vegetables,
oil, and sugar, where she has greater comparative advantage.

Egypt seems to have exploited most of the benefits of her first
agricultural revolution, which was based on cotton. A second revolution in the country's agriculture policy, now recommended, is to give
more emphasis to growing more profitable crops.[110] If such a policy
is adopted, a number of factors will necessitate greater state control
over the cultivation of the new land. First, the high capital costs of
growing fruits, vegetables, and other new crops, as well as the long
gestation period which must elapse before any return is obtained,
make such undertakings economically feasible only as government
projects. Second, the poverty of the population, which severely
limits the internal market, will necessitate the careful study of the
external market. Third, fruit and vegetable growing require technical
knowledge which the average farmer does not possess.

The decision which the government will take concerning growing
traditional crops or new ones will be of great relevance to the future
employment of the agriculture work force. The cultivation of the
traditional crops in the new land will mean that Egypt will be successful

only in keeping the man/land ratio at the same level it was when
work on the high dam first began. The shift to new crop cultivation
in the reclaimed land, on the other hand, would increase returns per
acre severalfold and absorb a large amount of labor. In addition, a
new employment horizon would be opened in the growing processing,
canning, refrigerating operations, as well as in the transportation
industry.

Aside from the use of the Nile, the prospect for extending the
nation's cultivated land centers on the use of underground water.
Several projects of reclaiming some areas of the desert with underground water were contemplated, such as the New Valley, the Wadi
Naturn, and the Quattara Depression.[111] The government has
launched small-scale pilot schemes but, in general, these projects
are targets for the distant future.

NOTES

1. The writer refers specifically to the drastic measures toward
women's emancipation in Turkey in the time of Ataturk.

2. Peter C. Dodd, "Youth and Women's Emancipation in the
U.A.R.," The Middle East Journal, XXII (Spring, 1968), 159-61.

3. U.A.R. Information Department, Draft of the Charter of the
Republic (Cairo, May 21, 1962), p. 63, Sec. 7.

4. These figures are taken from U.A.R. Central Agency for
Public Mobilization and Statistics, Statistical Yearbook, 1952-1966
(Cairo, June, 1967).

5. Charles Issawi, Egypt in Revolution (New York: Oxford
University Press, 1963), p. 102.

6. Peter Mansfield, Nasser's Egypt (Baltimore: Penguin Books,
1965), p. 116.

7. International Labor Office, Women Workers in a Changing
World (Geneva: La Tribune de Geneve, 1963), pp. 26-27, Table 11.

8. Morroe Berger, The Arab World Today (Garden City, N.Y.:
Doubleday and Co., 1964), p. 129.

9. U.A.R. Central Agency for Public Mobilization and Statistics,
Population Increase in the U.A.R. and Its Deterrents to Development
(Cairo, 1966), p. 170.

10. Donald C. Mead, Growth and Structural Changes in the Egyptian Economy (Homewood, Ill.: Richard D. Irwin, Inc., 1967), p. 33.

11. A. M. N. El-Shafei, "The Current Labor Force Sample Survey in Egypt (U.A.R.)," International Labour Review, LXXXII (1960), 438, Table IV; and Central Agency for Public Mobilization and Statistics, Population Increase in the U.A.R. and Its Deterrents to Development, p. 167, Table 69.

12. International Labour Office, Labor Survey of North Africa (Geneva: La Tribune de Geneve, 1960), pp. 244-48.

13. Frederick Harbinson and Ibrahim A. Ibrahim, Human Resources for Egyptian Enterprise (New York: McGraw-Hill Book Co., 1958), p. 156.

14. Issawi, op. cit., p. 103.

15. Ibid., p. 92. Also, Wendell Cleland, The Population Problem in Egypt (Lancaster, Pa.: Pennsylvania Printing Corp., 1936), pp. 82-87.

16. J. M. Weir, et al., "An Evaluation of Health and Sanitation in Egyptian Villages," Journal of the Egyptian Public Health Association, XXVII, 3 (1952), 90-91.

17. Ibid., 93.

18. Issawi, op. cit., p. 105.

19. Mead, op. cit., p. 303, Table 11-A-8 and comments.

20. Mansfield, op. cit., p. 111.

21. Issawi, op. cit., p. 104. Also, A. H. Shaban, "The Government and Medical Care in Egypt," World Health Journal, VIII, 2 (March, 1961), 112.

22. Mansfield, op. cit., p. 110.

23. This is so according to what is known in economics as Ingles Law, concerning the relationship between level of income and household expenditure on foodstuffs.

24. Shehata S. Shehata, "Cooperative Efforts and Food Consumption in the U.A.R.," L'Egypte Contemporaine, LV (January, 1964), 69.

25. U.A.R. Central Agency for Public Mobilization and Statistics, Population Increase in the U.A.R. and Its Deterrents to Development, p. 208.

26. Institute of Agrarian Affairs, "Contemporary Problems in the Economics of Agriculture," International Journal of Agrarian Affairs, III, 3 (London: Oxford University Press, September, 1962), 155.

27. Labor legislation: There are several English translations of the labor code without its amendments. The complete labor laws of the U.A.R. with all their amendments up to 1964 are published in French as part of the "Repertoire Permanent de Legislation Egyptienne," a private enterprise of the Bulletin de Legislation et de Jurisprudence Egyptiennes, published in Alexandria. For a comprehensive comment on the united law and its amendments, see U.A.R. Ministry of Labor, Public Relations Department, Egyptian Labor: New Horizons (Cairo, 1963); Trade Union Federation, Legal Department, Labor Legislation Past and Present in U.A.R. (Cairo: July, 1963); and Muhammed Hilmey Murad, "Modern Trends in the U.A.R. Labor Legislation," L'Egypt Contemporaine, LIII (October, 1962), 5-18.

28. L. Solovyov, "Reductions of Hours of Work in the U.A.R.," International Labour Review, LXXXVI, 1 (July, 1962), 69-70; and U.S. Department of Labor, Labor, Law and Practice in the U.A.R. (Washington, D.C.: Government Printing Office, 1965), Parts III, IV, and V, pp. 56-84.

29. International Labour Office, op.cit., pp. 122-24.

30. For a discussion of the social welfare legislation, see Robert J. Myers, Report on Social Security Systems in the U.A.R., Washington, D.C., Social Security Administration, U.S. Department of Health, Education and Welfare (November, 1961); and The International Office, "Recent Development in Social Insurance in U.A.R.," International Labour Review, LXXV (May, 1962), 522-27.

31. Patrick O'Brien, The Revolution in Egypt's Economic System (New York: Oxford University Press, 1966), p. 206f.

32. U.S. Department of Labor, op. cit., p. 60.

33. Ibid., p. 70.

34. This opinion was repeated in several parts of O'Brien's book: O'Brien, op. cit., p. 245; also, Issawi's remarks on the effects

of the law No. 113 of 1961 concerning the reduction of hours of work, Egypt in Revolution, p. 194.

35. See especially O'Brien's critics in his The Revolution in Egypt's Economic System, p. 259.

36. U.S. Department of Labor, op. cit., Chapter XI.

37. Cited in Mansfield, op. cit., p. 149.

38. U.S. Department of Labor, op. cit., p. 28 fn.

39. For the history of the labor movement in Egypt, see Issawi, Egypt at Mid-Century (New York: Oxford University Press, 1954), pp. 172-74; Ali El-Gritly, "The Structure of Modern Industry in Egypt," L'Egypte Contemporaine, Nos. 241-42 (1947), 534-54; M. T. Audsley, "Labor and Social Affairs in Egypt Middle East Affairs," St. Antony's Papers, No. 4 (1958), 102-09; Harbison and Ibrahim, op. cit., pp. 174-82; W. J. Handley, "The Labor Movement in Egypt," Middle East Journal, III, 3 (1949), 277-92; U.S. Department of Labor, Survey of the Labor Situation in Egypt (Washington, D. C., 1955); and "Labor Movement in the Arab World," Arab World, X (1963), 8-9.

40. Frederick Harbison, "Egypt," in Walter Galensen, ed., Labor and Economic Development (London: John Wiley and Sons, 1959), Chapter 4.

41. U.S. Department of Labor, Labor Law and Practice in the U.A.R., op. cit., pp. 47-49. Also, I. Abdelkadar Ibrahim, "Socio-Economic Changes in Egypt (1952-1964)," in Arthur M. Ross, ed., Industrial Relations and Economic Development (London: Macmillan Co., 1966), pp. 123-27.

42. O'Brien, op. cit., p. 198.

43. Harbison in Galensen, op. cit., especially p. 174f.

44. Ibid., p. 155.

45. Such opinion was expressed by Mansfield, op. cit., p. 151; by Issawi, op. cit., p. 196; and Harbison in Galensen, op. cit., Chapter 4.

46. Keith Wheelock, Nasser's New Egypt: A Critical Analysis (New York: Frederick A. Praeger, Publishers, 1960), pp. 127-29.

47. Mansfield, op. cit., p. 150.

48. Ibid., p. 152.

49. Mead, op. cit., Statistical Appendix, p. 301, Table 11-A-6.

50. Fahim I. Qubain, Education and Science in the Arab World (Baltimore: Johns Hopkins Press, 1966), p. 30.

51. Egypt's need for industrial workers has been emphasized by several writers: Harbison and Ibrahim, op. cit., pp. 131-43.

52. Qubain, op. cit., pp. 31-32.

53. Ibid., p. 32, Table 7.

54. See M. Al-Arabi, "A Modern Apprenticeship in the U.A.R.," International Labour Review, LXXXIV (1961), 478-98. Also, his "Experience of Apprentice Training in the U.A.R.," International Labour Review, XCII, 6 (1965), 490-505.

55. Qubain, op. cit., p. 71, Table 13.

56. Ibid., pp. 206-209 and Table 48.

57. Ibid., p. 215.

58. Ibid., p. 216. Here Qubain expresses the view that there is no restriction on the mobility of scientists between government and industry. O'Brien presents different views. He sees the elaborate system of jobs and wages classification as well as government directions of certain skilled manpower to add to the rigidity of labor market. See O'Brien, op. cit., especially pp. 176-77 and 197-98.

59. Qubain, op. cit., pp. 216-19.

60. Daniel F. Nugent, Jr., S. Lewis Land, and Carl S. Coler, "Development of Manpower Resources for Egyptian Industrialization" (Cairo: U.S. Agency for International Development, December, 1962), p. 60. (Mimeographed.)

61. Ibid., p. 61.

62. S. Lewis Land, "Industrial Teacher Education in the U.A.R." (Cairo: Institute of National Planning, 1963), pp. 26-27. (Mimeographed.)

63. Qubain, op. cit., p. 218.

64. Nugent, et al., op. cit., p. 60.

65. Qubain, op. cit., p. 219.

66. Malcolm H. Kerr, "Patterns and Problems of Educational Underdevelopment, Egypt," in James S. Coleman, ed., Education and Political Development (Princeton, N.J.: Princeton University Press, 1965), p. 169.

67. Morroe Berger, Bureaucracy and Society in Modern Egypt (Princeton, N.J.: Princeton University Press, 1957), pp. 80-81 and 82-84.

68. Frederick H. Harbison and Kurt A. Myer, Education, Manpower and Economic Growth (New York: McGraw-Hill Book Co., 1964), pp. 42, 47, and 103.

69. Harbison in Galensen, op. cit., p. 154.

70. Issawi, Egypt in Revolution, pp. 105-107.

71. Such observations have been reported by many. See Issawi, Egypt in Revolution, p. 180, and The Development of Modern Industry in Egypt, Israel and Turkey (New York: United Nations, Publication, 1958), pp. 64-67.

72. See Gamal Eldin Said, "Productivity of Labor in Egyptian Industry," L'Egypte Contemporaine, Nos. 259-60 (May-June, 1950), 501-509.

73. A Study made by Gamal Eldin Said showed that by comparison to the U.K., the proportion of salaried employees to the total labor force was higher in six out of seven industries. See Gamal Eldin Said, "Igt Sadiat MISR," p. 260. (In Arabic.)

74. See Harbison and Ibrahim, op. cit., Chapter IV; and Said, "Productivity of Labor in Egyptian Industry," 501-503.

75. For a discussion of the wage structure in the Egyptian industry prior to the revolution, see A. El-Gritly, op. cit.; Bent Hansen and Girgis Marzouk, Development and Economic Policy of the U.A.R. (Amsterdam: North Holland Publishing Co., 1965), pp. 287-90; and Mead, op. cit., pp. 115-120 and 225.

76. Hansen and Marzouk, op. cit., pp. 286-90.

77. U.N., op. cit., pp. 70, 72, and 75.

78. M. Wilmington, "The Middle East Supply Center," Middle East Journal, (June, 1952, p. 144.

79. Issawi, Egypt in Revolution, p. 191.

80. O'Brien, op. cit., p. 304.

81. See Berger, Bureaucracy and Society in Modern Egypt, pp. 82-84; and Issawi, Egypt in Revolution, p. 74.

82. Mead, op. cit., p. 145. Also, M. A. Anis, "A Study of the National income of Egypt," L'Egypte Contemporaine, CCLXI-CCLXII (1950), 806-807.

83. Mead, op. cit., p. 145.

84. Ibid., pp. 147-48.

85. Ibid., p. 150.

86. O'Brien, op. cit., pp. 256-57.

87. Mead, op. cit., p. 152.

88. For a discussion of the problem of this data, see Mead, op. cit., pp. 32-33 and 80-83. See also M. El-Tomy and B. Hansen, "The Seasonal Employment Profile in Egyptian Agriculture," Memo No. 501, (Cairo: Institute of National Planning, 1964), especially pp. 7-12.

89. Mead, op. cit., pp. 81 and 83.

90. United Nations Food and Agriculture Organization, Production Yearbook, 1963, XVII (Rome, 1964), Tables 1 and 5.

91. This opinion is expressed by most observers about the organization of labor in Egyptian agriculture. See Issawi, Egypt in Revolution, pp. 87 and 298. Also Mead, op. cit., Chapter 4 and Appendix; and M. A. W. Ezzat, "The Land Tenure System in Egypt," in K. H. Parsons, et al., eds., Land Tenure (Madison: University of Wisconsin Press, 1956). However, it should be noted that in spite of the agreement on the waste of labor use in agriculture in Egypt, there is considerable divergence of opinion, both in the theoretical literature on economic development and in the discussion of the Egyptian economy in particular, as to the existence and extent of under-employment of labor in the agricultural sector, a point which will be discussed later.

92.   For a good appraisal of mechanization of agriculture in Egypt, see National Planning Center Memo. 253, "Report of Committee on the Mechanization of Agriculture," 1959 (in Arabic). See also A. Fawazi El-Atar and Elidisoki A. El-Molahi, "Analytical Study of the Problems of Labor Resources in a Combined Center Area," L'Egypte Contemporaine, CCCXXXIII (July, 1968), 619-21.

93.   See U.N. Food and Agriculture Organization Production Yearbook, 1963, XVII (Rome, 1964) (for statistics on output per acre in Egypt and other countries).

94.   Fawazi El-Atar and Elidisoki A. El-Molahi, op. cit., 595-624.

95.   Mead, op. cit., p. 75.

96.   See A. A. El-Tonbary, "Measures of Efficiency in the Organization and Use of Farm Labor," L'Egypte Contemporaine, XXXXVIII (April, 1957), 64-76.

97.   See F. El-Atar and E. A. El-Molahi, op. cit., pp. 616-18. See also A. Mohiedien, "Agriculture Investment and Employment in Egypt Since 1935)" (unpublished Ph.D. dissertation; London, (1966).

98.   See G. Saab, "Motorisation de l'agriculture et developpement agricole en Proche-Orient," SEDEIS (1960), 6-7 and 327-28.

99.   See Abdel Mawls Bashier, "Price Policy for Agricultural Products," L'Egypt Contemporaine, Issue 334 (October, 1968), 911-14.

100.   For a Discussion of the alternatives open to achieve such labor economy, see A. A. El-Tonbary, "Comparative Standards in Farm Management Appraisal with Special Reference to Homogenity of Farm Type" (Ph.D. dissertation, University of Durham, England, 1954), I, 179-80.

101.   Issawi, in Egypt in Revolution, p. 127, expressed the opinion that the Egyptian agriculture awaits a second revolution based on mechanization and intensification.

102.   The two outspoken observers expressing this opinion are Mead, op. cit., pp. 74-80 and O'Brien, op. cit., pp. 117-18, 138, and 168.

103.   O'Brien, op. cit., pp. 188-89; and El-Tonbary, "Measures of Efficiency in the Organization and Use of Farm Labor," p. 67. 67.

104. See G. Saab, op. cit., pp. 188-95.

105. U.N. Food and Agriculture Organization and the International Labour Organization, Progress in Land Reform, Third Report (New York: United Nations, 1962), p. 45.

106. U.A.R. Central Agency for Public Mobilization and Statistics, Statistical Yearbook, 1962-1966, p. 263.

107. Mead, op. cit., p. 72.

108. Mohammad H. Haikal, Al-Ahram, January 8, 1967.

109. Sayed Marei, Al-Ahram, (March 7, 8, and 11, April 5, 6, 7, and 8, and May 11, 1965).

110. Issawi, Egypt in Revolution, p. 298.

111. U.A.R. Central Agency for Public Mobilization and Statistics, Statistical Yearbook, 1962-1966, pp. 55-59.

3

The purpose of this chapter is to analyze the major structural changes that have occurred in Egyptian society. First, the impact of urbanization and internal migration on the supply of labor and the mobility of workers are examined; second, the effects that industrialization has had on employment are considered; and finally, the land reform laws are reviewed in order to understand their relevance to the employment characteristics of the agricultural labor force.

INTERNAL MIGRATION AND URBANIZATION

The main source of information on internal migration is the population census, which since 1937 has included a question on "place of birth."[1] Despite their limitations, census figures enable us to make a number of important observations on the internal movement of population. For example, the percentages of the population enumerated outside the governorate of birth in successive censuses show an increase in mobility of both males and females since 1937. Migration from lower Egypt to urban governorates seems to have been of the family type. This is not the case in the four governorates in upper-upper Egypt.[2] In this part of the country, particularly around Aswan, there has been considerable out-migration of the individual type, particularly by males.[3] This situtation is caused by the tendencies among Nubian males to work in services in Cairo and Alexandria rather than in the construction and mining operations which they leave behind to workmen coming from Kena.

The governorates of upper-upper Egypt, Aswan, Kena, Sohage, and Asyut have also a high rate of out-migration compared to other parts of the country. The governorates of lower-upper Egypt,[4] on the other hand, have some of the lowest out-migration rates. The two governorates lying north of Cairo, namely Menoufia and Kalyubia, show a high rate of out-migration. The town of Damiatta, which was a separate urban governorate before the 1960 census, had the highest rate of out-migration in the country.

The excess in the rates of out-migration from upper-upper Egypt over those of lower-upper Egypt and of the Delta can be explained by economic conditions. Until recently, upper-upper Egypt had no resources except the land, most of which, in contrast to the rest of the country, can be irrigated only once a year. Population pressure on the land is also a main cause of out-migration from this section; population density in upper-upper Egypt in 1960 reached 990 persons per square kilometer of cultivated land and 635 persons per square kilometer of crop area. The corresponding densities in lower-upper Egypt were lower, only 750 and 420, respectively. Population pressure on the land seems also to be a main factor behind out-migration from the governorates of the Delta having heavy out-migration, namely Kalyubia and Menoufia.

Further information can be gleaned from available census figures on the areas of destination. The percentage of migrants going to urban governorates is largest in Aswan. These migrants are the Nubians who move to find employment in services, particularly in Cairo and Alexandria. A considerable number of out-migrants from Kena go to Aswan to work in the factories, quarries, or mines. Aswan is therefore experiencing not only heavy out-migration but also a fairly sizable in-migration. [5] Most of the out-migration from the three governorates surrounding Cairo (Giza, Kalyubia, and Menoufia) is directed toward the capital. Thus, Cairo's share of male out-migration from her three neighboring governorates, according to the 1960 census, ranged from 67 percent (Giza) to 45 percent (Menoufia). [6] Likewise, most of the out-migration from Behera is directed towards Alexandria. The highest rates of out-migration from an urban governorate to other urban governorates are observed in the governorates lying along the Suez Canal. Cairo is the governorate exporting the least population to other governorates; and Alexandria is the second. The reason for these low urban-bound percentages lies in the fact that these two cities offer all that urban areas can offer of employment, education, medical care, and all other urban facilities.

The effect of internal migration in altering the rural/urban composition of the Egyptian population has been increasing in the last half-century or so. [7] Table 22 reveals that the urban population has more than doubled during the present century, and accounted for 40 percent of the total population in 1966. Part of the increase in the urban population is attributed to the changes of several rural centers to urban units in the successive censuses, as a result of their increase in size. However, the bulk of the increase in the urban population resulted from internal migration.

TABLE 22

Urban and Rural Population, 1907, 1937,
1960, and 1966

Year	Urban	Percent	Rural	Percent	Total
1907	2, 125, 000	19	9, 058, 000	81	11, 183, 000
1937	4, 382, 083	28	11, 429, 001	72	15, 811, 084
1960	9, 651, 097	37	16, 120, 368	63	25, 771, 495
1966	12, 042, 030	40	17, 689, 630	40	39, 731, 660

Source: Central Agency for Public Mobilization and Statistics,
Population Increase in the U. A. R. and Its Deterrents to Development
in the U. A. R. (Cairo, November, 1966), pp. 115 and 45.

Not all urban areas have been growing at the same rate. Cairo,
Alexandria, and the Suez areas have continued to grow at a faster
speed than the other governorates of the country. Cairo continues
to occupy the first position as far as population size is concerned.
The percentage of the population in the capital to the total population
increased from 8. 2 percent in 1937 to 14 percent in 1966. [8]

Urban population density is highest in Cairo, which in 1960 had
38, 345 inhabitants per square mile. (Chicago, in the same year, had
15, 836 inhabitants per square mile). [9] The attraction of the large
cities lies mainly in their capacity to provide jobs. The service
sector and government administration provide most of the employment
opportunities in the large cities. Moreover, charity and welfare
organizations are more accessible in the cities than in the countryside.
Industrial centers which were created in and around these primate
cities (Cairo and Alexandria), also absorbed a good proportion of
unemployment. [10] Urbanization trends were not only limited to the
noticeable increases in the size and the rate of the growth of the
large urban centers. In every province, the urban population has
increased at a higher speed than the rural population since 1937. [11]

We have seen that Egypt is experiencing a heavy rural-urban
migration trend, and that population pressure on the land seems to be
a main cause of out-migration. Urban centers are growing at a much
faster rate than the rest of the country. Excessive population movement between urban centers, a characteristic of more developed

countries, has not yet developed in the Egyptian society. And finally, there is evidence which suggests that in-migration is moving parallel to industry in several governorates such as Aswan, Giza, and Kalyubia

The details of the population census permit us to go further in our examination of the nature of the relationship between population movement and the employment status of the adult male population as well as the economic transfer between the sectors of the economy. [12] The territory of Egypt falls into two clear and distinct sections. The first of these sections includes the five urban governorates of Cairo, Alexandria, the Canal Zone, Suez, and Damiatta. The urban nature of this group is made clear by the fact that within the five, the agricultural sector has accounted for no more than 3 to 5 percent of total employment over the last three censuses. The rest of the country is divided into provinces, where the agricultural sector has provided between 70 and 80 percent of total employment. In this case, then, the division between governorates and provinces is in fact tantamount to an urban-rural division.

In both rural and urban areas, the growth of industrial employment was relatively small. In percentage terms, the expansion of employment in the governorates was far greater than in the provinces. This expansion in the urban areas was substantially in excess of the natural increase in adult males in those districts and was made possible only by the influx of men from the countryside. [13] It is thus clear that during the 1937-60 period, it was the rapid expansion of employment in services that kept the country from facing more serious pressure from growing underemployment in agriculture, as well as more unemployment both in the cities and in rural areas.

Prior to World War II, the "not employed" (those looking for work and unable to find it, as well as those who were not in the labor force), stayed predominantly in the rural areas, where there were better prospects of finding some work, at least during certain peak seasons of the year, and where they could share in family work. During the postwar period, the "not employed" group continued to expand in both rural and urban areas. The absolute number approximated 500,000 persons in the provinces in 1960, where the demand for temporary agricultural laborers was falling off as a result of the land reforms. The continued expansion of this group is a measure of the frustration which Egypt faces in attempting to increase the number of jobs fast enough to keep pace with the supply of labor.

In this regard, it may be important to mention why Egypt is usually cited as a good example of an overurbanized country. [14] Egypt is believed to have a much higher level of urbanization than its level of economic development can sustain, and to be far more urbanized than its present structure would require. The large cities of Egypt have far more people than their economic technological base warrants. As a result of the impoverishment of the rural masses, migration to the cities by people seeking employment was intensified during the last three or four decades. Much of this migration was from the countryside where the growing population and family inheritance system have diminished the size of land holdings and created a considerable amount of unemployment among agricultural laborers. The densely settled and impoverished rural areas in Egypt seem to be pushing people out of the land into cities. The push from the land of this economically inactive population is considered the major process accounting for the observed overurbanization in Egypt.

INDUSTRIALIZATION

The trend toward industrialization in Egypt began immediately after World War I. The demand for industrial products increased during that war as a consequence of Egypt's position as an army base. In 1921 the government set up a Committee on Industry, which presented several recommendations. As a result of this committee's activities, a number of manufacturing industries were established. The most important step toward industrialization, however, came as a result of the government's encouragement to the founding of the all-Egyptian MISR Bank, as a private concern to promote industries.

The pioneer efforts of the MISR group, especially in the textile industry, are generally considered to be the first serious attempts toward Egyptian industrialization;[15] however, it is the tariff reform of 1930, which increased duties on imported goods, that really marked the beginning of large-scale industrialization. World War II greatly stimulated industry. During the war years, the restriction of imports was accompanied by large-scale expenditures by the allied armies stationed in the country. The development of large-scale industrialization was also reflected in the increasing number of workers who found employment in the newly established industries and in the British Army workshops or camps.

In the postwar years, industry--especially that in textiles, preserved foods, chemicals, glass, and cement and other building materials--continued to expand. The encouraging elements of the wartime situation persisted into the postwar era and Egyptian industry continued to grow until 1949. In the two years before the Egyptian revolution (1950-52), however, the rate of growth in industrial production showed a decelerating trend.[16] A prominent explanation of the stagnation of industry at midcentury centers on the ceiling reached on the demand for manufactured goods. The facts that mass markets remained in rural areas and that real output per capita in agriculture was almost stagnant prevented future diversion of rural income toward manufactured goods. Also, any expected increases in the propensity to consume manufactured goods with the increase in urbanization in this period were probably counteracted by the rising population and the diversion of a major part of families' expenditure toward basic foodstuffs. [17]

Undoubtedly, such demographic explanations for the stagnation that plagued industrial production in the early 1950's are not the only ones. For example, the country's political climate of turmoil and unrest, the tendency of the landed aristocracy to prefer foreign goods, the withholding of investment funds from industry in favor of investment in buildings, and the relapse which occurred in the prices of Egyptian cotton in the world market after the Korean War are among the many factors considered responsible for the decrease in industrial growth. [18]

The efforts of the government to promote industrial growth since 1952, as well as the changing policies adopted by the regime toward industrialization, have been presented in a number of excellent studies on Egypt's economic structure after the revolution. [19] The interested reader will no doubt find a broader account in these sources. What mainly needs to be mentioned here is that industrial production has been increasing since 1953, and has been increasing at a relatively faster rate since 1959.

Turning to a consideration of industrial location, the employment figures revealed by the census show an increasing concentration of industrial employment in the urban governorates, from 39 percent in 1937 to about 48 percent in 1960. [20] The regional distributions of workers in industry in 1961 are presented in Table 23. Forty-nine percent of all industrial employment was concentrated in urban governorates; 46 percent of all industrial employment was in Cairo and Alexandria alone. More than two-thirds of the industrial labor force was employed in the governorates of Alexandria, Cairo, Giza, and Kalyubia, the latter of which are actually suburbs of Cairo. In 1961, industrial employment in rural governorates was 48 percent. Thirty-three percent of all industrial employment was in the rural governorates of lower Egypt while only 15 percent was in upper Egypt.

The high concentration of industry in Cairo and Alexandria is due to many factors: among these are the high purchasing power in the large urban centers, the good communication systems, the relative abundance of both skilled and unskilled labor, the existence of sources of electric power and repair shops, and the early development of industry in these two cities. The continuation of this trend since the early 1920's until the early 1960's has been enhanced by government policies and inadequate planning for industrial location.

The changes which occured in the employment figures in industrial

TABLE 23

Regional Distribution of Workers
in Industry, 1961

Governorate	Percent of Workers
Total------------------100. 0	
Urban governorates	49. 0
Cairo	20. 3
Alexandria	26. 1
Port Said	. 6
Ismailia	. 1
Suez	1. 9
Rural governorates	47. 8
Lower Egypt	32. 8
Damiatta	. 4
Daqahlia	. 6
Sharqia	. 9
Kalyubia	12. 5
Kafer-el-Sheikh	. 1
Gharbia	10. 5
Menoufia	. 6
Beheira	7. 2
Upper Egypt	15. 0
Giza	8. 8
Beni-Seuif	. 2
Fayum	. 1
Mania	1. 0
Asyut	. 4
Suhag	. 4
Kena	1. 8
Aswan	2. 3
Desert governorates	3. 2

Source: U.S. Bureau of Labor Statistics, Labor, Law and Practice in the United Arab Republic (Egypt) (Washington, D. C.: U.S. Government Printing Office, March, 1965), BLS Report No. 275, p. 28, Table 13.

establishments (firms with ten or more workers) in all the governorates between 1954 and 1965 are presented in Table 24. While
these figures indicate the persistence of the dominant positions of
the Cairo-Alexandria complex, they also reveal a rapid growth of
industrial employment in other governorates such as Aswan and
Gharbia.

The location of industry by type of activities shows a substantial
decentralization in food and textile industries, which are widely
scattered in the countryside. [21] In each of these two industries, 55

TABLE 24

Employment in Industrial Establishments,
1954 and 1964

	1954	1964
Cairo	81, 917	156, 552
Alexandria	57, 199	116, 768
Port Said		8, 449
Ismailia	7, 609	2, 331
Suez	6, 740	11, 640
Damiatta	1, 217	3, 770
Daqahlia	3, 290	8, 324
Sharqia	1, 626	7, 302
Kalyubia	20, 570	57, 263
Kafer-el-Sheikh	963	1, 803
Gharbia	28, 908	43, 581
Menoufia	1, 308	6, 245
Beheira	19, 347	25, 633
Giza	13, 076	41, 170
Beni-Seuif	1, 154	2, 726
Fayum	1, 007	3, 253
Mania	3, 454	7, 936
Asyut	2, 325	4, 008
Suhag	1, 282	3, 687
Kena	5, 182	14, 729
Aswan	1, 640	17, 843
Border governorates	5, 214	9, 956
Total	265, 078	554, 979

Source: U. A. R. Central Agency for Public Mobilization and
Statistics, Statistical Indicators of the U. A. R., 1952-1966 (Cairo,
July, 1967), p. 31.

percent of employment in firms with ten or more workers was outside
the five urban governorates according to the 1960 census of industrial
production. [22] The recent government policy is to encourage further
growth of industrial centers such as Aswan and Helwan as well as the
textile center already existing in Mahla-Alkubra. The distribution
of the new major spinning and weaving establishments in the midst of
the cotton-growing areas of the Delta was another step in the decentralization trend.

With regard to size, industrial establishments in Egypt are for
the most part very small enterprises (engaging less than ten workers);
there are only a few very large establishments (employing 500 and
over). [23] The absence of middle-size industrial establishments and
the particular predominance of very small enterprises is clear from
the return of the several industrial censuses. While the return of
the several industrial censuses are not comparable for historical
purposes, Hansen and Marzouk have concluded that during 1947-60,
employment in small-scale industry continued to rise perhaps as
much as 35 percent compared to an employment increase of less than
30 percent for all industry during the same period. [24] The predominance
of small-scale establishments is attributed to the prevalence of handi-
craft industries and the inadequacy of providing loans to small firms.
The existence of the very large firms is primarily a reflection of the
modern, high-capital-investment textile industry and government
encouragement of the monopoly of large-size industrial firms. [25] As
regards the size of establishments by branches of industry, a United
Nations study indicated that large-size establishments comparable to
those in more industrialized countries prevail also in the sugar and
petroleum refining industries, and in the making of paper, fertilizer,
and cement. [26]

Perhaps the most relevant aspect of the industrialization policies
which affect labor and employment in Egyptian industry is the noticeable
tendency toward the use of capital-intensive techniques of production. [27]
A number of economists have singled out this paradoxical tendency as
the most serious shortcoming of Egypt's strategy of industrial development. [28] In their opinion, the failure to bring idle resources (labor)
into production represents a source of inefficiency. On the other
hand, the use of more capital-intensive techniques of production in
Egyptian industry is seen as a rational policy, since for Egypt to
benefit from automation in the long run, and in order not to sacrifice
productivity, the present course seems appropriate. [29] A compromise
position is voiced by O'Brien, who sees Egypt's development strategy
as being rational from other points of view, but as being unlikely to
make serious inroads into the employment problem. [30] At the present,
no attempt will be made to weigh the pros and the cons of the argument.
Instead, we find it more useful to follow the trends in the intensity of
capital investment in industry, and ascertain the underlying causes of

any shifts and changes, in order to better understand the effects of these changes in the expansion of industrial employment.

Despite a number of problems involved in estimating capital formation in industry, Robert Mabro presented an index of capital intensity in manufacturing industry for the period between 1937 and 1965 (see Table 25). According to these data, there was a decline in the capital/labor ratio during the war years. The heavy wartime usage of industrial equipment and the shortage of imports are estimated to have resulted in a fall of nearly 37-40 percent in the capital/labor ratio during the war years. [31] In the postwar years, 1947-54, a rapid rate of investment in industry took place, and during this period employment remained virtually constant. By the year 1954, the capital/labor ratio was 88 percent higher than in 1947, but only 19 percent higher than in 1937. This fact suggests that the heavy investment in the postwar period was partially due to replacement of the badly worn machinery. [32] Between 1954 and 1960, the capital/labor ratio rose at a slower rate than in the preceding period. During the 1950's, and especially between 1952 and 1958, the rise in capital intensity in industrial establishments of ten or more workers increased by 40 percent, while employment showed no increase in this six-year period. In the first five-year plan, industry continued to move towards more capital-intensive undertakings. The bias in favor of capital-intensive techniques is reflected not only in the allocation of investment

TABLE 25

Index of Capital Intensity in Manufacturing
Industry, Selected Years from 1937 to 1965

Year	Employment	Capital	Capital/Labor	
1937	100	100	100	
1947	159	100	63	100
1954	161	192	119	188
1960	202	249	123	195
1965	266	362	136	216

Source: Robert Mabro, ''Industrial Growth, Agricultural Under-Employment and the Lewis Model. The Egyptian Case, 1937-1965,'' The Journal of Development, 3, 1967, p. 341.

funds but also in the official policies adopted in the national charter. [33]

In spite of the prevailing tendency to use more capital-intensive techniques in Egyptian industry, Hansen and Marzouk have noted that industrial establishments in Egypt still lag considerably behind those in the most advanced industrial centers in terms of the capital/labor ratio. [34] For example, they estimated the capital intensity of Egyptian manufacturing industry to approximate 600 Egyptian pound workers in 1960 and 680 Egyptian pound workers in 1965, in comparison to 3,000 Egyptian pound workers for the whole industrial sector in Sweden.

It is interesting to note that the installment of the most modern laborsaving machinery begins with the very early development of industry in Egypt. [35] The MISR group that actually started the trend toward large-scale industrialization, [36] especially in the textile industry, adopted the use of modern machinery as a means of saving raw materials. While in principle these pioneer Egyptian entrepreneurs accepted the idea that machinery should not be used to replace manpower when manpower can do the job just as well, the low level of skills of the labor force and the high-quality targets of the products led in practice to economy in the use of labor. [37] It is also worth noting that in response to pressures from different groups, the government prohibited the importation of used machinery, which caused capital intensity to continue to rise as a result of purchasing up-to-date equipment. [38]

A number of facts explain the rise in the capital/labor ratio during the 1950's to a level that exceeds the prewar level. First, industries which developed more rapidly during the 1950's were those having to do with paper production, cement, oil refining, and fertilizers. All of these are capital-intensive industries. Second, not only did other capital-intensive industries develop during the 1950's but also the remaining industrial establishments underwent a replacement and modernization of machinery following the deteriorating effect of the war period, when there was no importation of capital goods. However, there is some evidence that the updating of the equipment of several industrial establishments led to actual labor substitution by machinery. [39]

Another factor which encouraged the continuation of capital-intensive methods of production was the monopolistic structure of the Egyptian industry, which tends to ignore the possibilities of an unlimited surplus of labor. [40] A lack of competition combined with a favorable movement of industrial prices relative to the cost of living made it possible for entrepreneurs to use more capital-intensive machinery without a noticeable reduction in the rate and shares of profits.

Probably, the degree of mechanization during the first five-year plan increased more than would be suggested by figures in Table 25. This is because employment in industry was suddenly affected by the government's drive to employ more workers and the restriction on the number of working hours to 42 a week. The rationale of the government's policies in the use of modern technological machinery centers on a number of arguments. [41] First, planners argue that the shortage of managerial talent able to exploit surplus labor prevents the establishment of the kind of small-scale manufacturing operations found to be successful in other poor countries. Second, they firmly and perhaps correctly believe that the quality of production, especially for export markets, is best ensured by the use of machinery. Third, the problem of convincing both the entrepreneur and the technician to reside in the village constitutes an obstacle which impedes the spread of rural industry. Finally, their most important argument is that capital intensity in industry promotes higher rates of net capital formation and long-run growth, since it minimizes the net output occurring for labor and maximizes returns to property.

Also, two simple but general factors underlie Egypt's choice of more capital-intensive techniques. First is the fact that Egypt imports all of its capital goods from highly industrialized countries, where such goods are originally designed to suit these countries (where labor is scarce). Second, industrialization in Egypt, as in most developing countries, is a symbol of national prestige. The allocation of investment and the choice of industrial techniques are thus subject not only to economic objectives but also, perhaps especially, to political and nationalistic demands.

In contrast to its use of relatively advanced technology, industry in Egypt is characterized by a primitive and wasteful use of manpower and resources. In Egypt, as in many other developing (industrializing) countries, the development of effective human organization lags far behind the introduction of modern technology. [42] Egypt's most abundant resource consists of uneducated, untrained, and unskilled manpower. The vast surpluses of underemployed agricultural labor, in addition to the vast pool of unemployed or partially employed labor in urban areas, plus the number of new entrants into the labor force each year resulting from the population increase, provide inexhaustible resources. Unfortunately, however, while labor surplus exists, only a small proportion of this sizable resource possesses any usable skills.

LABOR PROBLEMS OF INDUSTRIALIZATION

Labor problems of industrialization in Egypt are many and result from a number of factors. Three interrelated but analytically distinguishable sets of problems can be outlined: (1) the industrial worker, (2) the human organization of industry, and (3) the labor market.

Egypt is a latecomer to industry and industrial workers in Egypt therefore retain many of the attributes of nonindustrial society. Tradition, family ties, long-established customs, lack of aspiration, or sheer ignorance deter workers in the villages from entering industrial employment. However, conflicting trends are shown in the behavior of the fellahin (the peasants) when faced with employment opportunities. While some will willingly move away from their home territory to change their activity, others are willing to learn a new occupation but will not move away to enjoy better conditions. [43] Industrial employment is a way of life for only a very small percentage of the total labor force.

As a part of the larger society, the factory worker is coming to be recognized as an important--although still small--part of the labor force. In fact, he is already being envied by his peer workers in agriculture and the service sectors because he has benefited more than others from legislation designed to improve his conditions of employment and habitation, to protect him from exploitation, and to minimize the uncertainties of his urban-industrial environment. Once an ambiguous type of occupational person, the factory worker today receives more respect from society. [44] The distinction between him and the artisan, a distinction the latter used to insist on for prestigious purposes, has now almost disappeared. In fact, the crushing forces of large-scale industrialization are quickly turning the trend against artisian activities; and the factory worker, who was once an alien to the historical experience of the larger society, is coming to have an integrated role in the social structure.

Until recently, mobility of labor between jobs and certain kinds of employment was extremely high. Turnover of labor in the textile industry during the 1940's, for example, constituted such a serious problem that several companies customarily employed up to 30 percent more workers than needed simply to take care of turnover and absenteeism. [45] In recent years, however, turnover has been negligible because of the lack of employment opportunities elsewhere, as well as the continuous improvement in the wages and working conditions of the industrial worker.

While it is extremely difficult to describe the extent of labor commitment in a country where everything seems to be undergoing rapid change, it is nonetheless possible to outline the direction of the change. The lack of industrial tradition and industrial experience, and the little attention which managers gave to the importance of labor commitment because of the abundance of labor resources, have had economic costs as well as long-run implications for industrialization measures. The shortage of skills hidden behind the labor surplus was sharply disclosed in recent years when the need arose for skilled labor and technicians in large numbers. [46] This shortage derived not only from poor commitment to industrial work, but also from problems of motivation and incentive. For several reasons, financial incentives in the form of higher wages have not been operating freely in the Egyptian industry. The first and foremost reason is the oversupply of labor, which tends to keep wage increases at a moderate rate. Second, wages paid for unskilled workers are characterized by such a wide range that the highest-paid unskilled worker's wage in one industry may be higher than that of semiskilled and skilled workers in another. For example, in 1960 the average weekly wage for unskilled workers in the petroleum industry was higher than the average weekly wage of any skilled labor in more than 35 other branches of industry.

Still another reason why financial incentives have not operated successfully is that recent government intervention to grant minimum wages and put a ceiling on wage increases restrained managers in their use of higher pay to attract skilled workers. The generally low level of wages in Egyptian industry in general has also had its impact on management policies. Managers are primarily concerned not with the productivity of labor but with getting the maximum productivity per machine. For this reason alone it is estimated that six to eight workers per machine may be employed in Egypt for every one in the United States. [47]

It has been shown by experience that the bureaucratization of the labor force, a characteristic of all industrialized societies, provides transitional problems in developing areas. [48] In this regard, Egypt is not unique. The difficulties of this transition are not peculiar to the uneducated factory recruit who lacks the industrial tradition. Family and class favoritism, personal rather than organization loyalties, and haphazard management practices interfere with an efficient administrative process.

A pioneer study of the internal structure of the human organization of a textile center in Egypt was conducted by Frederick Harbison and Ibrahim Abdel Kader Ibrahim in the early 1950's. [49] Their observations may serve as a guideline to the labor problems resulting from the inadequacy of human organization in industry. According to these observers, management was isolated from the lower echelons of the salaried workers and laborers. Management's primary concern was with technical rather than organizational or human problems. The concentration of decision-making power in the managing director left very little downward communication and practically no upward communication between the various levels of management groups. Supervisors are graduates of trade schools who were hired mostly at the gate. Their learning in trade schools was of very little value on the job; their casual training on the job was a form of incidental help from their more experienced friends or kinsmen. Like workers, foremen had no orderly induction procedures or any formalized on-the-job training. However, the older workers were skillful in teaching the newer recruits how to behave during their probationary period.

Top management realized the deficiences of the labor force but blamed supervisors for the exaggerated feeling of their worth and the feeling of superiority over the workers they supervised. They charged that this group had little ability or feeling for handling problems of labor relations. For their part, members of the supervision groups criticized the lazy, untrained, and indolent workmen whom they had to supervise. Supervisors were also critical of the elite tendency of management. The workers were as discontented as their supervisors, and their morale was very low.

Harbison and Ibrahim made a number of sound conclusions about modern Egyptian industry from this study. These may be summarized briefly as follows: (1) Egypt is making immediate use of the more advanced technology of the higher industrialized countries; (2) recruitment and training of competent technologists should not be a substitute for efficient managerial organization; (3) the initially high turnover and low productivity of the working force may be more directly a result of underdeveloped management than the consequence of the adjustment of agricultural laborers to the routines of industrial employment; (4) in a cheap labor country such as Egypt, employers are interested in developing an obedient rather than efficient working force, and tend to increase the productivity of machines but not of manpower. In short, Harbison and Ibrahim regard labor problems of industrialization to be in large measure management problems. At the same time, the inadequacy of the foremen and other intermediary personnel is generally admitted to be one of the major weaknesses of Egyptian industry.[50]

The changes which occurred in the human organization of industry since the completion of the Harbison-Ibrahim study are in principle quite impressive. The inclusion of most industrial establishments in the public sector resulted in a noticeable managerial as well as administrative change. Today in factories and firms owned by the state, employees elect four of the nine members of the board of directors. Precisely how these employee representatives are nominated or what their power is in the determination of common policy is not yet clear. However, there are real government pressures to extend some forms of democratic participation to industrial enterprises. In this regard, human organization in Egyptian industry seems to be moving in the direction of a syndicalist organization similar to that in Yugoslavia.[51] Until case studies are published, nothing can be said about the effects of these changes on the aspects of labor problems stemming from the human organization in industry.

The principal fact affecting the unskilled or even the semiskilled industrial worker is the nature of the labor market. [52] It is not so large and well differentiated as it is in established industrial countries. There is not an abundance of alternative employment opportunities. In fact, the alternatives are often only two: either idleness or agriculture. Because of the absence of a developed labor supply for any given enterprise, industry does not recruit from a labor market but from the undifferentiated society. Since labor is overabundant in nearly all localities, employers tend to utilize it carelessly and wastefully. Further, since labor is so cheap there is little incentive to invest in its training or development. In the past, the practice was to hire unskilled workers at the factory gates. The main criteria of selection were subordinate characteristics rather than potential efficiency. Hiring today is controlled by government employment or "manpower offices." The employer has no choice of the unskilled labor he requires, but he may choose between workers in other categories. The system of registration for employment was completely reorganized in July, 1964. Three kinds of files are now kept by the manpower offices: one file for workers now unemployed but previously employed; a second file for new entrants into the labor force; and a third file for employed workers who seek to change their employment. This new organization will undoubtedly help to structure the labor market.

Government intervention in the labor market has been concerned with establishing minimum wages for industrial and agricultural labor and with fixing ceilings for the salaries of managers. The government has also limited the power of public enterprises to establish their own wage structures and to bid labor away from each other. Patrick O'Brien believes that the likely effects of these measures will be " to raise wage rates for unskilled labor above its scarcity levels and to restrain the pay of managerial staff and skilled workers at artificially low levels."[53] In this way, enterprises will be encouraged to economize on the use of the unskilled labor and to neglect to exploit the potentialities of labor-intensive techniques. He even believes that they might be more wasteful in their use of skilled labor.

Some observers believe that recent labor legislation will reduce the mobility of labor and the operation of an efficient wage system for the allocation of labor among enterprises in the public sector. [54] Also, the government's intention to impose similar regulations over the activities of small-scale producers and traders in the private sector will, if carried out, limit their efforts to utilize more labor.

EMPLOYMENT PROBLEMS DERIVING
FROM LAND REFORM

Four different approaches guided Egypt's policy of land reform: (1) the Land Reform Act of 1952, which set a ceiling on holdings, arranged for the distribution of the land in excess of these ceilings, and organized tenancy and fixed minimum wages for agricultural laborers; (2) the Land Reform Law of 1961, which lowered the ceilings set by the 1952 law; (3) the reclamation and distribution of state-owned land; and (4) the consolidation of land use and the adoption of uniform crop rotation procedures outside areas affected by the land reform legislation.[55]

The land reform laws of 1952 and 1961 are considered by most informed observers to be basically labor policies, as under these laws the redistribution of income and the raising of the agricultural wage were contemplated for a number of fellahin.[56] The 1952 land reform law was, in principle, the first wage legislation passed for agricultural laborers, and gave them the right to join trade unions for the first time. However, it is misleading to imply that an increase in employment opportunities was the only objective of the land reform laws. In fact, other declared objectives of the reform policies, such as redistribution of income, direction of investment to industry, and maximization of the rate of technological advance and productivity in agriculture, were not designed to increase employment opportunities. This is why the laws have had adverse as well as positive effects on the employment issue in Egypt.

It is unfortunate that few surveys have yet been undertaken to ascertain the trends of employment and wages after the introduction of land reform measures.[57] Statistical data are very scarce, and this constitutes an important aspect of the general problem of estimating underemployment and unemployment in the agricultural labor force. The inconsistency of the available statistics also leaves too much doubt about the actual trends. It is unavoidable that the effects of the land reform measures on employment and wages be presented here in a somewhat selective manner.

The problem of surplus agricultural population in Egypt pre-dates land reform and has as its basis the pressure of population on a limited surface of usable land. This fact led one observer to note that "No reform, even if it went further than the present measure, could provide land for all in this congested country, or could increase employment in agriculture. That the reform has not benefited the casual laborers is a result, not of a weakness in reform, but of population pressure."[58] The reduction in employment opportunites has been reported by various writers studying the effect of the 1952 law. Various estimates put the unemployment figure resulting from the first agrarian reform law at an average of 5 to 10 percent of the tenants and agricultural laborers formerly employed on the expropriated estates and not benefiting from redistribution. [59]

Another way of looking at the problem is to consider the changes that occurred in the wages of agricultural laborers as indicators of trends in the employment opportunities. Because of the tendency for some reduction in employment to take place following the implementation of the law, it was impossible to enforce the minimum wage law stipulating 18 piasters per day for men and 10 for women. The comparative wages of agricultural labor in 1953 and 1956 indicate a rise which does not even reach 10 percent, in comparison to a minimum rise stipulated by law at 50 percent. [60] In fact, available evidence suggests that nothing had been done as late as 1961 (the year of the second law) to ensure the payment of a minimum wage to agricultural laborers or to encourage formation of labor unions. [61] Some reports indicated that the wage law of 1952 was effective only in underpopulated villages and where an unusual demand for labor existed because of land reclamation projects. In the rest of the country wage rates are still at the mercy of supply and demand. [62]

Several factors account for the failure of the land reform laws to solve the problems of employment and wages for the hired agricultural laborer. First, the reduction of the employment of hired laborers resulted from the fact that new beneficiaries employed less hired farm laborers than the ex-landowners. They did so because most of their farm work was carried on by family labor, and the operations which required an intensive use of labor, such as upkeeping of the drainage and irrigation networks, were operated less vigorously than in the past. Second, there was a general slack in agricultural investment by medium-scale and large-scale landowners not directly affected by the laws. Many of these owners, unsure about the future of their holdings, slowed down the pace of agricultural activities and subsequently slowed down the hiring of agricultural laborers. Third, many of these medium-scale and large-scale farmers even preferred to break up their holdings and sell out to small farmers who were reported to be employing less hired labor than previously. The transference of land tenure from large estates into smaller holdings was not an actual transference from an extensive system of farming to another which required intensive labor technique. In fact, the transference may have entailed a movement in the opposite direction.

The establishment of cooperatives following the enactment of land reform legislation has been an important contributing factor in increased investment on the land. Such increases in investment could have favorable effects on employment. Yet, other activities of the cooperatives were labor-saving techniques. Among these are the

organization of cultivation in the most efficient manner by the use of
large-scale farming methods for small properties and the advancement
in the use of agricultural machinery, together with scientific and
mechanical operations of the use of fertilizers, pest control, maintenance, and improvement of irrigation methods. Some observers
have commented that the activities of the cooperative system in the
land reform areas and outside it may have favorable effects on reducing
the plight of seasonal employment in Egyptian agriculture.[63] While
such observations could be correct, the adverse effects caused by the
trend toward mechanization and other methods of labor-saving techniques adopted by the cooperatives cannot be ignored. The growth of
agricultural mechanization took a sharp rise during the postwar years
and after the first land reform. It should be noted, however, that the
expansion in machinery is to a large extent concentrated on the big
estates, the cooperatives, and the land reclamation areas where
newly reclaimed desert land is cultivated by capital-intensive methods.[64]

The second major experiment in methods of agricultural cultivation which started with the NAWAGE experience is the consolidation
of fragmented holdings with more viable economic units to permit the
use of more technical and scientific methods of cultivation.[65] The
noticeable success of these methods in increasing land productivity
led to their gradual application in the old agricultural supply and
credit cooperatives outside of the land reform areas. In 1963 a new
type of village organization which combined rotation and cooperative's
efforts toward higher investment, technical supervision, and methods
of production, helped to raise land productivity and to minimize costs.
More and more, the use of modern machinery became more possible
with the increase in farm size; and the purchasing of such modern
equipment came more within reach through the use of cooperative
funds. These two trends worked together to minimize the need for
hired labor except in certain seasons.

Thus far, we have seen how certain factors of the new agrarian
structure and the methods introduced by the land reform laws have
actually led to a worsening of the position of hired workers in agriculture. Other factors were also responsible for keeping this group
comparatively unaffected by the laws. The absence of a real bargaining
power (a trade union) on their behalf was, and continues to be, one of
the more serious drawbacks. Even enforcement agencies of the
government were not able to do too much to ensure minimum wages
in the absence of such trade unions. Effective labor movement has
not been able to take hold among illiterate masses because of communication difficulties. The formation of agricultural labor unions
appears to have been delayed for two reasons. The first was an
apprehension that the unions would be rapidly infiltrated by extremists.
The second was a fear of a quick rise in agricultural wages, which

would outprice Egyptian products on the world markets. [66] Another factor responsible for keeping the enforcement of labor laws very difficult, especially those pertaining to wages, was the nonmonitorized characteristics of some aspects of the Egyptian rural economy. In the typical village, a farm laborer may alternate between wage employment and cultivation of small holdings, on the one hand, and between agriculture and other pursuits, on the other. Money economy has not fully penetrated into some parts of rural Egypt and payment for labor is either made in kind or effected through a barter system. Whatever the cause, the low level of agricultural wages in the 1952-61 period seems to bear out the complaints of the landless peasants so far as reduced employment opportunities were concerned.

The reduction in employment resulting from redistribution has been partially offset by the use of agricultural labor in the land reclamation schemes, notably in the Liberation Province. In the early 1960's, 14,000 workers were employed in reclamation and construction. [67] They came from upper Egypt and from the provinces of Menoufia and Daqahlia. They were the only segment of the agricultural labor force which was paid according to the standard stipulated by the land reform law. Thus, in 1961 they were paid at the rate of 12 Egyptian pounds per month in comparison with existing rates in upper Egypt, which averaged only 3 Egyptian pounds per month.

The assessment of the effects which the land reform laws had on employment opportunities would be incomplete if one focused attention solely on the negative effects which these laws produced on hired labor. The 1952 and 1961 acts had a substantial effect on the economic conditions of these casual laborers and tenants who benefited from land distribution.

The structure of land ownership before 1952 and after the 1952 and 1961 laws is presented in Table 26. The first most obvious change to note here is the increase in the number of owners of less than 5 feddans from 2,642,000 before 1952 to 2,919,000 after 1961. The percentage these small plots represented of land ownership also increased from 35 to 52 percent of the total land area in Egypt. The second observable change is the increase in the numbers of holders of 20 feddans after the 1952 land reform act. The only explanation for this sudden rise seems to be the fact that some large owners sold some of their expropriated land to these middle-sized land owners, since the 1952 law permitted such a transfer of property.

The majority of new owners of less than 5 feddans have larger incomes than before the land reform. It is officially estimated that in the more successful land reform projects, the net increase of the cultivators has approximately doubled. [68] This increase in income is due to a number of factors: annual charges now paid by the cultivator,

TABLE 26

Land Distribution of Ownership before and after the Land Reform Laws

	Number of Owners (thousands)			Area (thousands of feddans)			Percentage of Land Owners			Percentage of Land Owners		
	Before 1952	After 1952	After 1961	Before 1952	After 1952	After 1961	Before 1952	After 1952	After 1961	Before 1952	After 1952	After 1961
Less than 5 feddans	2,642	2,841	2,919	2,122	2,781	3,172	94.3	94.4	94.1	35.4	46.6	52.1
5+	79	79	80	526	526	526	2.8	2.6	2.6	8.8	8.8	8.6
10+	47	47	65	638	638	638	1.1	1.6	2.1	10.7	10.7	10.7
20+	22	30	26	654	818	818	.8	.1	.8	10.9	13.6	13.4
50+	6	6	6	430	430	430	.2	.2	.2	7.2	7.2	7.0
100+	3	3	5	437	437	500	.1	.1	.2	7.3	7.2	8.2
200+	2	2	--	1,777	354	---	.1	.1	--	19.7	5.9	----
Total							100.0	100.0	100.0	100.0	100.0	100.0

Source: U.A.R. Central Agency for Public Mobilization and Statistics, Statistical Yearbook, 1952–1966 (Cairo, June, 1967), pp. 49, 50, 51, and 52.

consisting of installments of purchase price, are lower than the former rental charges paid to the landlord; technical management of land has improved; there is more incentive for the cultivator to work hard on his holdings and to improve his techniques of operation; such services as credit are now available more cheaply than before; and cooperative marketing societies now bring in a higher return to the cultivator.

The full impact of the 1961 law on the employment opportunities of the agricultural labor force cannot be ascertained precisely. Yet one suspects that the 1961 laws would have somewhat different results on wage labor in agriculture because of the following: the confiscated land would be transferred from land owners who have been employing a highly labor-saving method of cultivation to new land owners who would use relatively less capital intensive methods in favor of more labor intensive techniques; the 1961 law permits the distribution of orchards and land planted with highly productive crops, which require an intensive use of labor; and the timing of the laws came with the dramatic changes in the economic and fiscal policies announced on July 21, 1961. The most relevant of these was that working hours in factories were shortened to seven hours a day. However, to keep production constant, more shifts were scheduled and operated with additional workers specially recruited for this purpose. The ensuing increase in the labor force was in turn destined to reduce unemployment in all sectors and in the agricultural sector in particular.

In summary, although Egyptian land reform has not been able to relieve the severe pressure of population on land or to ensure full employment for the entire agricultural labor force, the quality and profitability of employment have improved, especially since outside forces (e.g., the reduction in the hours of work in industry and the government decline since 1961, the increase in the employment oppor-tunities in construction, the increase in educational enrollment in both rural and urban areas) helped somewhat to mitigate the depressed levels of employment and wages in agriculture.

NOTES

1. For a description of the sources of information on internal migration, see M. A. El-Badry, ''Trends in the Components of Pop-ulation Growth in the Arab Countries of the Middle East: A Survey of Present Information,'' Demography, II (1965), 140-85; Janet L. Abu-Lughod, ''Urbanization in Egypt: Present State and Future Prospects,'' Economic Development and Cultural Change, XIII, 3 (April, 1965), 313-43; and El-Badry, Abdu-Rahman ''Internal Migra-tion in the U.A.R.,'' L'Egypte Contemporaine, No. 319 (January, 1965), 31-44.

2. Upper-upper Egypt consists of the following governorates: Aswan, Kena, Suhag, and Asyut.

3. El-Badry, op. cit., p. 161.

4. Lower-upper Egypt consists of the following governorates: Mania, Beni-Seuif, Fayum, and Giza.

5. U. A. R. Central Agency for Public Mobilization and Statistics, Population Increase in the U. A. R. and Its Deterrents to Development (Cairo, 1966), p. 152.

6. El-Badry, op. cit., p. 162

7. According to the official definition of the Egyptian census, urban population here refers to those living in the capitals of the governorates and the districts in addition to the metropolitan population of the five urban governorates.

8. U. A. R. Central Agency for Public Mobilization and Statistics, op. cit., p. 124, Table 51.

9. U. S. Department of Labor, Labor, Law and Practice in the U. A. R. (Washington, D. C.: Government Printing Office, 1965), p. 26.

10. The author feels that the very rapid increase in the size of the capital (Cairo) could have some negative effects on the development of the countryside, which may justify the use of the term. Further investigation is needed to support this claim. For a discussion of the concept of primate cities, see Surinder K. Mehta, ''Some Demographic and Economic Correlates of Primate Cities: A Case for Reevaluation,'' Demography, I, 1 (1964), 136-47.

11. U. A. R. Central Agency for Public Mobilization and Statistics, op. cit., pp. 116-17, 46.

12. For more discussion of this relationship, see Donald C. Mead, Growth and Structural Changes in the Egyptian Economy (Homewood, Ill.: Richard D. Irwin, Inc., 1967), pp. 31-41.

13. For further information, see Mead, op. cit., p. 37, Table 2-10, and p. 39, Table 2-11.

14. See Kingsley Davis and Hilda H. Golden, ''Urbanization and the Development of Pre-Industrial Areas,'' Economic Development and Cultural Change, III (1954-55), 6-26.

15. For a brief historical account of the effects of this group in the industrialization of Egypt, see F. Harbison and I. A. Ibrahim, Human Resources for Egyptian Enterprise (New York: McGraw-Hill Book Co., 1958), Chapter 3; a detailed and more comprehensive treatment of this subject is in Ali El-Gritly, "The Structure of Modern Industry in Egypt," L'Egypte Contemporaine, Nos. 241-42 (November-December, 1947), 534-54.

16. For a more detailed discussion of this trend and its causes, see Patrick O'Brien, The Revolution in Egypt's Economic System (New York: Oxford University Press, 1966), pp. 18-19 and 32.

17. Ibid., p. 21.

18. For an extensive discussion of the failure of industry to grow more rapidly between 1948 and 1952, see the reports of the Chairman of the Federation of Egyptian Industries and the National Bank, Introduction to Federation of Industry in Egypt, 1951-52 and 1952-53. See also, National Bank of Egypt, Annual Report of the President 1949 and 1950 (Cairo).

19. A number of studies can be cited in this regard. For a theoretical discussion, see O'Brien, op. cit., pp. 86-87; Bent Hansen and Girgis Marzouk, Development and Economic Policy in the U.A.R., Egypt (Amsterdam: North Holland Publishing Co., 1965); and Mead, op. cit., pp. 111-14.

20. See Central Bank of Egypt, "Industrial Census for 1926," Economic Review, VII, 1 and 2 (1967), 15.

21. Ibid., pp. 10-22.

22. Ibid., p. 12.

23. Charles Issawi, Egypt in Revolution (New York: Oxford University Press, 1963), pp. 174-175; and Kurt Grunwald and Joachim Ronall, Industrialization in the Middle East (New York: Council for Middle Eastern Affairs Press, 1960), p. 200.

24. Hansen and Marzouk, op. cit., p. 125.

25. For a discussion of the government policies which tolerate and even encourage the monopolistic tendencies of some large industries, see Mead, op. cit., pp. 125-26; and Charles Issawi, "Egypt Since 1800: A Study in Lopsided Development," Journal of Economic History, XXI, 1 (March, 1961), 1-26.

26. United Nations, The Development of Manufacturing Industry

in Egypt, Israel and Turkey (New York: U.N. Publication, 1958), p. 37.

27. This tendency has been pointed out by several economists. See Robert Mabro, "Industrial Growth, Agricultural Underemployment and the Lewis Model: The Egyptian Case, 1937-1965," Journal of Development Studies, III, 4 (1967), 322-51; and Patrick O'Brien, "Industrial Development and the Employment Problem in Egypt, 1945-1965," Middle East Economic Papers (1962), pp. 90-120.

28. K. Raj, Employment Aspects of Planning in Underdeveloped Countries (Cairo: Nation Bank of Egypt Memorial Lectures, 1957).

29. The Deputy Minister for Industry of the U.A.R. stated that in order for Egypt to benefit from the Technological Stage, rise in employment should not parallel the rise in population. In his words, "Industrial sector cannot today or in the foreeable future absorb the excess rural labor," The Times (London), July 23, 1967.

30. O'Brien, The Revolution in Egypt's Economic System, pp. 279-80

31. Mabro, op. cit., pp. 340-41.

32. Ibid., p. 342, and Mead, op. cit., p. 114

33. The Charter of the Republic adopts the use of modern machinery in the following quotation: "We must put aside the assumption which says that using modern instruments does not give a full chance of work, on the grounds that modern machines do not need large labor power. This conception may prove sound at the beginning but it is not valid in the long run...." The Information Department, The Charter of the Republic (Cairo, 1962), p. 68.

34. Hansen and Marzouk, op. cit., p. 131.

35. See Harbison and Ibrahim, op. cit., p. 53.

36. The MISR group: nationalistic entrepreneurs who started that industrialization drive by forming the MISR Bank to lend financial support to the textile industry. A pioneer in this movement is Talat Harb.

37. For example, from the end of World War II until 1954, the Mehalla Company doubled its production and decreased its total labor force by 40 percent. Within eight years the Kafre El-Darvar Company tripled its output with no net addition to its labor force. See Mead, op. cit., p. 120f.

38. Under the pressure from the MISR Bank groups and other entrepreneurs in Egypt, the government prohibited the importation of secondhand machinery in 1944.

39. For example, employment in cotton ginning and processing shrank from 26, 390 in 1952 to 8, 209 in 1958. U. A. R. Central Agency for Public Mobilization and Statistics, Statistical Pocketbook, various issues.

40. Hansen and Marzouk, op. cit., p. 165; Mabro, op. cit., pp. 278-82.

41. For a more extensive discussion of these and other points, see O'Brien, The Revolution of Egypt's Economic System, pp. 278-82.

42. Frederick Harbison and Ibrahim A. Ibrahim, "Some Problems of Industrialization in Egypt," Annals of the American Academy of Political and Social Sciences, CCCV (May, 1956), 114.

43. U. S. Department of Labor, op. cit., p. 29.

44. See Thomas B. Stouffer, "The Industrial Worker," in S. Fisher, ed., Social Forces in the Middle East (New York: Cornell University Press, 1955), p. 85.

45. Harbison and Ibrahim, Human Resources for Egyptian Enterprise, p. 82-84.

46. The shortage in technicians and foremen for the newly developed industries was estimated at 10, 309 persons between 1961-65. U. S. Department of Labor, op. cit., p. 30f.

47. Harbison and Ibrahim, "Some Problems of Industrialization in Egypt," p. 117.

48. For a good discussion of these transitional problems, see W. E. Moore, op. cit., pp. 290-378, especially pp. 304-17; W. E. Moore and Arnold S. Feldman, eds., Labor Commitment and Social Change in Developing Areas (New York: Social Science Research Council, 1960); and Hassan El-Saaty, "Changes in the Industrial Organization of Egypt," International Sociological Association, Transactions of Third World Congress, II (London, 1956).

49. Harbison and Ibrahim, "Some Problems of Industrialization in Egypt," p. 114.

50. Ibid., p. 117.

51. O'Brien, <u>The Revolution in Egypt's Economic System</u>, pp. 198 and 286.

52. Stouffer in Fisher, <u>op. cit.</u>, pp. 83-99.

53. O'Brien, <u>The Revolution in Egypt's Economic System</u>, p. 250.

54. <u>Ibid.</u>, p. 322.

55. It would be impractical to attempt a list of complete bibliography. See, for example, Gabriel S. Saab, <u>The Egyptian Agrarian Reform 1952-1962</u> (London: Oxford University Press, 1967); Doreen Warriner, <u>Land Reform and Development in the Middle East</u> (London: Oxford University Press, 1962); Saad M. Gadella, <u>Land Reform in Relation to Social Development in Egypt</u> (Missouri: University of Missouri Press, 1962); Sayed Marei, <u>Agrarian Reform in Egypt</u> (Cairo: S.O.P. Press, 1957); M. Darling, "Land Reform in Italy and Egypt," <u>Yearbook of Agricultural Cooperation,</u> 1956; K. H. Parsons, "Land Reforms in the U.A.R.," <u>Land Economics,</u> XXV, 4 (November, 1959), 314-26; and S. Nakaoka, "A Note on the Evaluation Work of the Agrarian Reform in the U.A.R. (Egypt)," <u>The Developing Economics,</u> I, 1 (January–June, 1963).

56. U.S. Department of Labor, <u>op. cit.</u>, p. 42. See also Warriner, <u>op. cit.</u>, p. 27.

57. This deficiency of the statistics available has been emphasized by several writers. See G. Saab, <u>op. cit.</u>, pp. 9-10.

58. Warriner, <u>op. cit.</u>, p. 49.

59. <u>Ibid.</u>, pp. 27-40; Saab, <u>op. cit.</u>, pp. 122-123, 146-147; and Eva Garzouzi, <u>Old Ills and New Remedies</u> (Cairo: Dar El-Maaref, 1958), pp. 77-87.

60. Garzouzi, <u>op. cit.</u>, p. 24.

61. Saab, <u>op. cit.</u>, pp. 123 and 186-187.

62. U.N. Food and Agriculture Organization and the International Labor Organization, <u>Progress in Land Reform, Third Report</u> (New York: United Nations, 1962), p. 58.

63. See O'Brien's analysis of the cooperative use of labor in <u>The Revolution in Egypt's Economic System,</u> pp. 117, 143, 167, and 170.

64. For a brief but good account of the cooperatives in the provinces, see Keith Wheelock, Nasser's New Egypt (New York: Frederick A. Praeger, Publishers, 1960), pp. 94-102.

65. Nawage experience refers to the early experiment in land consolidation and rotation of crops, where organized rotation was first applied with success in the villages of Nawage.

66. Saab, op. cit., p. 147.

67. Wheelock, op. cit., p. 97.

68. U.N. Food and Agriculture Organization and the International Labor Organization, op. cit., pp. 37-42.

4

The principal demographic factors influencing the size and com-position of the supply of labor are age, sex, marital status, and size and type of household. Many, if not all, of these demographic deter-minants of labor supply could be as well treated as consequences of the structure and the employment of the supply of labor. However, most of the following analysis tend to emphasize their determinant effects.

AGE COMPOSITION

Detailed studies of age reporting in the Egyptian census have indicated that there is a consistent tendency toward age heaping and erroneous replies to the census questionnaires.[1] Perhaps the most relevant inaccuracy concerns males between the ages of twenty and twenty-nine, who were found to be consistently underreported in the last three censuses. Underreporting was estimated to be between 9 and 13 percent.[2] However, since most of the labor force analysis is concerned with adult males taken as a whole, this shifting should not be a major problem.

During the first half of this century the demographic development of Egypt shows how a relatively closed population, without significant migration and with relatively constant age-specific fertility and mortality rates, would attain a stable age structure after a number of years. In 1960, however, the relatively stable structure of the popu-lation was broken.[3] The rise in the rate of natural increase brought about by the marked decline in mortality resulted in a noticeable in-crease in the number and proportion of young people in the total popu-lation. Prior to the most recent census, the proportion of persons under fifteen remained fairly constant, around 38-39 percent, but in

1960 it rose to 43 percent. In contrast, the proportion of persons in
the age group encompassing those between fifteen and fifty-four,
which fluctuated between 53 and 56 percent from 1917 to 1947, fell to
51 percent in 1960. At the other end of the age cycle the small percentage of persons over sixty decreased from 8 percent in 1927 to
less than 6 percent in 1960. As a result of the continued high fertility
and the sharp decline in mortality rates after 1947, the Egyptian population has become younger than before. [4]

Even more dramatic are the numerical changes revealed in
Table 27. Here it is seen that out of a total population increase of
7.1 million persons between 1947 and 1960, 3.9 million (or 55 percent)
were persons under fifteen, and 2.8 million (or 39 percent) were
between fifteen and fifty-nine. Persons sixty and over increased by
less than 0.4 million, or less than 6 percent. This pattern of age

TABLE 27

Number of Persons by Age Distribution,
1937, 1947, and 1960
(in Millions)

| | Age Group: | | | |
	0-14	15-59	60+	Total
1937:				
Male	3.2	4.3	0.5	8.0
Female	3.1	4.3	0.5	7.9
Total	6.3	8.6	1.0	15.9
1947:				
Male	3.7	5.2	0.5	9.4
Female	3.6	5.4	0.5	9.6
Total	7.3	10.6	1.0	19.0
1960:				
Male	5.7	6.6	0.7	13.1
Female	5.5	6.8	0.8	13.0
Total	11.2	13.4	1.5	26.1
1960 increase over 1947:	3.9	2.8	0.4	7.1

Source: U.A.R. Central Statistical Committee, Population
Trends in the U.A.R. (Cairo, 1962), p. 4.

distribution shows that Egypt is characterized by a large number of children who are dependent on the adult population represented by the fifteen-to-fifty-nine age group. There were between eight and nine children under fifteen to every ten persons between fifteen and fifty-nine years old in 1960, whereas the figure for 1947 was only seven children per ten adults. This compared with a ratio in the economically most -advanced countries of Europe and North America of about four or five children for every ten active adults. 5

A particularly useful technique for evaluating the burden of dependency is to compute the age dependency ratio, which is generally defined as the number of persons under fifteen and over sixty-five per 100 persons between the ages of fifteen and sixty-four. Table 28 shows dependency ratios of Egypt for total and male population in the last three censuses. This table indicates a trend toward an increase in the overall dependency ratio. In 1960 it reached a level of 90 in comparison to 65 in 1947 and 75 in 1937. Considering just males, the observable pattern is also an increase in the dependency load, especially between 1947 and 1960. The heavy load of dependency characteristic of the Egyptian population in 1969 can be seen from further inter-national comparison, especially with a more highly developed nation such as the United States. In 1960, Egypt had 43 percent of its popu-lation age fourteen and under as compared to 27 percent for the United States. For the active adult ages (fifteen to sixty-four), the compara-tive figures were 53 and 65 percent, respectively.

The breakdown of the population into the three major age groups gives only a rough idea about the relationship between age structure of a population and its economic conditions. Therefore, a better pro-cedure toward this end is to estimate the productive capacity of the different age groups, as well as their needs for consumption patterns. 6

TABLE 28

Dependency Ratio (the Number of Persons Less Than
Fifteen Years of Age and Over Sixty-five Divided by
Persons Between Fifteen and Sixty-five)

1937		1947		1960	
Male	Total	Male	Total	Male	Total
64. 4	74. 8	70. 9	67. 7	91. 6	90. 5

Source: United Nations Demographic Yearbook (New York, annual), 1948, p. 106, Table 4; 1952, p. 132, Table 4; and 1967, p. 142, Table 5.

TABLE 29

Estimates of the Units of Production and Consumption
per 1,000 of the Population According to Age Group,
1960

Age Group	Population in Thousands	No. of Units of Production In Thousands	Percent	No. of Units of Consumption In Thousands	Percent
0-14	11,110	712	5.3	4,846	25.9
15-64	13,970	12,442	91.7	13,167	70.3
65+	902	404	3.0	712	3.8
Total	25,982	13,558	100.0	18,725	100.0

Source: U.A.R. Central Agency for Public Mobilization and Statistics, Population Increase in the U.A.R. and Its Deterrents to Development (Cairo, 1966), pp. 67 and 161.

TABLE 30

Percentage of the Share of the Major Age Group in
the Units of Production and Consumption, 1960

Age Group	Population	Units of Production	Units of Consumption
0-15	42.7	5.3	26.0
15-64	53.8	91.7	70.2
56+	3.5	3.0	3.8
Total	100.0	100.0	100.0

Source: U.A.R. Central Committee for Public Mobilization and Statistics, Population Increase in the U.A.R. and Its Deterrents to Development (Cairo, 1966), p. 162.

TABLE 31

Comparative Estimates of the Units of Production
and Consumption per 1,000 of the Population,
1960

Country	Number of Units of Production per 1,000 Population	Number of Units of Consumption per 1,000 Population	Number of Units of Consumption per 1,000 Units of Production
Egypt	521	720	1,382
India	561	756	1,347
U.S.A.	626	794	1,269
Sweden	671	821	1,224

Source: U.A.R. Central Agency for Public Mobilization and Statistics, Population Increase in the U.A.R. and Its Deterrents to Development (Cairo: November, 1966), p. 162, Table 67.

Such estimates are presented in Table 29. The population in Egypt roughly equalled 13.5 million units of production and 18.6 million units of consumption in in 1960. For every 1,000 persons there were 521 units of production and 720 units of consumption. For every 1,000 units of production there were 1,382 units of consumption. The significance of these differences becomes more apparent by an examination of Table 30, which presents the share of the three major age groups in Egypt's total units of production and consumption. The productive age group (fifteen to sixty-four), which constitutes about half of the population, contributed 92 percent of the nation's productive capacity and consumed only 70 percent of its consumption units, whereas the youthful dependency group (under fifteen) contributed 5 percent to production and consumed 36 percent of the consumption units. These figures clearly demonstrate the magnitude of the dependency load which falls on the shoulders of the population in the productive ages.

Egypt's relative disadvantage as far as the effects which the age structure of the population produces on economic conditions becomes even clearer when we compare the Egyptian figures with others from selected developed and less developed countries (see Table 31). When compared to Sweden, the United States, and India, Egypt has the highest number of units of consumption per unit of production. That is,

in this regard Egypt is in an even worse position than India, the country
that is most often cited in discussions of population in relation to
economic development.

SEX COMPOSITION

Sex ratios (defined as the number of males per 100 females)
indicate a very slight increase in 1960 compared to previous years.
While the sex ratio remained unchanged in rural areas, males tended
to increase more than females in the urban areas. This, of course,
reflects the selectivity of migration.[7]

Many married males leave their wives and children behind in
their home villages and move to cities to seek jobs. This kind of
migration is predominant in upper Egypt. Among the various governorates, sex ratios have fluctuated between 98 and 102 over the past five
censuses, which means that Egypt did not experience any problem of
sex discrepancy as in some other countries.[8] Sex ratio tends to be
higher in urban governorates of upper Egypt than in the rural governorates of lower Egypt. In upper Egypt, only the governorates of Aswan
and Beni-Seuif have shown a preponderance of females over males for
a long period of time. Male migration of the Nubians to work in Cairo
and Alexandria explains the low pattern of sex ratio in Aswan. The
border governorates, on the other hand, have always had a higher sex
ratio in comparison to the total republic because of the fact that more
of their population are male migrants who leave their families behind
and spend some time working in different industrial and quarry establishments in the desert.

An examination of the sex composition of the economically significant age groups in rural and urban population indicates that males
outnumber females in rural areas at young ages, but that the situation
is reversed at the older ages. The preponderance of young males in
rural areas could be either apparent (i.e., a result of female under-
enumeration in the census) and/or real (caused by differences in sex
mortality rates because of more medical attention given to males).
Most probably, the migration of young girls to cities to work as house
servants and in other personal services is also responsible.

The overall impact of the changes in sex ratio on the supply of
labor in Egypt seems to be minimal, since there was no large-scale
dislocation by migration or war in the country's recent history.
Nonetheless, the combined impact of sex and age composition of the
population, especially on the type and the magnitude of financial dependency, should be emphasized. The returns of a 1958-59 household
budget survey conducted in 1960 provide us with some information on

TABLE 32

Financial Dependency by Sex and Rural-Urban
Areas for Egypt and India, 1958-1959

Dependency Case	U.A.R.			INDIA		
	Male	Female	Total	Male	Female	Total
Independent:						
Rural	31.4	1.3	16.1	47.1	10.4	29.1
Urban	29.9	1.4	15.3	49.8	7.4	30.2
Total	30.6	1.3	15.7	47.6	9.9	29.3
Partially dependent:						
Rural	22.4	2.8	12.5	7.9	16.0	11.9
Urban	15.4	4.5	9.8	4.5	4.6	4.5
Total	18.8	3.7	11.1	7.3	14.1	10.6
Totally dependent:						
Rural	46.2	95.9	71.4	45.0	73.6	59.0
Urban	54.8	94.1	74.9	45.7	88.1	45.7
Total	50.6	95.0	73.2	45.1	75.9	60.1

Source: U.A.R. Central Agency for Public Mobilization and Statistics, Population Increase in the U.A.R. and Its Deterrents to Development (Cairo, 1966), p. 41, Table 15.

the financial dependency of the sexes in the rural and urban population.[9] In this survey, household members were classified as either financially independent or dependent. The financially independent persons are those individuals who are financially responsible for themselves and for other members of their household, either from work incomes or real estate. The persons described as financially dependent were classified further as partially dependent or totally dependent. The first group consists of those persons who were receiving auxiliary income but still depended financially on their family for support. The second group were those persons who were totally dependent on their families. Table 32 compares the returns of this survey with a similar one conducted in India at the same period. The figures clearly show that the percentages of the financially independent persons in Egypt are far less than those in India (15.7 in Egypt as compared to 29.3 in India), and that although there is little difference in the extent of partial dependency the percentage of total dependents is much higher in Egypt (73.2 percent) than in India (60.1 percent).

The percentage of partially independent males was higher in rural than in urban Egypt. In addition, totally dependent males were much more represented in the urban than in the rural population. Rural families seem to put their sons to work earlier. The simplicity of agricultural work permits such early entrance into the labor force. Further, urban families provide education for a larger number of their sons and for a longer period than do rural families, a factor which compounds the dependency situation in urban families. The number of females was much smaller proportionally in Egypt than in India; and, also in contrast to the Indian situation, there was no significant urban/rural differential.

The relevance of these figures becomes obvious when we realize that 95 percent of the approximately 13 million women in 1960 were totally dependent financially on other members of their families, and that only 1.3 percent were supporting themselves. It is also important to consider these figures in line with the fact that about two-thirds of all women in Egypt reside in rural areas. The very low percentage of those who were financially independent (1.3) could be a result of the fact that in spite of the Islamic laws of inheritance which entitle the girls to inherit their parents' property, in rural Egypt a daughter's share is frequently left with her brothers and, subsequently, her husband considers it beneath his dignity to claim it.[10] Such zeal for keeping the family property intact could be partly responsible for such very high dependency on the females' part. Employment policy should consider these facts as guidelines. Only successful schemes for developing rural industry where women can be employed in large numbers would provide a realistic solution.

MARITAL STATUS

The factors which determine age at marriage in a society are many, and include legal, social, and economic aspects. Changes in the average age at which women marry may in turn have profound effects on a number of socioeconomic as well as demographic factors. Among the latter is the size and composition of the female labor force. Marriage at an early age is generally recognized as an important demographic determinant of population increase in developing countries.[11] In this respect, Egypt is no exception. In Egypt, the minimum age at marriage is sixteen for girls and eighteen for boys. Recent figures indicate that the average age of marriage is rising; nevertheless, it

TABLE 33

Percentage Distribution of Females According to the Marital
Status and Participation in Economic Activities by Age,
1960

Age Groups	Never Married	Married	Divorced	Widowed	Economically Active
-15	----	----	----	----	7. 8
15-19	66. 88	31. 76	1. 13	0. 23	8. 6
20-24	22. 96	73. 50	2. 53	1.01	7. 3
25-29	6.73	88. 84	2. 39	2. 04	4. 8
30-34	3. 26	89. 93	2. 43	4. 38	4. 5
35-39	1. 88	89. 01	2. 01	7. 10	4. 4
40-44	1. 84	79. 51	2. 41	16. 24	5. 3
45-50	1. 24	76. 23	1. 97	20. 56	4. 4

Source: U.A.R. Central Agency for Public Mobilization and
Statistics, Population Increase in the U.A.R. and Its Deterrents to
Development (Cairo, 1966), pp. 62 and 169, Tables 23 and 72.

is still relatively low. Average age at marriage rose from 24.2 years
in 1947 to 25.9 in 1960 for males, from 18.6 years in 1947 to 19.8 in
1960 for females.[12] This rise in the average age at marriage corresponds to the general urbanization trend, the increase in the general
educational level of the population, and the growing role of women in
economic activities.

Unfortunately, census publications do not provide the necessary
tabulations which enable us to examine directly the economic activities
of women belonging to different marital status groups; nevertheless,
some useful inferences can be drawn from Table 33, which presents
the female population by different age groups according to their marital
status and participation in economic activities in 1960. These data

clearly indicate the relatively high percentage of married women in all ages and especially those years of potential maximum fertility (ages twenty-five through forty). Hence, it is not only that early marriage results in a greater number of children ever born, but also permits women who die at middle age to have as many children before they die (a factor which is not by any means minimal, especially in a country like Egypt, where female mortality at middle age, mostly from maternity-related causes, is still quite high).

The implications of early marriage on the fertility of Egyptian women needs no further discussion. A widely accepted conclusion is the fact that women with family responsibilities are known to be less prone to participate in work outside their homes, especially where household activities are still largely traditional and where technological equipment in the home is not advanced enough to free women to work. It is, therefore, customary for women in Egypt to cease outside work after marriage. Such observation receives support from the figures which show the percentages of the never married and the economically active in each age group. The noticeable drop in the percentage of the economically active females, from 8.6 percent of women between the ages of fifteen and twenty to 4.8 percent of women between the ages of twenty-five and thirty, was paralleled by another noticeable drop in the percentage of never-married women in these two age groups, from approximately 67 percent to only 7 percent. However, recent surveys indicate that in rural areas the female participation rate reaches its peak at ages twelve through sixteen, and then drops as statutory marriage begins for girls and childbearing starts. [13]

Change in the age of marriage is not by itself the only factor which affects the likelihood of women's participation in economic activities. Change in the proportion of women who eventually marry can also alter the size and composition of the labor force. In what follows, attention will focus first on the difference of the marital-status composition of the rural and urban population, in order to assess the impact of urbanization on the proportion of women who will eventually marry. Second, the relationship between education and marital status will be considered in order to ascertain the impact of education on marriage postponement.

Table 34 presents the percentage distribution of the rural and urban populations according to their marital status as of 1960. These figures clearly demonstrate the higher percentage of the never-married groups, males as well as females, in urban areas. Prolonged educational training, higher aspirations of urban life, and sheer economic reasons seem to foster the decisions of urban dwellers to postpone their marriages to later ages. Also, for the urban person, marriage

TABLE 34

Percentage Distribution of the Rural Urban Population
According to Marital Status and Sex, 1960

Marital Status	Sex	Urban		Rural		Total	
		Number	Percent	Number	Percent	Number	Percent
Never married	M	701, 604	27. 3	909, 479	22. 3	1, 611, 083	24. 3
	F	409, 703	15. 5	474, 961	10. 2	884, 664	12. 1
	T	1, 111, 307	21. 3	1, 384, 440	15. 8	2, 495, 747	17. 9
Married	M	1, 772, 746	69. 1	3, 012, 044	73. 9	4, 784, 790	72. 0
	F	1, 764, 510	66. 9	3, 163, 613	67. 8	4, 928, 123	67. 5
	T	3, 537, 256	67. 9	6, 175, 657	70. 6	9, 712, 913	69. 6
Divorced	M	30, 788	1. 2	41, 862	1. 0	72, 650	1. 1
	F	60, 801	2. 3	86, 393	1. 9	147, 194	2. 0
	T	91, 589	1. 8	128, 255	1. 5	219, 844	1. 6
Widowed	M	49, 480	1. 9	91, 307	2. 2	140, 787	2. 1
	F	8 30, 404	14. 4	885, 893	19. 0	1, 266, 297	17. 3
	T	429, 884	8. 3	977, 200	11. 2	1, 407, 084	10. 1
Not stated	M	12, 342	0. 5	22, 781	0. 6	35, 123	0. 5
	F	24, 187	0. 9	52, 875	1. 1	77, 062	1. 1
	T	36, 529	0. 7	75, 656	0. 9	112, 185	0. 8
Total	M	2, 566, 960	100. 0	4, 077, 473	100. 0	6, 644, 433	100. 0
	F	2, 639, 605	100. 0	4, 663, 735	100. 0	7, 303, 340	100. 0
	T	5, 206, 565	100. 0	8, 741, 208	100. 0	13, 947, 773	100. 0

Source: U.A.R. Central Agency for Public Mobilization and Statistics, Population Increase in the U.A.R. and Its Deterrents to Development (Cairo, 1966), p. 60, Table 27.

is becoming more of a personal rather than a family affair. In light of these differences between the rural and urban populations, increased urbanization is expected to lead to further increases in the average age at marriage and in the proportion of women who are not married.

In an earlier discussion it has been noted that at later stages urbanization is also expected to increase women's role in economic life. Therefore, in Egypt as in many other parts of the world, delayed marriages as well as female entry in service occupations seem to be two manifestations of urbanization.

The percentage distribution of the population according to their marital status and educational attainment in 1960 is presented in Table 35. The reported figures show a striking difference in the never-married category. While only 13.4 percent of the illiterate people were never married, about 37 percent of those with higher education were never married. Those with the equivalent of a high school education showed a pattern closer to those with a university degree. Two general conclusions can be drawn from these data. First, there is a clear tendency toward marriage postponement with an increase in education. Second, educational expansion will very likely lead both to a rise in the average age of marriage and to an increase in the percentage

TABLE 35

Percentage Distribution of the Population According to
Marital Status and Educational Attainment, 1960

Marital Status	Illiterate	High School or Equivalent	University or Equivalent
Never married	13.4	30.7	37.1
Married	71.3	65.6	60.7
Divorced	1.7	1.1	0.9
Widowed	12.7	2.1	1.0
Not stated	0.9	0.5	0.3

Source: U.A.R. Central Agency for Public Mobilization and Statistics, Population Increase in the U.A.R. and Its Deterrents to Development (Cairo, 1966), p. 64, Table 25.

of never-married persons in the aggregate. [14] In fact, more than any other factor, education may work to raise the age of marriage in a relatively short time, since the emphasis is directed toward the education of the young (those twenty years old or less). This group constitutes a sizable portion of the total population and any delay in marriage among them will be felt on the aggregate level.

During World War II, crude marriage rates rose, reflecting the country's economic boom. The favorable economic conditions of the war years continued throughout the period which followed the cessation of hostilities; this helped to keep the marriage rate at a high level up to 1947, when it started to undergo a declining trend. By 1952 the crude marriage rate had reached a level below that of 1938. From 1952 to 1965, with the exception of the years 1961 and 1962, crude marriage rates fluctuated between 9.1 and 10.8. The exceptionally low crude marriage rates during the years 1961 and 1962 (8.6 and 8.5) resulted mainly from a great loss in the cotton crops of these years, a loss caused by a plague of cotton worms. In this respect, it is of interest to note that in rural areas, marriage rate takes on a seasonal nature, reaching a peak around October and December (the cotton season). [15]

The lower marriage rates that have prevailed during the 1960's will probably increase further the number of never-married women, thus increasing the number of potential female workers. Counterbalancing this, however, the fall in the number of divorced women and the decline in the percentage of widowed women are expected to continue. In part, this is because widowed and divorced persons remarry more now than they did earlier. The fall in the percentage of widowed is also most probably related to the fall in mortality.

Divorce is generally recognized to be widespread in Egypt. The country's divorce rates are among the world's highest. Divorce is more common in the city than in the village, and more prevalent in the major cities than in the provincial towns. A possible explanation for the high rates of divorce may be the ease by which divorce can be accomplished and the manner in which marriage is arranged, without appreciable intervention on the part of the couple concerned. A second cause is the higher standard of education, culture, and social development that exists among men more so than among women. A third cause is the widespread nature of revocable divorce, where marital life is usually resumed after a short period of separation. Divorce rates, however, showed declining trend during the 1950's, and by 1965, were only two-thirds of those in 1947. The average divorce rate, which was 9.8 percent in the period between 1947 and 1951, declined to 7.1 percent in the years between 1962 and 1965. [16] Legal restrictions on divorce, the rise in the level of education (especially of women),

and the continued rise in the economic cost of supporting a divorced
wife and children helped to sustain this trend.

In spite of its fairly widespread nature, divorce in Egypt has
little direct effect on fertility because of two facts. First, a great
portion of the divorce cases, as has been pointed out, are revocable
divorces and have little or no effect on marriage duration. Second,
the remarriage of divorced women is common. In 1960, approximately
66 percent of the divorced women between the ages of twenty-five and
forty remarried. [17] However, the high rate of divorce is not totally
without impact on fertility. Ironically, divorce's net effect is to increase rather than to decrease the fertility of married women. Because
of the ease by which husbands can divorce their wives, and because of
women's total financial dependency on their husbands, young women
are taught early in their life that once they get married they should
have as many children as soon as they can in order to protect themselves
against divorce. Even if divorce should take place, they would at least
assure themselves and their children of financial support from their
husbands. Thus, the high divorce rate in Egypt works as one of the
institutional patterns favoring high fertility. [18] Perhaps a more active
role of women as bread winners will give them the security needed
to direct their emphasis away from a family building pattern which
encourages maximum fertility. [19]

HOUSEHOLD SIZE CHARACTERISTICS

The available data indicate a tendency for the average size of the
household to increase, on the aggregate, at least between 1947 and 1960.
During this period, the average size of the household increased in all
governorates with the exception of Suhag, where it decreased slightly
from 5.2 to 5.1 persons. In rural governorates, the largest increase
was recorded for the newly established governorate of Kafer-el-Sheikh
(from 5.0 persons in 1947 to 5.8 in 1960). Among urban governorates,
those in the Suez area (Port Said, Ismailia, and Suez) recorded the
largest increase in the size of the household. Alexandria ranked second,
and Cairo showed very little change, from 4.7 persons in 1947 to 4.8
in 1960. [20]

A closer look at the distribution of households by size may throw
some light on the nature of these trends in the average size of the household. Table 36 indicates that the changes which occurred in the average
household size between 1947 and 1960 resulted primarily from an increase in the percentage distribution of households with large numbers
(7 persons and over). Such a trend toward a large-size household cannot easily be explained in the face of the urbanization trend and increasing movement and mobility of the population. However, there is

TABLE 36

Average Size of Private Household and Its Distribution
in Size Groups, 1947, 1957, and 1960
(in Percentages)

	Percentage Distribution of Households in Households with Size					Average Size of Household
Year	1	2-3	4-6	7-9	10 and Over	
1947	7.0	36.6	43.1	15.8	4.5	4.7
1957	7.2	33.5	42.7	17.7	5.4	4.8
1960	7.8	34.0	41.4	19.9	5.6	5.0

Source: U. N. Economic Bulletin for Africa, V (January, 1958),
53, Table 18; and U.A.R. Central Agency for Public Mobilization and
Statistics, Basic Statistics, 1964 (Cairo, 1965), p. 27.

some evidence to suggest that there is probably a close relationship
between the level of infant mortality and the size of the household.
The governorates which recorded a substantially low level of infant
mortality, whether rural or urban (Kafer-el-Sheikh and Beheira, as
well as Ismailia and Damiatta), are the ones that reported the largest
average size of the household. [21]

Two other factors which are sociological in nature are also
necessary if the changes which occurred in the size of the household
are to be understood. These are the availability of housing units and
the pattern of family living arrangements. There is no doubt that the
availability of housing units is a limiting factor on the number and
size of households, especially in the large urban centers. [22] Furthermore, the fact that the Egyptian definition of a household adheres to
the housekeeping unit concept rather than the household housing unit
concept would result in smaller size households. [23] Not the number
of dwellers in a given household, but other criteria (such as being
under the authority of the same head of household, sharing of meals,
etc.) are actually the limiting factors in the Egyptian definition.

The second sociological factor which has some bearing on the
size of the household is the pattern of family living arrangements. As
one observer has commented, "The typical form of the extended

family is considerably less common in Egypt than in the other parts
of the Middle East because, in Egypt, the average life span of the
father is lower, which means that he often dies before his sons
marry."[24] While this observation could be true, the increase in
life expectancy in the last two or three decades leads one to be cautious
in accepting this interpretation. More important, perhaps, are a
number of socioeconomic factors which actually encouraged the movement away from the extended family. First, the city has new living
prospects which enable sons to break away from their dependence on
the family property and the traditional family occupation. Second,
the spread of education among sons and daughters has introduced new
aspirations toward financial independence. Third, the nature of the
extended family in Egypt is largely a social rather than an economic
unit, and the unity of the extended family is demonstrated in public
and on formal occasions but not in day-to-day work activities.[25]

The percentage distribution of manpower and labor force in the
total population, along with the average size of the household in each
governate around 1960, is shown in Table 37. No clear-cut relationship between the average size of the household and the percentage of
the population in the labor force can be ascertained from the data.
Nevertheless, the data do suggest two observations: First, in rural
areas, household size seems to be associated with the percentage of
the population in the labor force. For example, the three governorates
which have noticeably larger percentages of their population in the
labor force (Kafer-el-Sheikh, Beheira, and Daqahlia) also recorded
the largest average size of the household among rural governorates.
Second, the pattern was quite reversed in urban governorates. The
Suez, area governorates, with the smallest percentage of their population in the labor force, recorded a relatively larger size of the
household.

Such rural-urban differentials are largely due to the nature of
the household in each of the traditional and modern sectors of the
economy. In the rural sector, household members find work easily
on the family farm and/or in other family enterprises. In the urban
sector, however, the definition of labor force membership is more
restricted and denotes participation in economic activities outside the
household. The relatively young age structure of the Suez governorates,
as it is reflected in the lower percentage of their population in the
manpower classification, is probably a contributing factor to household
size, as well as a limiting factor on the percentage of the population
reported in the labor force.

The information which can be obtained from census returns on
the relationship between size of household and the labor supply are
scant and inadequate for historical analysis. However, a number of

TABLE 37

Percentage Distribution of Manpower and the Labor Force
in the Total Population of Each Governorate Along with
the Average Size of Household, 1960

Governorates	Labor Force (Percent)	Manpower (Percent)	Average Size of Household
Cairo	23.9	61.1	4.8
Alexandria	24.1	60.9	5.0
Port Said	21.8	60.0	5.2
Ismailia	22.0	55.0	5.3
Suez	20.3	56.4	5.0
Damiatta	27.0	57.6	5.4
Daqahlia	28.6	60.3	5.4
Sharqia	25.3	60.0	5.2
Kalyubia	26.0	60.2	5.2
Kafer-el-Sheikh	29.6	60.0	5.8
Gharbia	25.4	60.6	5.1
Menoufia	27.0	63.1	5.0
Beheira	30.0	58.4	5.6
Giza	27.0	62.2	4.8
Beni-Seuif	26.6	61.2	4.3
Fayum	27.6	61.5	4.5
Mania	28.1	64.4	4.5
Asyut	25.9	60.2	4.9
Suhag	25.3	60.0	5.1
Kena	25.3	58.9	4.7
Aswan	26.2	61.3	4.4

Source: U.A.R. Central Agency for Public Mobilization and Statistics, Basic Statistics, 1964 (Cairo, 1965), Ref. 1151/65, pp. 26, 27 and 70.

observations can be gleaned from other recent surveys such as the family budget sample surveys (1958-59) and the rural employment surveys (1964-65). Unfortunately, the findings of the last survey cannot be generalized, since the sample was not representative of the rural population as a whole; nonetheless, some of the findings should be given some attention because of their suggestive nature. For instance, Table 38 shows there is some evidence to indicate a strong association between size of household and income and also between income and the number of labor units per household.

It is relevant to note that the ability to read and write seems to greatly increase the chances of women to find work outside the house-hold. In contrast to the illiterate population, where only about 5 per-cent of the women were actively employed, nearly 10 percent of the literate females were employed. Analysis of these findings supports the assumption that the medium certificate[26] represents the minimum educational attainment that can afford its holders a reasonable chance to work either in the technical, administrative, and clerical fields, or in certain agricultural work, like supervision and marketing, which for most advanced positions requires special qualifications that cannot be met except by those who hold medium or high certificates. This assumption is further supported by statistics on educational status by professions.[27] For instance, the proportion of crafts and construction workers is 7. 6 percent among illiterates, while it is 11. 1 percent among those who can read and write. For salesworkers, the proportion is 2. 2 percent among illiterates while it is 8. 8 percent among those who can read and write. The great majority of those who hold medium certificates (83. 3 percent) work in technical, administrative, and clerical occupations.

Turning to a specific consideration of the rural work force, the 1960 census returns indicate that 80 percent of the labor force in rural areas is engaged in agricultural activities. It is customary to classify this category into two groups; the farmers (those who own the land) and farm laborers (those who do not own land). The remaining 20 percent are usually classified as nonagricultural operators. However, such a classification by itself is not sufficient in understanding the nature of rural employment. The fact that in rural Egypt specialization is almost nonexistent, and that a division of labor is almost completely lacking, makes it extremely difficult to classify the rural labor force by occupation. However, the Institute of National Planning, in co-operation with the International Labor Organization, adopted a simplified classification by types of work which distinguished between five major groups of work: field work, animal husbandry, processing farm pro-ducts, other agricultural work, and nonagricultural work. Table 39 gives the distribution of annual working hours spent in the different types of work according to the type of household and age-sex groups.

TABLE 38

Distribution of Household by Annual Family Income, Household
Size, and Number of Labor Units per Family, 1964-65

	Under a 50 LE[a]	50-99 LE	100-149 LE	150-199 LE	200 LE and more	Unknown	Total - 100
Household size: (Members)							
1	71	16	5	4	1	3	77
2	51	31	9	6	2	1	91
3	43	36	11	4	4	2	127
4	35	30	22	8	3	2	156
5	29	37	17	8	7	2	144
6	24	27	31	8	8	2	131
7	19	30	31	10	5	5	83
8	12	40	25	14	9	-	65
9	23	20	23	14	18	2	49
10 and more	6	15	28	13	38	-	71
Labor Units:							
Less than 0.50 units	3	76	13	1	4	3	68
0.50 - 0.99 ,,	47	29	13	6	4	1	129
1.00 - 1.49 ,,	37	36	17	7	4	1	281
1.50 - 1.99 ,,	30	31	24	5	9	1	184
2.00 - 2.49 ,,	23	23	27	14	10	3	121
2.50 - 2.99 ,,	15	35	35	6	14	5	81
3.00 - 3.99 ,,	18	25	28	15	12	2	85
4.00 - 4.99 ,,	7	36	32	7	15	3	28
5.00 - 6.99 ,,	6	12	18	18	40	-	17
Total	32	30	20	8	8	2	994

[a]LE - Egyptian pound

Source: U.A.R. Institute of National Planning, Final Report on Employment Problems in Rural Areas, U.A.R. (Cairo, 1968), p. 56, Table 34.

TABLE 39

Distribution of Annual Time Worked According to Type of
Work, 1964-65

Type of Household	Sex-Age Groups	Recorded Annual Working Hours	Field Work	Animal Hus-bandry	Process-ing Farm Products	Other Agricul-tural Work	Non-Agri-cultural Work
Farmers:	Men	871,682	53	21	3	13	10
	Women	166,811	19	63	11	3	4
	Children	164,511	49	39	3	5	4
	Total	1,203,004	48	30	4	10	8
Farm laborers:							
	Men	164,462	58	13	3	11	15
	Women	36,617	31	35	4	8	22
	Children	44,671	55	23	2	7	13
	Total	249,750	53	18	3	10	16
Non-agricultural operators:							
	Men	171,263	8	4	3	3	82
	Women	21,963	14	29	6	2	49
	Children	30,989	25	26	2	1	46
	Total	224,217	11	10	3	2	74

Source: U.A.R. Institute of National Planning, Final Report on Employment Problems in Rural Areas, U.A.R. (Cairo, April, 1968), p. 36, Table 19.

The first two categories, the farm owners and farm laborers, are similar in that almost 50 percent of the total working hours of men, women, and children was devoted to field plantation work. They differed, however, in the annual time worked in animal husbandry and non-agricultural work. Animal husbandry absorbed more of the annual time worked by farmers than farm laborers. This is because farmers are more financially able than laborers to invest a portion of their income in animal husbandry.

It should be noted, however, that animal husbandry absorbed a comparatively high proportion of the women's and children's work. That nonagricultural work received 16 percent of farm laborers' time in comparison to only 8 percent of farmers' time was due to the larger proportion of farm laborers who usually work in construction, transport, and maintenance work. The table also shows that the nonagricultural operators spent about 26 percent of their time in agricultural work, an indication of a considerable interrelationship between the agricultural and nonagricultural sectors in rural areas.

In order to ascertain the relative contribution of the members of the different types of rural households in the total working hours, the type of work by age and sex has to be considered. Table 40 shows the contribution of men, women, and children in the different types of household, to the annual labor input according to type of work. The figures show that most of the work, 73 percent, was done by men, while the contribution of women was 13 percent, on the average, and that of children was 14 percent. The table also shows that the contributions of women and children were greater in the category of farm laborer household than the other two types.

While those observations suggest the relative contribution of rural household members in annual labor input, they are not, as indicated earlier, applicable to the rural population as a whole. The contribution of women and children has to be reconsidered in light of three factors: (1) the traditional ban on the exact reporting of the working hours of women and children; (2) the possibility that the survey did not include some temporary operations which are usually performed by hired women and children; and (3) the existence of sufficient regional variations in the percentage of women's labor input in the different types of agricultural work.

As far as urban areas are concerned, the effect of industrialization on the ways of life and on the social characteristics of the rural population seems to be far greater than that indicated by mere migration from rural to urban areas. On the aggregate, rural-urban migration between 1937 and 1960 did not result in any decrease in the size of household. On the contrary, such population mobility, combined with

TABLE 40

Contribution of Men, Women, and Children to the
Annual Labor Input According to Type of Work,
1964-65

Type of Household and Sex-Age Groups	Field Work	Animal Husbandry	Processing Farm Products	Other Agri-cultural Work	Non-Agri-cultural Work	Total
Farmer:						
Men	81	52	52	89	86	72
Women	5	30	38	4	7	14
Children	14	18	10	7	7	14
Total	100	100	100	100	100	100
Farm laborer:						
Men	73	49	71	75	64	67
Women	9	28	18	12	21	15
Children	18	23	11	13	15	18
Total	100	100	100	100	100	100
Non-agricultural operator:						
Men	57	32	68	89	85	76
Women	12	30	22	8	7	10
Children	31	38	10	3	8	14
Total	100	100	100	100	100	100
Grand Total:						
Men	79	51	56	86	82	73
Women	6	29	34	6	9	13
Children	15	20	10	8	9	14
Total	100	100	100	100	100	100

Source: U.A.R. Institute of National Planning, Final Report on Employment Problems in Rural Areas, U.A.R. (Cairo, April, 1968), p. 37, Table 20.

limited expansion in housing and especially low-rent housing in the
large urban centers during World War II, and during the postwar
period up to the late 1950's, resulted in an actual increase in the size
of the household. The effect of industrialization on the size of the
household and other living arrangements can be seen from the findings
of a study which was undertaken in 1956 in the area adjacent to Kafar
El-Dawar, the major industrial center for cotton spinning and weaving. [28] This study clearly revealed that the establishment of industrial
centers in the rural areas results in a big increase in the total population of the area surrounding the center due to migration from other
villages: the total population of the study area increased by 146.7
percent in the nine years from 1947 to 1956.

The number and size of households in the area also witnessed
some major changes. During the 1937-56 period the number of households increased by 383.2 percent while the average family size decreased
from 6 persons in 1937 to 4.9 persons in 1956. This compares to an
average family size of 6.8 persons for agricultural families. Furthermore, comparisons with the agricultural families reveal that the bi-
ological family system was prevalent in the area studies. Also, the
agricultural families consisted of more persons, more children, and
more relatives than did nonagricultural families. Not only has industrialization brought about a noticeable change in the size of the household and the structure of the families, but it has also influenced changes
in age composition. For example, the population under five years of
age constituted a larger proportion in 1956 than in 1947. The survey
findings also revealed that industrialization has a great effect on the
educational status of the people. For example, illiteracy among agricultural family heads was 73.3 percent compared to 48.5 percent among
nonagricultural family heads, and the proportion who had five years or
less of education was 49 percent for agricultural heads as compared to
2.8 percent for nonagricultural heads.

NOTES

1. For a discussion of this problem see: U.A.R. Central Agency
for Public Mobilization and Statistics, Population Increase in the U.A.R.
and Its Deterrents to Development (Cairo, 1966), pp. 41-49.

2. Donald C. Mead, Growth and Structural Changes in the Egyptian Economy (Homewood, Ill.: Richard D. Irwin, Inc., 1967), p. 24.

3. For a discussion of the stability of age composition in Egypt until 1947 census, see: M. A. El-Badry, "Some Demographic Measurements for Egypt Based on the Stability of Census Age Distribution," The Milbank Memorial Fund Quarterly, XXXIII, 3 (July, 1955), 268-305.

4. U.A.R. Central Statistical Committee, Population Trends in the U.A.R. (Cairo, 1962), p. 4.

5. Bent Hansen and Girgis Marzouk, Development and Economic Policy in the U.A.R. (Amsterdam: North Holland Publishing Co., 1965), p. 28.

6. For further information on the computation procedures, see: U.A.R. Central Agency for Public Mobilization and Statistics, op. cit., pp. 165-169.

7. United Nations, Economic Bulletin for Africa (New York: United Nations, 1965), V, January, 1965, p. 45, Table B. 13; and United Nations, Demographic Yearbook, 1948, (New York: United Nations, 1948), Table 8, p. 213.

8. The writer has in mind as an example of the discrepancy in sex ration, the U.S.S.R. after World War II, where the sex ratio was 83, and West Germany, Poland, and Austria where sex ratios were 89, 90, and 88, respectively. See Donald J. Bogue, Principles of Demography (New York: John Wiley and Sons, 1969), p. 168.

9. U.A.R. Central Statistical Committee, "Family Budget Sample Survey, 1958, 1959," (Cairo, 1961).

10. Gabriel Baer, Population and Society in the Arab East (New York: Frederick A. Praeger, Publishers, 1964), p. 39.

11. Bogue, op. cit., pp. 316 and 364.

12. U.A.R. Central Agency for Public Mobilization and Statistics, op. cit., p. 63.

13. Institute of National Planning, Final Report on Employment Problems in Rural Areas, U.A.R. (Cairo; April 1968), p. 39.

14. The effect of education on raising the age of marriage was anticipated by many writers. See Hansen and Marzouk, op. cit., p. 40.

15. U.A.R. Central Agency for Public Mobilization and Statistics, op. cit., p. 67.

16. Ibid.

17. Ibid., p. 66.

18. See K. Davis for a discussion of "The Institutional Patterns Favoring High Fertility in Underdeveloped Areas," Eugenics Quarterly, II (March, 1955), 33-39. The writer, however, presents the idea that the threat of divorce combined with females financial dependency is one of the institutional factors favoring rather than discouraging high fertility.

19. U.A.R. Central Agency for Public Mobilization and Statistics, loc. cit.

20. U.A.R. Central Agency for Public Mobilization and Statistics, Basic Statistics, 1964 (Cairo, 1965), p. 27.

21. Ibid., pp. 40-41.

22. For statistical information on housing problems and development see U.A.R. Statistical Yearbook, 1952-1966 (Cairo, 1967), pp. 169-72.

23. For the distinction between "household housing unit" concept and "household housekeeping unit" concept, see: United Nations "Demographic and Social Characteristics of the Population," Handbook of Population Census Methods, III, pp. 70-71.

24. Baer, op. cit., pp. 58-59.

25. Morroe Berger, The Arab World Today (Garden City, N.Y.: Doubleday and Co., 1962), p. 113.

26. The minimum certificate referred to here is the Preparatory School Certificate or its equivalent.

27. Institute of National Planning, op. cit., p. 73

28. This field study was undertaken in 1956--a survey report of this study is given in <u>Ibid.</u>, pp. 32-33.

Thus far we have discussed the socioeconomic and demographic determinants of the supply of labor. In this chapter, attention is focused on the economic activities of the Egyptian population. The main purpose of this discussion is to see how the size and structure of the labor force and employment are related to the various socioeconomic and demographic factors discussed earlier. Such information can best be provided by studies of long-term trends in the nation's labor force.

TRENDS AND DIFFERENTIALS IN ECONOMIC ACTIVITY

The simplest way of determining quickly the relative extent of participation in economic activities over time is to compute the crude activity rate (i.e., the number of economically active persons expressed as a percentage of the total population).[1] The crude economic activity rates for Egypt at the three most recent censuses reveal a decline in economic activity from 38.3 percent in 1937 to 30.6 percent in 1960. The decline was most pronounced for females, whose crude economic activity rates dropped from 11.3 to 4.8 percent.

Although other sources give slightly different figures, all available evidence, as shown in Table 41; clearly points to a decline of 6 or 7 percent in the crude economic activity between 1937 and 1960.

A similar picture of the overall labor-force situation is revealed by the returns of the labor-force sample surveys. Long-time comparison of the return of these surveys may be questioned because of their exclusion of certain unpaid females in agricultural fieldwork in later rounds.[2] Nonetheless, for short-term analysis the sample return are comparable.

142

TABLE 41

Crude Economic Activity Rates by Sex--Percentage Economically Active Among Population of All Ages of Given
Sex, 1937, 1947, and 1960

Year	Age of econo- mically Active	Total Population	Economically Active	Percentage
1937	5+	15,970,694	6,094,982	38.3
1947	5+	18,966,767	6,476,897	34.1
1960	6+	25,840,789	7,769,067	30.6
		Male Population		
1937	5+	7,966,675	5,198,032	65.2
1947	5+	9,391,728	5,827,774	62.1
1960	6+	12,992,036	7,154,867	55.1
		Female Population		
1937	5+	7,954,019	896,950	11.3
1947	5+	9,575,039	649,123	6.8
1960	6+	12,838,753	614,200	4.8

Source: Computed by author from U.N. Demographic Yearbook,
1960 (New York: United Nations, 1960), p. 456, Table 12; International
Labour Office, Yearbook of Labour Statistics, 1958 (Geneva, 1958),
p. 7, Table 1; and Yearbook of Labour Statistics, 1963 (Geneva, 1963),
p. 6, Table 1.

Between 1957 and 1960 the proportion of population which constituted manpower remained constant, around 77 percent.[3] In contrast,
the size of the labor force experienced some significant changes between
1957 and 1960. The labor force declined both in absolute and in relative
proportion of manpower and of the total population. Compared with
30 percent of the population in 1957-58, the labor force constituted
only 25 percent of the total population in 1960. The labor force constituted 39 percent of the total supply of manpower in 1957-58 but only
33 percent in 1960.[4]

The Central Statistical Committee attributed this noticeable
decline in economic activity to two factors. First is the April, 1959,
law prohibiting the employment of juveniles under the age of twelve.
This prohibition was estimated to have resulted in a decline of 209,000
persons in the labor force in 1960. Second is the restrictive interpretation of the definition of the labor force in the last rounds. While
the definition of the labor force did not change in all of these rounds,
it is suspected that the later rounds excluded females who gave

incidental help on their farms, since the number of females included in the labor force declined by 465, 000, and most of this decline was in rural areas. 5

So far, the census returns (1937-60) and the labor force sample surveys (1957-60) indicate a declining trend of participation in economic activities. However, determinants of both the long-term trend (the census) and the short-term trend (the surveys) are not the same. Socioeconomic changes seem to be mainly responsible for short-term changes in the size of the labor force. As indicated before, the decline shown by the sample surveys' returns resulted primarily from child-labor legislation and a more strict procedure of enumeration. The percentage of manpower in the total population remained constant, around 77 percent, an indication that demographic factors were not mainly responsible for such changes. The impact of demographic changes on labor force participation in the total population, in addition to socioeconomic determinants, is seen from the long-term trends revealed by the census.

Crude economic activities rates are normally affected by the age composition of the population. Table 42 shows age-specific activity rates for males and females. The figures indicate a substantial decline in the proportion of males working at the upper and lower levels of the age span and a substantial decline of female workers at all ages.

TABLE 42

Trends in Age Specific Activity for Males and Females--
Percentage Economically Active of Given Age Group,
1937, 1947, and 1960

Age	1937		1947		1960	
Male Female	Male	Female	Male	Female	Male	Female
15-19	91.1	16.3	77.8	10.5	68.4	8.6
20-64	97.4	16.9	94.6	8.4	94.8	4.9
65+	89.7	14.1	83.5	8.8	62.5	1.9
Total	65.2	11.3	62.1	6.8	55.1	4.8

Source: 1937: International Labour Office, Labour Statistics Yearbook, 1947-1948 (Geneva, 1948), p. 22; 1947: International Labour Office, Labour Statistics Yearbook, 1958 (Geneva, 1958), p. 10; and 1960: International Labor Office, Labour Statistics Yearbook, 1963 (Geneva, 1963), p. 10.

Additional information on changes in the age-sex composition of the Egyptian labor force is presented in Table 43. A number of obser-vations can be drawn from these statistics on the trends in the dis-tribution of the economically active population by age and sex in the last three censuses. First, the percentage of the economically active male population under twenty declined from 24 to 20 percent. Second, only a slight decline was reported in the percentage of the economically active population aged sixty-five and over. The middle age groups, which constitute the bulk of the labor force, increased from 71 to 76 percent. The reduction in the proportion of the labor force under twenty resulted primarily from child labor legislation, an intensifying campaign toward universal education, a prolonged training period, and vocational preparation before entering the work force. It is in-teresting to note that, between 1937 and 1960, while the Egyptian population as a whole was moving toward a juvenile age structure, the age structure of the labor force was changing toward middle age predominance. This is another indication of how the load of dependency was being further compounded by a number of nondemographic measures (e.g., prolonged educational and training period, child-labor pro-hibition) which were taking place during this time.

Considering the female labor force, the first thing to note is the marked increase that has occurred in the rate of economic activity

TABLE 43

Trends in Distribution of Economically Active Population
by Age, Male and Female, 1937, 1947, and 1960

Age	1937		1947		1960	
	Male	Female	Male	Female	Male	Female
-15	11.6	11.9	10.1	19.6	9.6	36.5
15-19	12.5	11.5	13.1	14.8	10.6	14.4
20-64	71.4	73.9	72.8	61.0	76.2	47.6
65+	4.5	2.7	4.0	4.6	3.6	1.5
Total	100.0	100.0	100.0	100.0	100.0	100.0

Source: 1937: International Labour Office, Labour Statistics Yearbook, 1956 (Geneva, 1956), p. 9, Table 3; 1947: International Labour Office, Labour Statistics Yearbook, 1960 (Geneva, 1960), p. 9, Table 3; and 1960: International Labour Office, Labour Statistics Yearbook, 1962 (Geneva, 1962), p. 15, Table 3.

of girls under fifteen, from 12 percent in 1937 to 37 percent in 1960. In sharp contrast, the economic activity rate of females in the middle age groups decreased from 74 percent in 1947 to 48 percent in 1960, which indicates an opposite trend from that observed for the economically active male population. The most plausible explanation of this trend lies in the structural transformations taking place in Egyptian society. Urbanization trends seem to have worked out to reduce the employment opportunities for middle age women, most of whom are illiterate. It is reasonable to assume that in the last three decades or so, and probably in the coming decade or two, there will continue to be a decreasing trend in female labor-force participation, especially at the middle and older ages.

The 1960 census returns give a clearer picture about the extent of the participation of the different sex-age groups in economic activities (Table 44). Participation rates for males increased from 12 percent in the young age group (under fifteen), reaching a peak in the middle age group (from thirty-five to fifty), after which a gradual decline set in. Several features of these figures ought to be expressed. First, there was still a considerable portion of child labor under the age of fifteen in Egypt in 1960 (12 percent for males and 8 percent for females). Second, the very marked increase in the rate of labor force participation from 12 percent for boys under fifteen to 68 percent for boys between fifteen and nineteen was due to the fact that a large proportion of boys do not go to school after the elementary level but go back to work instead, especially in rural areas. Third, the participation rate for those between twenty and twenty-four was somewhat less than for the subsequent age groups (twenty-five to sixty) in part because of the intensive programs of training and higher education which had been taking place and which delayed somewhat the age of labor force entry of a portion of males between the ages of twenty and twenty-four. Fourth and finally, it is worth noting that a relatively high percentage of males sixty-five and over were participating in the labor force in 1960. Most of these older men were working in agriculture.

The percentage of the labor force in the population was substantially smaller for females than males for each group. The peak of female participation in economic activities was reached between the ages of fifteen and twenty and was followed by a noticeable drop, starting with age twenty-five. The percentage of females at the older ages (sixty-five and over) in the labor force was very small.

Table 45 shows the percentage of the population in the labor force by age and urban-rural residence in 1960. The rates clearly show that rates of labor force participation are higher in rural areas for all ages, but especially for the very young and the very old. For the age group comprising those between six and fourteen, the percentage of the

TABLE 44

Percentage of the Population in the Labor Force
By Age and Sex, 1960

Age Group	Percentage in the Labor Force	
	Male	Female
Under 15	12.0	7.8
15 - 19	68.0	8.6
20 - 24	86.7	7.3
25 - 29	96.0	4.8
30 - 34	97.8	4.5
35 - 39	98.2	4.4
40 - 44	98.0	5.3
45 - 49	97.8	4.4
50 - 54	96.4	4.6
55 - 59	94.5	3.4
60 - 64	85.2	3.1
65+	62.5	1.8

Source: U.A.R. Central Agency for Public Mobilization and Statistics, Population Increase in the U.A.R. and Its Deterrents to Development (Cairo, 1966), p. 169, Table 72.

population in the labor force in rural areas was almost four times as great as that in urban areas (20.7 percent in comparison to only 5.3 percent). For the following age group, fifteen to nineteen, the rate in rural areas was twice that in urban areas (49.3 percent in comparison to 24.3 percent). From age fifty on, the participation rate of the urban labor force again falls substantially behind the corresponding rates in rural areas. In rural areas, people go to work at an earlier age than in urban areas and continue to work longer. This is partially a reflection of the types of economic activities performed. The high participation rates in rural areas for the younger and older age groups may be due to the fact that such persons can still help in some agricultural activities which do not require special skills.

The comparison between urban governorates and other urban areas reveals a striking difference in the percentage of the population in the labor force. In fact, the figures indicate that the pattern of participation in the labor force in rural areas was very similar to that of urban governorates. The corresponding rates in each age group in "other" urban areas were less than those of the urban governorates as well as of the rural areas. This low level of participation in economic activities characteristics of other urban areas in Egypt in comparison

TABLE 45

Percentage of the Population in the Labor Force According
to Age Group, 1960

	6-14	15-19	20-29	30-39	40-49	50-64	65+	Total
Urban governorates	6.7	30.7	46.0	53.1	55.2	47.0	2.5	33.9
Other urban areas	3.5	15.6	24.4	28.7	29.4	25.6	12.1	17.9
Total urban areas	5.3	24.3	37.0	42.8	43.9	37.4	16.4	27.0
Rural	20.7	49.2	52.7	54.3	56.0	52.2	35.5	42.9
Total	14.7	39.3	46.5	49.9	51.6	47.1	29.6	36.9

Source: U.A.R. Central Agency for Public Mobilization and Statistics, Population Increase in the U.A.R. and Its Deterrents to Development (Cairo, 1966), p. 167, Table 69.

to both urban governorates and rural areas is an interesting phenomenon, one which needs further discussion because of its theoretical implication for the concept of overurbanization.[6]

In areas of an intermediate transition from rural to urban, urbanization often refers simply to an agglommeration of population in relatively large-size localities having some primitive characteristics of urban life.[7] In these areas, urbanization is not accompanied by industrialization and/or bureaucratization of the labor force. Concentration of government and business services as well as other enterprises in the large urban governorates makes them the centers of employment and hinders the development of other urban areas as nonagricultural employment centers.[8] In these other urban areas, the economic and technological base is neither wide nor diversified enough to provide nonagricultural jobs to their residents. Yet because of the various urban comforts they provide, these towns attract certain segments of the population who are economically inactive, such as students and semilandlords (who do not farm the land by themselves). With the decentralization of government, which began in the early 1960's, it is hoped that this paralytic effect of the large primate cities of the urban governorates, especially Cairo and Alexandria, on the growth and the structural transformation of the smaller urban centers will be ended.

THE STRUCTURE OF THE LABOR FORCE

Table 46 shows the distribution of the labor force according to major economic sectors in the census years from 1907 to 1960. The figures reveal a long-term decline in the proportion of the labor force engaged in agriculture and corresponding increases in the proportions engaged in industry, service, and commerce and transportation. The bulk of the decline in the percentage of the agricultural labor force was compensated for by an expansion in the nonindustrial sector (services and commerce and transportation).

Between 1907 and 1927, agriculture was the principal sector, absorbing 60 percent of all increments to the working force.[9] Services absorbed slightly less than one-third of the increase in the labor force, and industry's share was less than one-tenth. In the following decades, from 1927 to 1947, agriculture continued to be the sector with the largest absorptive capacity for additional work force. However, its relative rate of increase declined from 60.3 to 46.7 percent. Services and commerce and transportation increased their rate of expansion from 30.0 percent in 1907-1927 to 35.2 percent in 1927-1947. From 1927 to 1947 industry almost doubled its rate of increase, from 9.7 percent in 1907-1927 to 18.1 percent in 1927-47. This was very likely due to the war economy and to the accompanying expansion in industrial

TABLE 46

Distribution of the Labor Force by Sector, Census Years
from 1907 to 1960

Year	Agriculture		Industry		Commerce and Transportation		Services		Total	
	Total	Percent	Total	Percent	Total	Percent	Total	Percent	Total	Percent
1907	2,244,003	70.5	380,453	11.0	262,346	7.6	375,816	10.9	3,458,645	100.0
1917	2,936,352	68.5	492,388	11.5	431,195	10.0	426,563	10.0	4,286,498	100.0
1927	3,525,206	67.0	555,969	10.6	655,322	12.5	523,337	9.9	5,259,834	100.0
1937	4,002,444	69.0	609,733	10.6	598,986	10.4	578,062	10.0	5,789,225	100.0
1947	4,244,951	62.4	835,102	12.3	823,623	12.1	897,565	13.2	6,801,241	100.0
1960	4,402,945	58.0	958,188	12.6	886,410	11.7	1,347,894	17.7	7,595,337	100.0

Source: U.A.R. Central Agency for Public Mobilization and Statistics, Population Increase in the U.A.R. and Its Deterrents to Development (Cairo, 1966), p. 150, Table 64.

employment. The period between 1947 and 1960 saw services expanding at a much faster rate than before, and also more so than both industry and agriculture. Between 1947 and 1960, services absorbed about two-thirds of all increments to the labor force, agriculture absorbed about one-fifth, and industry's share was relatively modest at only 15 percent.

These structural transformations in the absorptive capacity of the different sectors for additional employment give some confirmation to Colin Clark's thesis concerning economic growth and occupational structure. 10 The relative distribution of the gainfully occupied population proceeded from agriculture to industry and lastly to tertiary activities. However, the lack of further expansion of employment in industry after 1947, coupled with continuous population pressure on the land, meant that the only outlet for further employment was in services. Thus, since 1947, a great deal of the redistribution of workers between economic sectors seems to have proceeded directly from primary to tertiary activities.

Colin Clark considers the movement of the working population from agriculture to manufacture to commerce as "the most important concomitant of economic growth."11 From empirical data collected for several countries, he shows that "the different levels of economic advancement are very closely associated with the proportions in which the working population is distributed."12 Clark believes that economic progress is characterized by the redistribution of the gainfully occupied population out of primary production into the production of services and tertiary industries (e.g., commerce, transport, public administration, and all other activities producing a nonmaterial output).13 Looking back at Table 46, the following figures on the percentage distribution of the labor force by economic sector can be derived:

	1927	1937	1947	1960
Primary	67.0	69.0	62.4	58.0
Secondary	10.6	10.6	12.3	12.6
Tertiary	22.4	20.4	25.3	29.4

These figures reveal an increase in the percentage of workers in tertiary activities, and a decline in the percentage of workers in primary production between 1927 and 1960. These results only partly confirm Clark's thesis. 14 In other words, there was an increase in the tertiary production during the development period of 1937-60 but there was no marked transition through secondary production. It should be noted further that the rise in the percentage of the labor force in tertiary activities in the 1937-47 decade was due mainly to the increase in the production of services needed for the armed forces stationed in Egypt during World War II.

Actually, three important conclusions could be derived from the Egyptian development experience. First, the precentage of the working population in the production of tertiary services is considerably higher for the underdeveloped Egyptian economy; tertiary activities absorb almost one-third of the working force, which is relatively higher than that which existed in the early days of development of the now-industrialized countries. Second, the percentage of the working population in secondary activities has been relatively low and stagnant over a very long period of time, in spite of the large increase in the share of industry to the national income. Third, the redistribution of workers between economic sectors in the process of economic progress does not necessarily imply the movement of labor from primary to secondary and then to tertiary activities as Clark postulated. The Egyptian experience shows that tertiary rather than secondary activities worked as the real outlet for the unemployed manpower in agriculture. In brief, the experience of Egypt seems to lend some support to the recent hypothesis that a relatively small industry (in terms of numbers of employees) could have a favorable radiating effect on creating employment opportunities in the other sectors of the economy and especially in the production and administration of services. [15]

It may be worthwhile to compare the returns of the census with those of the labor force sample surveys. According to the surveys (see Table 47) more than 50 percent of the labor force was engaged in agriculture in 1960; however, the 52.9 percent given is considerably less than the 58 percent reported in the census. It is not easy to explain such divergence, except by resorting to what has already been said about the probability that later rounds of the survey were carried on with a stricter definition of unpaid females working on their farms. In fact, according to Hansen and Marzouk, the return of the 1957-58 rounds of the surveys have confirmed the total number of persons occupied in agriculture in 1960, after an adjustment in the bias introduced by the population count of 1957. [16] The important thing to note, however, is that both the census returns and the labor surveys indicate an increase in the size of the labor force engaged in almost every branch of economic activity. Further, both sets of data show that the share of agriculture in the labor force is declining in relative terms.

Between 1937 and 1960, the trend was more or less toward a stabilization in the number of agricultural workers. Hansen and Marzouk even believed that because of different timing of the census in 1947 and 1960, there might have been actually a slight fall in the size of the population occupied in agriculture between the 1947 and 1960 censuses. Further light on this issue is provided by Table 48. This table shows the rural population together with the number of active persons in agriculture, the cultivated areas, and the cropped areas for the years 1937, 1947, and 1960. [17] These figures show that while the population increased by 40 percent between 1937 and 1960, the average cultivated area per active individual increased only 8 percent. However, because of improved agricultural methods, the

TABLE 47

Distribution of Labor Force by Main Types of Economic Activity, 1957–58, 1959, and 1960
(in Thousands)

Type of Activity	1957–58	Percent	1959	Percent	1960	Percent
Agriculture	3,930	55.9	3,681	55.8	3,202	52.9
Mining and quarrying	13	0.2	26	0.4	21	0.4
Manufacturing	592	8.4	577	8.7	570	9.4
Building and construction	146	2.1	133	2.0	124	2.1
Electricity and gas	8	0.1	15	0.2	18	0.3
Commerce	668	9.5	610	9.2	595	9.8
Transport and communications	244	3.5	271	4.1	225	3.7
Civil service	1,288	18.3	354	5.4	417	6.9
Other services			816	12.4	739	12.2
Not stated (including also persons under 12 years)	140	2.0	118	1.8	140	2.3
Total	7,029	100.0	6,601	100.0	6,501	100.0

Source: National Bank of Egypt, " Economic Bulletin" Population and Manpower, XVI (Cairo, 1963), p. 14, Table VIII.

crop area per active individual increased by 16. 3 percent. Nevertheless, even this increase was still substantially less than the 40 percent increase in population that took place in the same period.

The breakdown of the agricultural labor force according to age and sex illustrates clearly the difficulty of considering the labor force in agriculture as if it were homogeneous. As of 1960, young boys (under fifteen) and women accounted for about one-fifth of the agricultural labor force. [18] It should be noted, however, that this represents a marked decline from 1937, at which time these less productive groups composed nearly one-third of the agricultural labor force.

Some observers have speculated that the drop in farm employment of females between 1937 and 1960 is merely a statistical phenomenon to which no analytical significance should be attached. [19] The problem of enumerating farm wives with precision and consistency from one census to another may be the major factor behind the apparent decline in the number of females from 673, 000 in 1937 to only 270, 000 in 1960. Considering the employment of young persons under fifteen, the drop between 1937 and 1960 was less pronounced than in the case of females. Part of this trend may be a reflection of an actual downward trend and part of it may also be due to the timing of the last census enumeration, where the peak of child employment was missed. [20] Thus, the declining number of females and boys between 1937 and 1960 is in large part an outcome of the changing interpretation on the part of the census takers.

In view of the uncertainty about the available statistics of women and children in Egyptian agriculture, the discussion of the trends in the adult male employment figures become extremely relevant. Adult males in the agricultural labor force increased by more than 500, 000 between 1937 and 1960. It is not actually clear, at least from the census information, whether this increase in the number of adult males (from 2. 9 million in 1937 to 3. 5 million in 1969) had an effect on the decline in the number of women and children or not. Our guess is that it did not, for at least two reasons. First, the work contributions of women are largely restricted to animal husbandry and farm-products processing, two types of work still largely performed by women. Second, the employment nature of young people is seasonal in character and recent labor record surveys indicate that children still constitute about 14 percent of the annual labor input in agriculture. [21] The primary concern when considering the changes in the number of adult males employed in agriculture is the availability of land. In this respect, the man part of the man/land ratio has risen much greater than the rise in the aggregate man/land ratio.

At this point, it should be noted how observers of the structural changes in the Egyptian economy are divided on their assessment of the actual trend in the size of agricultural employment between 1937

TABLE 48

Population, Active People in Agriculture, Cultivated Land,
and Crop Area in Rural U.A.R., 1937, 1947, and 1960
(in Thousand)

Year	Rural Pop-ulation	No. of Active People in Agriculture	Cultivated Land	Age Workers / Cultivated Land	Crop Area Feddans
1937	11,484	4,121	5,281	78.0	8,358
1947	12,704	4,215	5,761	73.2	9,167
1960	16,120	4,406	5,879	74.9	10,397

Source: Institute of National Planning, Final Report on Employment Problems in Rural Areas, U.A.R.
(Cairo, 1968), p. 23, Table 15.

and 1960. On one side, Hansen and Marzouk see the stagnation period as real; in fact, they believe that an actual trend toward a decrease in the absolute size of the agricultural labor force may have taken place. [22] Their assessment is based on a consideration of an aggregate which includes figures of men, women, and children in the agricultural labor force. Mead, on the other hand, argues that since the 1960 population census showed less than 5 percent of all women fifteen and over as being economically active, and since there is a definite trend toward the reduction of child labor, and because of serious doubt on the validity of statistics of women and children in agriculture, the concept of agricultural employment most relevant to consider, at least as far as land use is concerned, should be the adult male part of the agriculture labor force. [23]

Table 49 presents statistics on the number and proportions of the population in industrial occupations according to the three most recent population censuses. [24] In Chapter 1, it was noted that the economically active population rose much less from 1937 to 1960 than the total population. The percentage increases were 33 and 65 percent, respectively; however, the economically active population in industrial occupations increased by 75 percent, or more rapidly than either the economically active population or the total population. As a result, the share of the economically active population occupied in industry rose from 7.5 percent in 1937 to 10 percent in 1960.

Bent Hansen and Girgis Marzouk estimated that employment in very small scale industry increased by only 42 percent from 1937 to 1960. In the rest of industry, however, employment increased by 136 percent. [25] If these estimates are correct, they actually indicate that the frequently expressed notion of a stagnation period in small-scale industry between 1937 and 1960 is without support. Although small-scale industry has increased less than the rest of industry, it has continued to undergo an expansion in employment. However, the expansion in small-scale industry seems to have taken place outside establishments proper (i.e., as handicrafts), as a result of population pressure. [26] In any case, from an employment point of view, small-scale industry is still predominant. In 1960, more than half the population occupied in industry was employed in establishments with fewer than ten persons. On the other hand, the concentration in big establishments is also noteworthy: 171,000 workers, or about one-fifth of the total population occupied in industry (770,000), was employed in establishments with 500 employees and more in 1960. [27] It is in these two extreme groups that the employment increase has taken place.

The available information on gross value added by size of establishments clearly reveals that larger establishments are of greater importance when the contribution to production measured in terms of value

TABLE 49

Economically Active Population in Industrial
Occupations, 1937, 1947, and 1960

	1937	1947	1960
Total population in thousands	15,924	19,021	26,089
Economically active population (adjusted) in thousands	5,838	6,995	7,734
In industrial occupation (adjusted) in thousands	440	610	770
As percentage of total population	2.8	3.2	3.0
As percentage of economically active population	7.5	8.7	10.0

Source: Bent Hansen and G. Marzouk, Development and Economic Policy in the U.A.R. (Egypt) (Amsterdam: North Holland Publishing Company, 1965), p. 122, Table 55.

added is considered.[28] To illustrate, those establishments which employ more than 500 persons (27 percent of all persons occupied in industry) produce about 47 percent of total value added. Very-small-scale industry, on the other hand, employs 54 percent of these engaged in industry, yet produces only 34 percent of value added. This suggests an average productivity of labor that is two or three times larger in big establishments than in small ones. However, this fact does not minimize the importance of small-scale industry as far as production is concerned, let alone employment.

Figures on employment in manufacturing since 1937 are shown in Table 50. As these data show, total employment and employment of adult males developed in about the same way. The figures also show the relatively little increase recorded between 1947 and 1954, in comparison to earlier and later periods. As was indicated earlier, the seven years which followed World War II were a period of significant re-equipping and modernization rather than of expansion, a factor which might explain the virtually constant state of employment during those years.

In 1960 more than 50 percent of all workers in manufacturing were employed by the textile industry. 29 Food processing ranked as the second largest category, with about 11 percent of the total employment in manufacturing. Chemical products occupied the third position (6 percent).

TABLE 50

Manufacturing Employment, Selected Years from
1937 to 1960
(in Thousands)

Year	Employment Total	Employment, Adult males	Percent
1937	353	320	91
1947	561	502	89
1954	569	n.a.	--
1960	713	658	92

Note: Percentages computed by author.

Source: Donald C. Mead, Growth and Structural Change in the Egyptian Economy (Homewood, Illinois: Richard D. Irwin, Inc., 1967), p. 111, Table 4-5.

Together these three accounted for approximately two-thirds of the manufacturing workers. As with the case in total industry, both from the employment and the value added points of view, manufacturing is dominated by very small and very large establishments.

Information about employment in the various services is given in Table 51. From 1937 to 1960, the number of persons working in this sector nearly doubled, rising from approximately 1.4 million workers at the earlier date to 2.7 million in 1960. 30

In 1937 the government sector accounted for only 16.1 percent of total employment in services. During and immediately after World War II, however, employment in the government sector expanded quite rapidly, rising by 70 percent during the decade between the two censuses. From 1947 to 1960, employment in the government sector more than

TABLE 51

Employment in Services, 1937, 1947, and 1960

	1937	Percent	1947	Percent	1960	Percent
General government	222,417	16.1	376,848	19.6	896,396	33.8
Commerce	436,074	31.5	587,848	30.5	641,408	24.2
Transport and communication	137,148	9.9	201,582	10.5	260,210	9.9
Construction	116,525	8.4	111,693	5.8	158,885	5.0
Personal services	326,699	23.6	473,808	24.6	567,027	21.4
Paid domestics	130,073	9.4	234,645	12.2	191,627	7.2
Other services	147,187	10.6	175,787	9.1	131,865	4.0
Total	1,386,050	100.0	1,927,260	100.0	2,655,791	100.0

Note: Percentages computed by author.

Source: Donald C. Mead, Growth and Structural Change in the Egyptian Economy (Homewood, Illinois: Richard D. Irwin, Inc., 1967), p. 132, Table 6-1.

doubled, as some 500, 000 workers were added to the sector. Coming at a time when total employment in the economy was gaining rather slowly, the striking result was that over 40 percent of all new jobs in the economy during thus period were in the government sector. 31 The result of this expansion is readily indicated by the fact that the share of general government of the total employment in services reached more than one-third in 1960.

The commerce branch of the services covers a wide range, from the big export merchants to those engaged in petty merchandise. Also included are large commercial activities such as financial institutions, insurance companies, and real estate organizations. Employment in commerce rose by 35 percent between 1937 and 1947. This was the same as the total employment growth, however, so that the share of employment in commerce in the aggregate services remained about constant between 1937 and 1947, at 31 percent. During the most recent intercensal period, however, the pattern of employment was quite different. Between 1947 and 1960, employment in commerce increased much more slowly, rising by less than 10 percent in a time where employment in aggregate services was expanding at a fast rate, thus reducing the share of commerce to only 24 percent. This means that in the postwar period, the commerce sector has been able to handle a large increase in the quantity of goods traded with very little increase in employment in that sector.

The figures on employment in transportation and communication indicate a relatively stable proportion of employment in this sector between 1947 and 1960 (roughly 10 percent). In order to understand fully the nature of employment in this sector, it is meaningful to distinguish between the modern and traditional sectors. 32 During the years between 1947 and 1960, the largest employment increase in both absolute and relative terms was in the modern sector. Thus, the apparent stability of employment in this sector marks some very real changes.

The construction sector is usually divided into three parts; residential housing, other building (primarily government offices and facilities), and all other construction work (transport, dams, and irrigation work). In terms of total employment, over 80 percent of those working in this sector in 1960 and close to 70 percent in earlier censuses, were engaged in the construction of buildings. 33 Until 1958, most of the activities of the construction of residential housing were directed toward the building of relatively expensive ''luxury'' houses. 34 The work done on the irrigation system from 1949 to 1954 indicates that a large proportion of employment in construction work was primarily for irrigation work. 35 In general, the share of construction in the total services employment declined from 8. 4 percent in 1937 to only 5 percent in 1960.

Turning to personal services, the recent trend has been a decline in the economic importance of this sector. After remaining relatively stable at about 24 percent between 1937 and 1947, the proportion of service workers in this sector declined to 21 percent. 36 This is in large part a reflection of the pronounced decline (absolute as well as relative) in employment of paid domestics. Part of the decline of the employment in domestic services reflects the increased use of modern household equipment, especially in urban centers and among families in the higher socioeconomic status groups. Increased enrollment of boys and girls in elementary school accounts for a large part of the declining trend in domestic services employment. In addition, a large number of paid domestic workers who worked as servants, maids, car drivers, cooks, gardeners, housekeepers, and other categories of personal services with the aristocratic families were laid off following the 1952 revolution.

With regard to the category ''other services'' the 1960 figures include religious organizations, business services (including law), and recreation. This category is a residual figure in the early census (before 1960) and for this reason, no significance should be attached to the fluctuating level of employment in this group.

To summarize, we have seen that employment in the services has almost doubled between 1937 and 1960. Thus, in terms of employment, the services were the fastest growing sector in the economy. An examination of employment in the various components of the services sector revealed that employment in the government and in personal services has expanded substantially more than in the other areas. In fact, between 1937 and 1960, nearly 50 percent of the total employment increase in the whole economy was in these two areas. 37

The distribution of the labor force according to the international standard of classification of occupations is presented in Table 52. These data reveal, first of all, that as of 1960 more than half (53 percent) of the labor force was engaged in agricultural occupations. About 16 percent were craftsmen, working in the production process and related occupations, and another 9 percent were engaged in service occupations. White-collar occupations, which include professional and technical, managerial, clerical, and sales people, constituted a relatively small percentage of the work force (15 percent), which indicates the still-rural character of the occupational structure in Egypt.

Closely related to the classification of the labor force according to occupation is the distribution of the labor force according to education. Considering the basic features first, Table 53 shows that the degree of illiteracy is very high; 63 percent of the total labor force in 1960 was illiterate. The second largest group is composed of people with

TABLE 52

Distribution of the Egyptian Labor Force By
Occupation, 1960 Census

	Number (Thousands)	Percent to Total
Professional and Technical	214	3. 1
Managerial	74	1. 0
Clerical	248	3. 6
Salesmanship	550	8. 0
Agricultural	3, 666	53. 2
Mining and quarrying	12	0. 2
Transport	206	3. 0
Crafts, production, and process	1, 080	15. 6
Services	635	9. 2
Unidentifiable	39	0. 6
Unemployed	174	2. 5

Source: International Labour Office, Yearbook of Labour Statistics, 1966 (Geneva, 1966), p. 146-147, Table 5.

less than middle - level education who form somewhat less than a third of the total labor force. From a quantitative point of view, each of the other more educated groups is fairly insignificant.

Further examination of the figures in Table 53 reveals some of the changes which have taken place since 1957. Despite the fact that this period is relatively short, some notable changes in the educational status of the labor force did occur. That is, there was a noticeable decline in the number of illiterate members of the labor force as well as a small but definite upward shift in the educational level. Thus, the number of persons in the various literate categories (categories 2 through 5) increased both absolutely and relatively. The largest increase occurred in Category 2, which comprises those who can read and write even though their level of attainment is less than middle-level. Part of the increase in the relative importance of the educated is, of course, due to the fact that the total labor force in 1960 was smaller than in 1957-58. This, however, does not account for all the increase in the literate and educated part of the labor force, from 30. 2 percent in 1957-58 to 36. 6 percent in 1960.

One characteristic of the labor force which needs special comment

TABLE 53

Labor Force Classified According to Educational
Status, 1957-60
(in Thousands)

Education Status	1957-58	Percent	1959	Percent	1960	Percent
1. Illiterate	4,892	69.6	4,378	66.3	3,797	62.8
2. Below middle-level education	1,839	26.2	1,898	28.7	1,898	31.4
3. Middle-level education	184	2.6	192	3.0	204	3.4
4. University education	94	1.4	97	1.5	105	1.7
5. Post-graduate education	5	0.0	8	0.1	5	0.1
6. Not stated (1)	15	0.2	28	0.4	42	0.6
Total	7,029	100.0	6,601	100.0	6,051	100.0

Source: National Bank of Egypt, "Economic Bulletin," Population
and Manpower (Cairo, 1963), XVI, Nos. 1 & 2, p. 12, Table VI.

is the employment status of the workers. The most obvious change
(as revealed in the last three censuses) is the decrease in the number
of employers. The category classified as self-employed, although
experiencing a slight absolute increase, also declined in proportion to
the total economically active population. The two categories which
recorded any substantial increase were the employee and the unemployed. [38] The increase in the employee category reflects the growing role of government, industry, business, and other service institutions as job providers and employers of an increasingly large share
of the economically active population. It also reflects the bureaucratic
trend where the state is becoming increasingly the sole employer of
the majority of the economically active population. The very substantial
increase in the number classified as unemployed, about five fold between
1947 and 1960, is indicative of a very serious unemployment problem
in Egypt.

The analysis of the labor force by employment status indicates that roughly two-thirds are employees, with or without pay. The categories of self-employed account for roughly one-fourth of the total labor force. According to the available survey data, [39] the 1957-60 period did not witness any noticeable changes in the distribution of the labor force by employment status. That the number of persons in the various categories declined (except for the unemployed) is largely due to the exclusion of juveniles under twelve and peasant women performing light agricultural jobs.

The figures in the 1960 census give some indication about rural-urban differences in the employment status of the working force. Table 54 presents the percentage distribution of the labor force according to employment status in both rural and urban areas in 1960. The figures are revealing. Those classified as employers, self-employeds, or unpaid family workers decrease in proportion with the increase in urbanization. As is expected, the paid-employee group is perhaps the only group, along with the unemployed category, which increases in percentage with the increase in urbanization. Such rural-urban differences result primarily from the nature of work in the different economic sectors dominant in rural and urban Egypt. Work on family farms, whether as employees, self-employeds, or unpaid family workers, is much more common in rural areas. In services and industry, the prevalent economic activities are paid jobs.

TABLE 54

Labor Force Distribution According to Employment
Status in Rural and Urban Areas,
1960

Status	Urban Governorates	Other Urban Areas	Rural	Total
Owner-manager	4.0	6.2	8.7	7.4
Self-employed	14.2	22.0	25.0	22.4
Paid employee	73.9	61.6	38.9	49.2
Family-employee	2.2	6.8	26.0	18.5
Unpaid employee	0.3	0.5	0.3	0.3
Unemployed	5.4	2.9	1.1	2.2

Source: U.A.R. Central Agency for Public Mobilization and Statistics, Population Increase in the U.A.R. and Its Deterrents to Development (Cairo, 1966), p. 186, Table 7.

It is interesting to note that in 1960, paid employees constituted over 28 percent of the agricultural labor force. It is, therefore, reasonable to assume that the notion of the typical laborer as being engaged in peasant agriculture on family farms working exclusively with family labor is at least partially accurate in Egypt.

UNEMPLOYMENT AND UNDEREMPLOYMENT

Perhaps no other aspect of the characteristics of the Egyptian labor force has received as much discussion as the extent of unemployment and the nature of underemployment, especially in the agricultural labor force.[40] In spite of the multitude of opinions and estimates that have been expressed, there is no consensus as to the precise nature of the problem. Rather, it remains a controversial issue. Influential theoretical models (e.g., that of W. A. Lewis)[41] in the literature of economic development are built on the possibility of development with an "unlimited supply of labor" in agriculture. Those who favor the Lewis theory always refer to Egypt as a typical case. However, a number of economists have recently doubted whether this theory of surplus labor in agriculture and an unlimited supply of labor actually applies to Egypt.[42] The relevance of this theoretical argument no doubt goes far beyond the Egyptian case to other underdeveloped, over-populated countries where disguised unemployment is believed to exist.[43]

The most reliable data available on the extent of unemployment in Egypt are those collected by the labor sample surveys. According to the most comparable survey rounds, only about 4 percent of the Egyptian labor force was unemployed.[44] This is a very low figure and must be interpreted with a great deal of caution. For example, it should be noted that the survey defined a person as unemployed only if he had no occupation whatsoever during a whole week previous to the day the sample was surveyed. In other words, if a person happened to be occupied for one day only during that week, he was counted as employed. To get a more realistic measure of unemployment, then, some attention should be given to the number of days worked per week. In this regard, it is worth noting that a coefficient of underemployment can be calculated as the number of man-days forgone by those working a shorter week related to the total capacity of the occupied population. Considering the normal length of the working week to be six days, it has been estimated that the employed were working up to some 90 percent of their capacity; this means that out of a total labor force of 7 million persons, only 6.1 million were fully occupied. This would bring the unemployment rate to nearly 14 percent of the total labor force.[45]

Information on unemployment in rural areas is provided by a

study conducted on rural employment during 1964-65. In spite of the
fact that this survey was carried out during the main slack season, in
which labor requirements drop sharply to the lowest level in rural areas,
the percentage of the civilian labor force which was unemployed during
the week of reference reached only 4 percent among males and 5 percent among females. 46 Since these figures should present the upper
extreme of unemployment in rural areas, an examination of its validity
seems desirable. In this case, a discussion of the categories of those
persons not working during the week of reference would illustrate the
low bias of the 5 percent figures.

Table 55 shows the percentage distribution of those unable to
work or unavailable for work, and those unemployed who were able
and available to work. It is our judgment that the final figure of only
5 percent unemployed was deflated, since a large portion of the 30
percent classified as unable or not available for work because of home
work are probably a group of discouraged persons. 47 This group is
not looking for work because of repeated failures and rebuffs, or because
of the mere belief that active jobseeking would be futile. Probably a
part of the 18 percent of those not available because of age (both young
and old) are also included in this discouraged group. Further, the
9 percent classified as prevented from employment by tradition or not
in need of employment should be considered as a part of institutional
unemployment, and according to the international standards, not to
be considered as members of the civilian labor force. Nevertheless,
this category is not fixed, and the changing tradition concerning women's
work probably supports our inclination to view the 5 percent unemployed
as low.

The seriousness of the unemployment problem in rural Egypt is
not only reflected in the percentage figures of unemployment as much
as it is in the data on the duration of unemployment. In this respect,
Table 56 presents the duration of unemployment by sex. Here it is
shown that 53 percent of the unemployed males in the sample remained
in a state of unemployment for a duration of one to three months. Since
the slack season starts in rural areas in October, three months before
the survey took place, the state of unemployment of these 53 percent
unemployed males could be considered seasonal. The serious category
of unemployment (three months or longer) covers 30 percent of the
males and 46 percent of the females.

Egypt is generally cited as a classic example of a country with
substantial underemployment, especially in the agricultural sector.
Official and unofficial estimates of underemployment in Egypt have
ranged from 20 percent to over 50 percent. 48 As early as the 1930's,
several observers argued that with relatively small increases in investment or minor alterations to productive organization, a large proportion
of the agricultural working force could have been withdrawn without

TABLE 55

Distribution of Rural Unemployment by Reason,
1964 (March) - 1965 (February)

	Percent
A. Percent unable to work or not available for work in the following order:	
Home work	30
School attendance	28
Old age	12
Young age	6
Physical handicaps, mental disease, illness or injury	3
Military service or other reasons	2
Subtotal	81
B. Percent able and available:	
Employers and own account workers	1
Lack of adequate employment opportunities or suitable work	4
Females prevented from employment by tradition	9
No answer	5
TOTAL	100

Source: Institute of National Planning, Final Report on Employment Problems in Rural Areas, U.A.R. (Cairo, 1968), p. 47-48.

affecting output.49 In the past, there was wide agreement that underemployment was quite substantial and was increasing. In recent years,
however, some observers have presented evidence they feel points in
the opposite direction. Thus, on the one hand the International Labor
Office in Geneva expressed the view that the general picture in Egypt
"is one not merely of considerable unemployment in rural areas, but
of an immense amount of disguised unemployment in the sense that
the same output could be achieved with a smaller labor force without
any improvement in technical methods."50 Hansen and Marzouk, on
the other hand, represent a different view in asserting that "if disguised
unemployment is taken to mean that the marginal productivity of labor
is near zero, so that labor can be removed permanently without detri-
mental effects on production, there is good evidence for the opposite

TABLE 56

Duration of Unemployment by Sex, 1964
(March) - 1965 (February)

Duration	Percentage of Unemployed	
	Male	Female
Less than one month	40	1
1-3 months	13	-
3-6 months	4	19
6 months and more	26	27
Looking for first job	9	-
No answer	9	53
Total	100	100
N	-53	-37

Source: Institute of National Planning, Final Report on Employ-ment Problems in Rural Areas, U.A.R. (Cairo, 1968), p. 47, Table 31.

view, viz., that there is not disguised unemployment in Egyptian agriculture, but there is some open unemployment, and a large seasonal underemployment. "51

We have no new definition or measurement techniques to add to the immense theoretical literature on this subject; however, we would here like to bring together and evaluate some of the empirical evidence which the conflicting observers have presented to support their arguments Mead argues that there is a substantial amount of disguised unemploy-ment in the agricultural sector. 52 He concedes that rapid expansion of employment outside the agricultural sector caused wage rates to increase sharply in the mid-1960's. Mead argues, however, that in spite of this development in the 1960's, "the agricultural sector has more workers than it can use; . . . there are considerable numbers in the sector whose marginal physical product is virtually zero, who could be permanently withdrawn from the sector with no loss of output and only minor organizational changes in the production process."53

Let us examine briefly the empirical evidence Mead advances to support his conclusion.54 First, he examines the man/land ratios since the late 1930's and shows how the agricultural labor force has been stagnant while the cultivated has been extended. He then discounts such evidence as inaccurate because it treats the agricultural labor force as if it were homogeneous. He sees the drop in the number of female agricultural workers and probably a part of child labor, between 1937 and 1960, as resulting from changing interpretations of the census takers; thus the drop is more apparent than real. There-fore, the concept of underemployment, which is more relevant to the economy, should refer to the man part of the man/land ratio, not to the total agricultural labor force since the level of economic activity of women is very low in Egypt, and the tendency is toward the abolition of child labor.

Second, Mead questions the results obtained from the various calculations of the production function of Egyptian agriculture which seem to present a challenge to those who believe that there is a signi-ficant amount of disguised unemployment in Egyptian agriculture.55 Again his criticism focuses on the heterogenity of the agricultural labor force. However, his computation of similar production functions for the adult male in the agricultural labor force still shows a significant coefficient for labor, which indicates a highly significant relationship between changes in labor input as measured by the number of adult males in the agricultural labor force and total output. He points out some basic problems of using the calculation of production function as an index of underemployment in Egyptian agriculture. For example, the estimation of such a function for the agricultural sector as a whole ignores the fact that agriculture comprises a number of different crops, each of which may in fact respond quite differently to an increase in a given factor of production. Also, he sees no way of finding out from the use of production function figures whether the relationship between labor and output was becoming more or less significant in time. By breaking the data into subperiods of ten years, the labor coefficient became insignificant. He also questions the use of labor input series since it is basically a capacity concept (labor available for use, rather than labor actually employed).

Mead examines two other sets of data which bear on the question of labor redundancy in Egyptian agriculture. These are the seasonal agricultural employment data provided by a special study of the Ministry of Agriculture, and the Agricultural Wage Rates produced by Bent Hansen. He admits that these two sets of data do not point clearly to one conclusion. The first set shows that during periods of peak demands, not more than 85 percent of the agricultural labor force was actually used. The other study says that during periods of peak seasonal demand there was some shortage in the supply of paid agricultural laborers, reflected in substantial seasonal increases in agricultural daily wage rates. Mead's interpretation of this conflicting evidence is that the market has been tightening only for paid agricultural workers in recent years, leaving considerable disguised unemployment on family farms. He concludes that there is no evidence to suggest that there was an overall shortage, but only a shortage in the specific category of paid laborers.

The major opponent of the view that there is considerable disguised unemployment in Egyptian agriculture is Bent Hansen. In a series of articles and research monographs, Hansen, with the collaboration of others, has challenged the orthodox views of the existence of disguised unemployment in the agricultural sectors in Egypt.56 His conclusion is based on a number of empirical findings. First is the fact that production funtion studies for field crops indicate that the value of the marginal productivity of labor, measured on a yearly basis, is on the same magnitude as current money wages for agriculture laborers. Second, his calculations of labor requirements indicate that the more permanent farm labor force is fully employed at certain times of the year and that there is a seasonal demand for outside labor. Third, the increase which has occurred in the cultivated areas and even more in the cropped areas relative to the number of persons occupied in agriculture since 1937 makes it likely that disguised unemployment as well as seasonal underemployment has diminished during the last 30 years.

It might be apparent by now that these two largely conflicting conclusions arrived at by Mead and Hansen stem from a number of conflicting assumptions rather than from procedural computations. First is the issue of homogenity versus heterogenity of the agricultural labor force. While Mead makes use of the adult male portion of the agricultural labor force only in his calculations of the man/land ratio, Hansen includes all men, women, and children. Mead's omission of women and children, as we have indicated earlier, stems from the unreliability of the census data on these two categories of the agricultural labor force. Such an omission, he seems to imply, is justified by the negligible role contributed by women in agriculture to the economy. Since child labor is on the decline, especially in recent years, Mead is also inclined to consider the discussion of the underemployment or unemployment of these groups as economically irrelevant.

Second is the categories of workers included in the agricultural labor force. Mead is critical of Hansen's exclusion of "seasonal and occasional workers" in the estimates of the agricultural labor force. The same criticism he believes applied to the 1950 agricultural census estimate of "permanent agricultural laborers," which was 30 percent below the level shown in the 1947 population census. The exclusion by

the Ministry of Agriculture of the marginal workers in agriculture
disturbs the real picture of disguised unemployment as well as seasonal
unemployment. In brief, Mead's approach to the problem of underemployment considers the full agricultural labor force, not just permanent workers. Yet he fails to notice that the same criticism could
apply to his exclusion of women and children from his consideration
of the full agricultural labor force. In fact, women and children constitute a large portion of the marginal and occasional workers he sees
as necessarily included.

Third is the relative confusion concerning the distinction between
paid agricultural laborers and family farmers in respect to underemployment. Mead seems to imply a larger distinction between the
two groups than does Hansen, who lumps them together. This disagreement also extends to the discussion of seasonal underemployment
in Egypt. Thus, on the one hand, Hansen believes that there is a large
seasonal underemployment, which may very well correspond to about
25 percent of the total present labor force calculated on an annual
basis.[57] Mead, on the other hand, expresses the view "that the extent
of purely seasonal unemployment is probably small in Egypt relative
to many other countries, such as the United States and England because
of multiple croppings. "[58] Ironically, the two writers agree on the
necessity to distinguish clearly between seasonal unemployment in
agriculture and year-round unemployment, whether open or disguised,
since the economic implications of these are different and must be
analyzed separately.

It should be clear that what Mead is arguing for is that the bulk
of underemployment in Egypt is one form or another of disguised
unemployment, with little seasonal underemployment. Hansen, on the
other hand, advances some evidence to support his argument that there
is a large seasonal surplus of labor in agriculture with little or no
disguised unemployment.

The theoretical and policy implications of the present disagreement on the extent and the nature of underemployment in agriculture
are important for the development of Egypt in general and for labor
market policy in particular. Those who, like Mead, believe there is
widespread disguised unemployment in Egypt point to the Lewis theory
of "development with unlimited supply of labor" as a suitable framework for Egypt's economic development. According to this theory,
in those overpopulated, underdeveloped countries with disguised unemployment in agriculture, industrial expansion can take place with
little or no increase at all in money wages. The low incomes for the
agricultural working force tend to fix the level of money wages in
industry at a low level, also. A very rapid expansion of industrial
employment may result in a certain increase in agricultural money
wages, but as long as there remain reserves of labor in agriculture

and in domestic and public service, industrial wages must stay at a low level and increase very slowly if at all. 59

Proponents of the seasonality of agriculture underemployment, on the other hand, point to the idea that industrial expansion cannot be based on a seasonal surplus of labor in agriculture, apart from special cases where counterseasonal industries can be established. Accordingly they discredit the applicability of the theory of development with surplus labor in agriculture in Egypt.

Unfortunately, we have no way to judge the reasonability of each argument except to turn once more to the more detailed information on unemployment and underemployment gathered from the 1964-65 survey conducted in Egyptian villages by the Institute of National Planning. It should be stated from the outset that this study was not conducted with the purpose of testing any of these theoretical arguments, but rather to examine a wide range of employment problems. Therefore, any inferences regarding seasonal and disguised unemployment should be regarded as tentative.

Also, it might be wise to point out to the reader that the survey findings should not be generalized to the situation in all Egypt since the sample survey was not representative of the rural population as a whole, and in fact, did not cover all fields of work. Nonetheless, these findings provide what is perhaps the most reliable empirical evidence so far on the subject. The findings of this study, which have some bearing on understanding the extent and the nature of underemployment, will be discussed more fully below. The intensity of the employment of the rural labor force measured by the annual working days indicates that men worked more days per year than women and women worked more days than children. 60 The average annual working days for men, women, and children were as follows: men, 286 days per year; women, 188 days per year, and children, 159 days per year. The majority of the men (89 percent) worked more than six months during the year of the survey, compared with 54 percent for women and only 38 percent for children. The number of those who have been recorded as working less than one month was 3 percent for men, 25 percent for women, and 34 percent for children.

Measured by daily working hours, the intensity of rural employment shows a somewhat different pattern. Men worked more hours per day than women but women worked less hours per day than children. The average daily working hours were 8.1 for men, 4.6 for women, and 7.5 for children. The most probable explanation for the relatively fewer working days per year--but longer working hours--for children in comparison to women is the type of work which they most often perform. The employment of children reaches a peak in the two seasons of pest control and cotton harvest, both of which require longer daily working hours.

Seasonal fluctuation was pertinent between men, women, and children, not only in the level of worktime per person, but also in the seasonal distribution of work as well as the extent and duration of both the peak and slack periods.[61] Analysis of this phenomenon indicates that men's fluctuation curve of work starts at a relatively high level in March and April, and reaches its peak from mid-May until the end of June. The curve then declines during July and August. A second but lower peak takes place in September; the curve then declines gradually to reach a low level in January. Thus, the curve shows two peak periods for men; the first in May-June and the second in September. Men's slack season extends from October to January. Women's fluctuation curve indicates a fairly balanced activity all around the year because most of the work performed by them--such as animal husbandry and the processing of farm products--tends to be evenly spread all over the year. In the case of children, as already indicated, there are two distinct peaks in June and September. The first takes place in the season of pest control, while the second occurs during the cotton harvest.

So far, the measurement of the intensity of rural employment points toward the existence of a wide seasonal underemployment. Also, the figures on annual working days could be safely interpreted as in-dications of the existence of disguised unemployment. The fact that about 11 percent of the men, 46 percent of the women, and 62 percent of the children worked less than six months in the year of the survey is no doubt clear evidence that disguised unemployment constitutes a real problem for the Egyptian agricultural labor force.

Further evidence to support the seasonal unemployment and disguised underemployment is available from the findings of the survey concerning labor utilization. Labor utilization was different from one governorate to another because the man/land ratio was not uniform among the governorates which were studied. Furthermore, the cropping pattern was not the same all over Egypt; labor input per feddan crop areas varied widely among the governorates.[62] Further evidence of the variations in agricultural employment is clear from seasonal fluctuations of employment and the movement of temporary workers.

The survey results also revealed large differences in the conditions of labor employment in agriculture according to the cropping system and the size of land holdings. For example, the study indicated that the average yearly work hours decrease sharply with the increase in size of holding. The study also indicated that vegetables, rice, sugar cane, cotton, wheat, and maize follow this rank in the use of the total annual work hours per farm, controlling for farm size.

In the final analysis, the Institute of National Planning estimated

the degree of underemployment in the agricultural labor force to be
12.5 percent for men, 25.4 percent for women, and 64.7 percent for
children. The resulting overall underemployment has been estimated
at 31.2 percent for the year 1964-1965.[63]

What do the findings of this field study tell us of the actual
existence of a substantial degree of both disguised and seasonal underemployment in Egyptian agriculture? The conflicting conclusions
arrived at by Mead and Hansen, as we have indicated earlier, reflect
largely conceptual differences, and not substantial differences; depend-
ing on who one defines as being in the labor force, there is or there
is not widespread underemployment in Egyptian agriculture.

Unfortunately we have no actual measure of the extent of underemployment in services in the Egyptian economy, nor did we encounter
any such empirical measurements. However, a large number of
observers have commented on the possibility that "the problem of
underemployment was transferred--or at least spread--from the
agricultural sector into the services."[64] As we have seen before,
the number of men working in this sector approximately doubled, during
the 1937-60 period, rising by more than 1 million and accounting for
well over half of the new jobs in the economy. This substantial increase
in employment being matched by a very much smaller increase in real
output would substantiate the belief that there was a spillover of underemployment from the agricultural sector to the services. In the discussion of labor productivity (Chapter 2), it was shown that labor productivity in some branches of the service sector has risen noticeably
in the last decades; in others, specifically in the government and in
personal services, it seems likely that employment has risen substantially more than the services which were provided. Some observers
even argued that "if zero productivity of actually employed labor is
to be found anywhere in Egypt, it is most probably in government
administration."[65]

A similar trend, but a relatively recent one, can be seen developing in the industrial sector. For example, in their account of the low
productivity of labor in the industrial sector during the first two years
of the planning period, Hansen and Marzouk offer two explanations.
First is the employment drive, which began in 1961-62 and which may
have led to underemployment within the enterprise concerned; and
second is the nationalizations, which may have influenced productivity.[66]
It is certainly clear that the two explanations are not mutually exclusive.
During the planning period, the attitude of the government concerning
the employment pattern seems to have changed somewhat. Employment
for social reasons seems to be accorded larger value than at the time
when the five-year plan was drawn up. The 1961 great employment
drive took place in the newly nationalized industries, among other
sectors. Such overemployment in industry was also connected with
the reduction in the working week from 48 to 42 hours.

Will the overemployment trend turn out to be a temporary phenomenon? The answer seems to be no, since the public sector (which absorbed the large portion of the new employment) consists mostly of industry and services; also, because the government has committed itself to employ all college graduates.

NOTES

1. United Nations, Demographic Aspects of Manpower, Sales No. 61, XIII. 4 (New York: United Nations; 1962), p. 3.

2. National Bank of Egypt, "Population and Manpower," Economic Bulletin, XVI, 1-2 (1963), 10.

3. Ibid., p. 9. Manpower is that part of the population which can be employed in economic activities. Manpower is divided into two sections, namely, the labor force and those not included in the labor force. The labor force comprises all persons who either actually participate in, or are capable of and looking for, any job which is related to the production of goods and services. The labor force comprises the employed as well as the unemployed.

4. Bent Hansen and Girgis Marzouk, Development and Economic Policy in the U.A.R. (Egypt) (Amsterdam: North Holland Publishing Co.; 1965), p. 35, Table 2.9.

5. National Bank of Egypt, op. cit., p. 11.

6. For a theoretical discussion of the relationship between urbanization and industrialization, see Bert F. Hoselitz, "The City, Factory and Economic Growth," American Economic Review, Papers and Proceedings, XLV (May, 1955), 166, 171. See also Philip M. Hauser, ed., "Urbanization in Asia and the Far East," Proceedings of the Joint UN/UNESCO Seminar on Urbanization in the ECAFE Region (Calenta: UNESCO Research Center on the Social Implications of Industrialization in Southern Asia, 1957), pp. 313-343.

7. Janet Abu-Lughod, "Urbanization in Egypt: Present State and Future Prospects," Economic Development and Cultural Change, XIII, 3 (April, 1965), 313-43.

8. Mark Jefferson, "The Law of the Primate Cities," Geographical Review, XXIX (April, 1939), 226-32. See also Rhoads Murphy, "New Capitals of Asia," Economic Development and Cultural Change, V (April, 1957), 216-43. See also Surinder K. Mehta, "Some Demographic and Economic Correlates of Primate Cities: A Case for Reevaluation," Demography, I, 1 (1964), 136-47.

9. U.A.R. Central Agency for Public Mobilization and Statistics, Population Increase in the U.A.R. and Its Deterrents to Development (Cairo, 1966), p. 151, Table 64.

10. Colin Clark, The Conditions of Economic Progress (London: Macmillan, 1940), Chapter V.

11. Ibid., p. 176.

12. Ibid., p. 177.

13. Bauer and Yamey disputed the empirical and analytical basis of the widely accepted Clark thesis. See P. R. Bauer and B. S. Yamey, "Economic Progress and Occupational Distribution," Economic Journal, LXI (December, 1951), 741-45; and their "Economic Progress, Occupational Distribution and Institutional Wage Rigidities; A Comment," Review of Economics and Statistics, XXXII (November, 1954), 461-62.

14. A different conclusion on this point was arrived at by Magdi M. El-Kamash in his Economic Development and Planning in Egypt (New York: Frederick A. Praeger, 1968), pp. 172-75. It is important to note that the different conclusions arrived at by the quoted author were mainly due to his use of the 1947 census figures before the adjustment, which was undertaken in 1960 published census figures. The figures used by the quoted author showed a decrease in the proportion of working population in the services between 1947-1960.

15. C. Hsieh, "Underemployment in Asia: 11. Its Relation to Investment Policy," International Labor Review, LXVI, I (July, 1952), 34.

16. Bent Hansen and G. Marzouk, Development and Economic Policy in the U.A.R. (Amsterdam: North Holland Publishing Co., 1965), p. 60.

17. Due to the richness of the land and the existence of water for irrigation all year round, the cultivated land in Egypt produces more than one crop per year, (three or four in rare cases). Therefore, the cropped area is larger than the cultivated area because of the system of multiple cropping.

18. Mead, op. cit., p. 82, Tables 4-13.

19. Ibid., p. 32.

20. The 1947 census was taken in March, a period of slack in the demand for young people in agriculture. The 1960 census was taken in September, a month of public demand for the work of young people in cotton harvesting.

21. Institute of National Planning, <u>Final Report on Employment Problems in Rural Areas, U.A.R.</u> (Cairo, April, 1968), p. 36.

22. Hansen and Marzouk, <u>op. cit.</u>, pp. 60-64, especially p. 61.

23. Mead, <u>op. cit.</u>, pp. 60-63 and 80-84.

24. a.) Persons employed in industrial occupations include those who are employed in industry. Those persons are usually carried by the census and labor force sample survey. The number of persons employed in industrial occupations are usually larger than the number of persons engaged in industrial establishment, since the first includes persons employed outside of recorded establishments.

b.) Persons employed in industrial establishments include those who work in all the industrial establishments employing ten or more persons and owned by both the public and private sector. Those are carried by the census of establishments.

c.) According to '' The Standard Classification of Economic Activities, April, 1961,'' which was based on the <u>International Standard of Industrial Classification of all Economic Activities</u> (published by the United Nations in 1959), economic activity was classified under eleven main sectors, e.g., ''Agriculture,'' ''Mining and Quarrying,'' and ''Manufacturing.'' In 1964 for example, the manufacturing sector, which accounted for 18 percent of the total number of establishments, employed 44 percent of the total number of employees as compared with 40 percent in 1960. These are carried by the industrial census.

25. Hansen and Marzouk have concluded that small-scale industry is continuing to expand, with employment rising perhaps by as much as 35 percent from 1947 to 1960, compared to an employment increase of less than 30 percent for all industry over the same period. See Hansen and Marzouk, <u>op. cit.</u>, p. 125. Mead, on the other hand, seems to believe that weakness of their data could lead to exaggerate the growth of small scale industry; see, Mead, <u>op. cit.</u>, pp. 123-24.

26. Hansen and Marzouk, <u>op. cit.</u>, p. 126, Table 58.

27. <u>Ibid.</u>, p. 127,. Table 59.

28. National Bank of Egypt, ''Industrial Census for 1961,'' <u>Economic Bulletin</u>, V (1962), 56, Table III.

29. Mead, <u>op. cit.</u>, p. 123, Table 5-11.

30. In the discussion of employment in the services sector we relied heavily on the work of Mead, <u>op. cit.</u>, Chapter 6.

31. <u>Ibid.</u>, pp. 134, 138 and 139.

32. For further information on the distinction between the modern and traditional sectors, see Ibid., p. 146-48.

33. Ibid., p. 150.

34. Patrick O'Brien, The Revolution in Egypt's Economic System (New York: Oxford University Press, 1966), pp. 219 and 256. S.H. Abdel Rahman estimated that 8.5 percent of all private construction between 1947 and 1950 was residential. See S. H. Abdel Rahman, "A Survey of the Foreign Trade of Egypt in the Post-War Period With Special Reference to Its Impact on the National Economy," (unpublished Ph.D. dissertation, Faculty of Commerce, Cairo University, 1959), Appendix B.

35. O'Brien, op. cit., pp. 78-79.

36. Mead, op. cit., p. 152.

37. Ibid., p. 132, Table 6-1 and p. 153, Table 6-11.

38. Ibid., p. 154.

39. National Bank of Egypt, "Population and Manpower," op. cit., pp. 10 and 16.

40. We have cited many references in this respect throughout this study; see, for example, footnotes No. 116 and No. 117, Chapter II; No. 20, Chapter II; No. 111, Chapter V; No. 12, Chapter VII; and footnotes No. 40 and No. 41 of this chapter.

41. W.A. Lewis, Economic Development With Unlimited Supplies of Labor: Readings in Economic Development (Belmont, Calif., 1963).

42. The major proponent of this view is B. Hansen; see his "Marginal Productivity Wage Theory and Subsistence Wage Theory in Egyptain Agriculture," Institute of National Planning, Memo. No. 547 (March, 1965). B. Hansen and G. Marzouk, op. cit., pp. 61-161. M. El-Tomy and B. Hansen, "The Seasonal Employment Profile in Egyptian Agriculture," Memo. No. 501 (Cairo, October, 1954). H. Kheir El-Dine, "The Cotton Production-Function in the U.A.R. and Its Relation to Technical Progress and to Disguised Unemployment," Memo. No. 370 (Cairo: Institute of National Planning, September, 1963).

43. See, for example, Yong Sam Cho, Disguised Unemployment in Undeveloped Areas With Special Reference to South Korean Agriculture (Berkeley: University of California Press, 1963).

44. M. El-Shafei, " The Current Labor Force Sample Survey in Egypt," International Labor Review, LXXXII, 5 (November, 1960), 441, Table IX.

45. National Bank of Egypt, "Statistics of the Labor Force in the Southern Region, "Economic Bulletin, XIII (1960), 91.

46. Institute of National Planning, op. cit., p. 47.

47. For a discussion of the relevance of the category labeled as " discouraged group" in the definition and measurement of the labor force concept, see R. L. Rowan and Herbert R. Northrup, Readings in Labor Economics and Labor Relations (Homewood, Ill.: Richard D. Irwin, Inc., 1968), pp. 21-24.

48. The conceptual procedures of defining underemployment as compared to unemployment is quite apparent in the literature of economics. Underemployment could be visible or invisible. Visible underemployment includes seasonal, chronic, and occasional under-employment. Invisible underemployment includes disguised and potential underemployment. The type most controversial in discussing the Egyptian setting is disguised underemployment. Disguised underemploy-ment is usually taken to mean that the marginal productivity of labor is near zero, so that labor can be removed permanently without detri-mental effects on production. From the demographic point of view, disguised unemployment makes the effective labor input smaller than the figures disclosed by census, and makes the effective amount of work done grow more slowly than the census figures may lead us to believe. On the other hand, census figures depict the extent of un-employment.

49. See, among others, W. Cleland, The Population Problem in Egypt (Pennsylvania: Science Press Printing Co., 1936), pp. 104-106; C. Issawi, Egypt in Revolution: An Economic Analysis (New York: Oxford University Press, 1963), pp. 298-99; (United Arab Republic, presidency of the republic), National Planning Committee, General Frame of the Five-Year Plan for Economic and Social Develop-ment, July 1960-June 1965 (Cairo, 1960), p. 118.

50. International Labour Office, Labour Survey of North Africa (Geneva, 1960), p. 101.

51. Hansen and Marzouk, op. cit., pp. 61-63.

52. Mead, op. cit., Chapter 4.

53. Ibid., p. 63.

54. For an extensive analysis of these evidences, see Ibid.,
Appendix to Chapter 4.

55. Production function is a statistical and mathematical computation for the coefficient for any factor or production. The type production function most suitable for agriculture experts is Cobb-Douglas.
This Cobb-Douglas method of production-function can tell the ratio of
the marginal production of any factor of production to its average product.

56. Hansen, op. cit., pp. 61-63

57. Hansen, and Marzouk, op. cit., p. 64.

58. Mead, op. cit., p. 91

59. See, W. A. Lewis, "Economic Development with Unlimited
Supplies of Labor," in A. Agarwala and S. Singh, eds., The Economics
of Underdevelopment (New York: Oxford University Press, 1963).

60. Since the discussion of the survey findings is actually an
attempt to summarize the relevant points, no attempt will be made to
make specific reference to the figures cited in this sector. All of the
information was taken from The Institute of National Planning, op. cit.
pp. 34-51.

61. Hansen and El-Tomy, op. cit., p. 4.

62. Labor input here is measured as the work hours provided by
similar age sex groups in eight-day periods per feddan crops areas.

63. Institute of National Planning, op. cit., p. 82

64. Mead, op. cit., p. 131.

65. Hansen and Marzouk, op. cit., p. 298.

66. Ibid., p. 135.

6

LABOR FORCE
AND EMPLOYMENT
IN THE 1960's:
THE PLANNING YEARS

The rapid growth of population coupled with the apparent shortage of productive resources has remained the crux of economic problems confronting Egypt. Prior to the 1952 revolution the Egyptian economy operated largely as a free enterprise economy. Since the revolution the economy has moved from the free enterprise phase, which lasted until 1956, to a stage of what is described as ''guided capitalism.'' This phase lasted from 1957 until 1960. Beginning in 1960, the Egyptian government launched an overall development plan aimed at doubling the national income in real terms over a period of ten years. The ten-year span was to be divided into two equal stages, starting from July, 1960, and taking 1959-60 as the base. In addition to planning, the nationalization measures of most of Egypt's industrial and commercial property in July, 1961, ushered in an era now referred to in Egypt as the ''social revolution.''[1]

As offically stated, the main objectives of the ten-year development plan were three: first, to double the national income in ten years; second, to achieve more even distribution of income and property; and third, to expand employment opportunities.[2]

As to the first target, national income was to rise from 1,282 million Egyptian pounds in 1959-60 to 1,795 million Egyptian pounds in 1964-65, and to 2,564 million Egyptian pounds in 1969-70.[3] The projected contributions of the different sectors of the economy to the national income before and during the planning period are shown in Table 57. Here it can be seen that the relative importance of each sector to the growth of the national income was expected to undergo significant changes during the ten-year period. Despite the continuous growth of agriculture, the plan called for a decline in its proportionate share of the national income. Both the absolute figures and the proportionate share of industry and construction were intended to increase considerably. The contribution of other sectors to the national

TABLE 57

Projected Contributions to National Income,
by Sector, in the Planning Period, 1959-60, 1964-65, and 1969-70

	National Income		
	1959-60	1964-65	1969-70
Agriculture percent	31.2	28.5	24.5
Industry and construc- tion percent	25.4	32.9	34.2
Other sectors percent	43.4	38.6	41.3
Total	100.0	100.0	100.0

Source: National Bank of Egypt, "The Next Ten Years," Economic Bulletin, XI (1962), 7.

income were to stay, on the average, at about the same level of importance.

The production targets assigned for various economic sectors called for heavy industry to increase substantially its production over the base year (See Table 58). The agricultural sector, on the other hand, was planned to show the least increase in production. This reflects the fact that productivity of Egyptian agriculture was already at a relatively high output. To achieve the targets of the plan it was estimated that 1,576.9 million Egyptian pounds would have to be invested in different economic sectors during the first five years, and another 1,717 million during the second five years. The bulk of this investment would be in industry and electricity. [4]

As a second major objective, the plan called for income redistribution without really discussing the means by which it was to be achieved; however, the broad government policies seemed to focus on the agrarian reform laws for the improvement in the distribution of farm income. In the urban industrial sector, minimum wage laws, coupled with more employment opportunities in industry and other economic activities, as well as profit-sharing laws for workers, paved the way for improvement in income distribution in favor of workers. Measures to break up private monopolistic enterprise in refining and trade limited the value of holdings by any one individual to 10,000 Egyptian pounds in 1960. Certain income tax reforms, including

TABLE 58

Production Targets Under The Ten-Year Plan, by Economic
Sector, 1960, 1965, and 1970

	(In millions of Egyptian pounds)		
Economic Sector	1960	1965	1970
Agriculture	100	128	159
Commerce	100	128	196
Heavy industry	100	310	445
Light industry	100	137	185
Services	100	128	213
Transport, housing, public utilities, and defense	100	122	160

Source: U. S. Bureau of Labor Statistics, Labor, Law and
Practice in The United Arab Republic (Egypt), BLS Report No. 275
(Washington, D. C.: U. S. Government Printing Office, March, 1965),
p. 9, Table 2.

increased rates of taxation on high incomes, also showed a definite
and consistent pattern of action towards income redistribution.[5]
Apart from these measures, income redistribution and the Socialistic
type of economy planned for depended mainly on the control of public
investment and would lead to the government's being the main source of
employment, especially outside of the agricultural sector.

The third objective of the plan was to employ nearly all the
projected increase in manpower. The civilian labor force in 1959-60
had been estimated at 7,547,000 persons, of whom 5,975,000 were
fully engaged. Of the remainder, 975,000 were persons working in
agriculture, who were thus classified as disguised unemployment,
and 597,000 were unemployed persons (about 7.0 percent of the total
labor force). This, in addition to an expected growth of 832,000 persons in the labor force during the first five years, urged the government
to consider employment as one of the main objectives of the plan.[6]
To achieve the planned targets, employment would have to increase

by about 1 million persons during the first stage and by another 2 million persons during the second stage. At the end of the two stages of the plan, it was planned that disguised unemployment would have disappeared and that the existing number of unemployed together with the expected growth in the labor force would be fully employed. The labor surplus estimated that 1,572,000 persons in 1959-60 (or 20.8 percent of the total labor force) would diminish to 1,378,000 in 1964-65 (16.4 percent of the labor force estimated for that year), and to less than 400,000 persons (only about 4 percent of the labor force) at the end of the plan (1969-70).[7]

Since employment increase during the planning period is the major concern of this study, the following section contains detailed analysis of projected employment targets and growth of the labor force.

EMPLOYMENT TARGETS AND LABOR FORCE PROJECTIONS

The projected rates of labor force growth and the planned rates of increase in employment are presented in Table 59. The figures show that employment objectives in each of the five-year plans were higher than the projected growth rate of the labor force, a fact which indicated a concern not only with minimum employment targets (i.e., not to let the employment situation become worse than it was before), but also to take care of a good part of already existing unemployment and underemployment. In the first five-year period, employment was planned to increase at a rate approximately one and a half times as great as the increase that was expected in the labor force. In the second five-year period, employment was planned to increase nearly twice as fast as the projected increase in the labor force. These figures reveal a number of points that are worthy of comment. First, the low annual rate of population increase projected during the second five-year plan (1.9 percent) proved to be too optimistic. A drop in the annual rate of population growth from 2.3 to 1.9 percent in a relatively short time appears to this writer to be unrealistic. There is no explanation in the frame of the plan as to how it was supposed to be achieved. Such optimism becomes even more striking when we compare Egypt's plan with plans of other developing countries such as India, Pakistan, and Turkey.[8] In all these countries, population was expected either to increase at a higher rate from one planning period to another or to remain constant.

Second, despite a projected slowdown in the rate of population increase the labor force was expected to increase at a greater rate in the second five-year plan (2.3 percent per year) than in the first (2.1 percent per year). Such an expectation seems quite reasonable in light of the age structure of Egyptian population, especially

TABLE 59

Planned or Projected Annual Compound Rates of Increase in
National Income, National Income per Head, Population,
Labor Force, and Employment, 1960-70
(in Percentages)

Plan	G.N.P. (R_o)	Employ-ment (R_e)	Labor Force (R_e)	Popu-lation	G.N.P. per Head	$\dfrac{R_n}{R_o}$	$\dfrac{R_n}{R_o}$
U. A. R. 1960-65	7.0	3.2	2.1	2.3	4.9	0.46	1.52
U. A. R. 1965-70	7.4	4.9	2.3	1.9	5.3	0.66	1.80

Source: C. Hsieh, "Planned Rates of Employment Increase in Development Plans," International Labour Review (Geneva: International Labour Office, January, 1968), LXXXXVII, 1, 37, Table 1.

considering the fact that a sizable proportion of the young population would be joining the labor force in the second half of the decade. If the projected rate of population increase were higher than the projected 1.9 percent, as suspected, it would not necessarily offset the employment targets of the second five-year plan, but would definitely have later repercussions.

Thirdly, as planned, employment objectives were significantly higher in the second five-year plan than in the first (4 percent as opposed to 3.2 percent). To begin with, it is difficult to see how such a high target could be achieved. What the planners seemed to have in mind was that the high planned annual rates of increase in employment would be possible as a result of a combination of a high planned annual rate of increase of the gross national product (7 percent between 1960 and 1965) and a greater elasticity of employment with respect to output.[9] Such an objective seems unrealistic, however, without a considerable sacrifice in the average output per worker.

In order to see how the aggregate employment targets were reached, it is necessary to examine the projected employment targets by major sectors.[10] Therefore, the following analysis is concerned

TABLE 60

Planned or Projected Annual Compound Rates of Increase in Output and Employment, by Sector, 1960-70

	U. A. R. I 1960-65	U. A. R. II 1965-70
Aggregate		
$R_o{}^a$	7.2	7.4
$R_n{}^b$	3.2	4.9
$\dfrac{R_n}{R_o}$	0.5	0.7
Agriculture		
R_o	5.1	4.1
R_n	3.2	3.2
$\dfrac{R_n}{R_o}$	0.6	0.8
Industry		
R_o	14.5	8.2
R_n	6.0	4.4
$\dfrac{R_n}{R_o}$	0.4	0.5
Construction		
R_o	0.4	8.0
R_n	1.2	6.8
$\dfrac{R_n}{R_o}$	3.0	0.9
Other sectors (services)		
R_o	4.4	8.9
R_n	2.7	7.9
$\dfrac{R_n}{R_o}$	0.6	0.9

[a]R_o = planned or projected compound annual rate of increase in output.

[b]R_n = planned or projected compound annual rate of increase in employment.

Source: C. Hsieh, "Planned Rates of Employment Increase in Development Plans," International Labour Review (Geneva: International Labour Office, January, 1968), LXXXXVII, 1, 52, Table III.

with the planned sectoral rate of employment expansion. For this purpose the economy is divided into four broad sectors: agriculture, industry, construction, and services.

The projected annual compound rates of increase in output and employment by sector are presented in Table 60. During the first stage of the plan, the projected rate of increase in employment was highest for the industrial sector (6 percent). At the other extreme, the planned sectoral rates of employment change in the construction sector was negative (-1. 2 percent). Comparing the two periods of the plan shows the following: the planned rate of increase in employ-ment in the agriculture sector remained constant at 3. 2 percent the planned rate of employment increase in industry slowed down from 6 to 4. 4 percent; and the planned rate of increase in employment in both the construction and service sectors accelerated substantially during the second five-year plan. Probably what the planners had in mind was the fast promotion of employment in the production of goods during the first five years of the plan and acceleration of employment in the service sectors during the second five years.

The percentage distribution of planned additional employment by sector is shown in Table 61. The main features of this distribution were five: (1) the largest contribution to planned additional aggregate employment came from agriculture; more than half the increase in employment in the first stage was allotted to agriculture; (2) the planned percentage contribution of agriculture to additional employ-ment diminished from 54. 1 to 34. 1 percent during the second five-year period; (3) the contribution of the construction sector to the planned additional aggregate employment was negative in the first five-year plan and relatively low in the second period; (4) the propor-tion of additional employment contributed by industry was about one-fifth of the total employment increase in the first phase, but decreased sharply to only 10 percent during the second phase; and (5) the com-bined contribution of agriculture and industry to the planned increases in aggregate employment approximated three-fourths of the planned total increase during the first half of the decenium, but their combined contribution was only 44 percent in the second phase of the plan. This is another indication that the major outlet for employment in the first five-year plan lay in the production sectors, but that the services sectors provided such outlets in the second phase.

The size of planned additional aggregate employment is usually determined by the allocation of planned investment among sectors. Thus, the larger the percentage of total planned investment allocated to sectors with a lower average amount of planned investment per additional worker, the greater will be the planned additional aggregate employment. From this point of view, one prominent feature of the plan takes on particular significance. As shown in Table 61, productive

TABLE 61

Sectoral Percentage Distribution of Planned Investment,
Additional Output, and Additional Employment, 1960-70

		U. A. R. I 1960-65		U. A. R. II 1965-70
Planned additional employment				
Agriculture		54. 1		34. 1
Industry		21. 0		10. 2
Construction		-1. 1		3. 2
Other sectors (services)		26. 0		3. 2
Planned investment				
Agriculture		24. 8		24. 0
Industry		23. 6		22. 7
Other sectors (services)		51. 6		53. 3
Power	31. 1		9. 6	
Transp. and commu- nications	17. 3		14. 9	
Housing	11. 0		16. 0	
Other (education, etc.)	10. 1		12. 8	
Planned additional output				
Agriculture		21. 8		15. 0
Industry		52. 0		34. 0
Construction		-0. 2		3. 0
Other sectors (services)		26. 4		48. 0

Source: C. Hsieh, "Planned Rates of Employment Increase in
Development Plans," International Labour Review, LXXXXVII, 1
(Geneva: International Labour Office, January, 1968), 54, Table IV.

investment in agriculture and industry together accounted for less
than half the total planned investment during both five-year periods.
More than half (52 percent the first five-year period and 53 percent
the second) was allotted to investment in the infrastructure or economic or social overhead services. Almost 80 percent of this investment went to three subsectors; power, transport and communication,
and housing. Normally, in these subsectors, investment per additional

permanent worker employed was considerably higher than in most other sectors. [11] The large amounts of investment allotted to these subsectors was, therefore, not expected to create much direct permanent employment.

As between investment in power and transport and investment in housing, there is one important difference that deserves mention in this connection; whereas the former is essential to the country's productive capacity and helps to generate permanent employment in agriculture and industry and elsewhere in the economy when the construction phase is over, the latter has little indirect permanent employment creating effect of this kind. However, the fact that a great deal of investment in housing is of a type that is complementary to direct production investment (workers' housing) seems to accord somewhat with the objectives of creating productive employment of a permanent nature. [12] The great drop in the planned additional investment in power and transportation sectors from 48.4 percent to only 24.5 percent between successive phases of the plan, and the increase in the planned additional investment in housing from 11 percent to 16 percent, would no doubt reduce the employment in the economy; yet, paradoxically enough, the planned or projected compound annual rate of increase in employment in the service sector (see Table 60) was projected to rise from 2.7 to 7.9 percent from one phase of the plan to the other.

The low percentage of total planned investment allotted to "other" (e.g., the production projects in economic and social fields such as education and health) needs a special comment. Had this part of investment been enlarged, it would have been more conducive to the allotment of the employment objectives and to the development of human resources. [13]

Having made the above general observations, it might be useful to consider how the average amount of planned investment per unit of additional output and the average amount of planned output per additional worker in the given sector would combine to yield the average amount of planned investment per additional workers in that sector. [14] Since the latter is a product of the first two variables, the same value of planned investment per workers might be arrived at by a higher output per worker with a lower per unit investment, or by a lower per worker output with a higher per unit investment. With the same amount of combination the former (output per workers) will bring about a greater additional output than the latter, though the additional employment created will be the same. As it stands, the relatively low percentage contribution of the industrial sector to additional employment in the second five-year plan results primarily from a relatively high planned output per additional worker. [15] This is so, since the planned investment per unit of additional worker results from a relatively very low average output per additional worker in agriculture. [16] From this fact we can clearly see the limited capacity of the agriculture sector to employ additional workers and to maintain at the same time a substantial increase in additional output per worker. In other words, a great part of the employment in agriculture could be described as "demographic employment" (i.e., employment for employment's sake because of population pressure), where future increase in the additional output per worker becomes limited. This latter type of employment stands in contrast to the type of "economic employment" as planned in industry, where substantial increases in additional output per worker are expected. [17]

The above discussion has brought to light some of the problems concerning employment increases in the development plan of Egypt. Planned aggregate employment depends on a very high growth rate of the gross national produce (7 percent). It is doubtful whether Egypt can attain and maintain such a high level of increase in its GNP under present conditions. This raises the problem of seeking alternate courses of action designed to create more productive employment, which could enable a more productive use of the presently underutilized labor.

The need for seeking alternatives also appears from the sectoral distribution of planned additional employment opportunities. Both the agriculture and the service sectors in Egypt are already overcrowded with underemployed, seasonally unemployed, and unproductively employed persons. It seems quite possible then, that a large portion of additional employment targets set for these sectors adds to these broad, unsatisfactory categories.

To review briefly the methods of calculating the total employment to be generated in each sector may help in understanding not only the methodology involved but also the planners' operating conceptions of the employment problems in each sector. It may also throw some light on the shortcomings of these methods. [18]

In agriculture, separate estimates were made for employment in crop operations, livestock, farming, fishing, and agricultural management. The methods used for estimating the number of persons required for all crop operations involved the following steps: (1) calculation of the number of operations for each crop; (2) assessment of the equivalent man-days required for each operation per acre for each crop; (3) calculation of total man-days required for each area under each crop by multiplying the number of areas under each crop by the above estimates of man-days; (4) aggregation of total man-days required for all crops; and (5) calculation of the number of persons required for all crop operations by dividing the estimated man days required for all crops by a norm of 195 working days per year. Thus, the method of estimating employment to be generated in agriculture takes care not only of the newly permanent jobs to be generated but also of the cases of reduction in underemployment as a result of increases in the hours of work. Such methods cause the researcher a great deal of confusion in interpreting the figures on the increases in the size of the agricultural labor force. There is no easy way to decide their relative distribution between the completely new jobs on one hand and the expansion of employment to the already underemployed workers on the other.

The volume of employment in different industries in the final year of each five-year period was calculated from the estimates of the annual wage bill and the average annual wage per worker to be paid by the industry in question that year. The annual wage bill was obtained by dividing the estimated value added envisaged for the industry by an empirically ascertained ratio of wages to value added adjusted for consideration of social desirability and economic feasibility, while the average annual wage was estimated after examining past trends where data existed.

The employment targets in services seem to have been estimated largely from the projected output and some assumed quantitative relationship between increases in output and in labor productivity in this sector. Both magnitudes are susceptible to a wide margin of error. Such crude methods applied to the service sector would tend to exaggerate the number of full-time new jobs to be created, since in Egypt, as in most developing countries, the service sector is already overcrowded.

In summary, the methods of estimating the volume of employment to be created in the first five-year plan seem to have been based largely on economic considerations related to fixed investment and output targets. The work of the manpower planning unit of the National Planning Committee appears to have exercised no influence on the choice of projects by different departments. [19] However, in the implementation phase, employment for social reasons seems to have taken place. The government drive in 1961 to speed up employment of the educated people seems to have caused some structural as well as individual dislocations. The net effect was an overstaffing in many cases, and hiring of unqualified personnel in others. This employment drive, as we shall see later, caused productivity to lag behind the planned targets.

The comparative figures of the planned and actual employment targets, aggregate and sectoral, are presented in Table 62. The very slight differences in the base year figures of the planned and the actual phases are due to the fact that the labor force estimates and/or projections are often in the process of revision. For all practical purposes, however, the differences are negligible.

TABLE 62

Planned and Actual Employment by Sector, 1960-65

| | (in Thousands) | |
	Planned	Actual
Agriculture		
Base year[a]	3, 245	3, 245
Target year[b]	3, 800	3, 780
Planned increase	555	535
Industry		
Base year[a]	632	613
Target year[b]	847	843
Planned increase	215	229
Construction		
Base year[a]	170	185
Target year[b]	159	345
Planned increase	-11	160
Other sectors (services)		
Base year[a]	1, 928	1, 962
Target year[a]	2, 195	2, 365
Planned increase	267	403
Total		
Base year[a]	5, 975	6, 006
Target year[b]	7, 001	7, 333
Planned increase	1, 026	1, 327

[a]1959-60

[b]1964-65

Source: U. A. R. Central Agency for Public Mobilization and Statistics, Population Increase in the U. A. R. and Its Deterrents to Development (Cairo, 1966), p. 185, Table 81; and C. Hsieh, "Planned Rates of Employment Increase in Development Plans," International Labour Review (Geneva: International Labour Office, January, 1968), LXXXXVII, 1, 54, Table IV.

The total net employment increase (1, 327) exceeded the planned increase (1, 026), by the end of the plan period. Judging from this achievement alone, one might conclude that the plan was a success. However, in comparing the planned and the actual figures sector by sector, it becomes apparent that only the agriculture and industrial sectors showed any real agreement between the achieved and the planned employment targets. The case was quite different in the construction and services sectors. In the construction sector, employment was originally projected to decrease by 11,000 workers; instead, it increased by 160,000 workers. This very substantial increase, which signifies a serious failure of employment planning in this sector, is associated with the rapid expansion of the industrial sector, along with heavy investment in transportation--particularly in roads and railroad construction. The reason behind the projected decline in construction employment lies in the fact that only the private sector was considered, and in making the projection for the private sector it was assumed that a slowdown of building activities would occur during the first five-year period as a result of government control over private investment. [20] The unplanned increase in construction employment, on the other hand, reflects changes in the public sector that had the effect of generating new employment opportunities (e.g., it was during this period that construction activities connected with the High Dam at Aswan began to assume some importance). The increase in service employment, on the other hand, is a reflection of expanding job opportunity in such areas as transportation and housing.

Employment trends by detailed sector for each year of the first five-year plan are presented in Table 63. As these figures show, employment increased at a slightly higher rate in the commodity-producing sectors than in the service sectors. At the end of the plan period, employment in the commodity-producing sectors had increased by 23 percent over the base line figure as compared to an increase of 21 percent in the services. Among the goods-producing sectors, construction increased by 87 percent. It was followed by electricity (51 percent) and industry (37 percent). Agriculture, with only 16.5 percent increase in employment over the base year, was the slowest growing sector.

In the services, employment in housing increased substantially faster than any other subsectors (31 percent). Transportation and communication occupied the second place (27 percent), whereas commerce and finance were the least growing in terms of employment (only 15 percent).

In terms of absolute numbers, the figures indicate an aggregate increase of 1.33 million workers during the plan period, with an average annual increment of nearly 266,000 workers. The share of the commodity-producing sectors in the total increase in employment was more than twice as high as that of the service sectors. In the former sectors, employment increased by 925,000 workers, thus accounting

TABLE 63

Trends in Employment in the First Five-Year Plan by Sector, 1959-60 to 1964-65

(In thousands)

	1959-60	1960-61	1961-62	1962-63	1963-64	1964-65	Total Increase	Percent Increase Over Base Year	Percent Contribution to Total Increase
Agriculture	3,245.0	3,600.0	3,600.0	3,632.0	3,673.0	3,780.0	535.0	16.5	40.3
Industry	601.8	625.6	679.1	725.9	789.7	825.0	223.2	37.1	16.7
Electricity	11.9	13.1	15.1	17.4	17.9	18.0	6.1	51.3	0.5
Construction	185.0	166.0	263.0	315.7	334.2	345.2	160.2	86.6	12.1
Total Goods	4,043.7	4,404.7	4,557.1	4,691.0	4,814.8	4,968.2	924.5	22.9	69.6
Transportation communication	218.7	252.7	239.2	249.2	258.3	277.7	59.1	27.0	4.5
Commerce and finance	635.7	663.0	680.9	702.2	719.0	729.7	94.0	14.8	7.0
Housing	16.0	16.0	18.0	18.1	18.5	21.0	5.0	31.2	0.4
General utilities	25.2	24.3	27.1	28.7	29.5	30.3	5.1	20.2	0.4
Other services	1,066.8	1,151.2	1,134.6	1,179.0	1,244.9	1,306.5	239.7	22.5	18.1
Total services	1,962.3	2,107.2	2,099.8	2,177.2	2,270.2	2,365.2	402.9	20.5	30.4
Grand total	6,006.0	6,511.9	6,656.9	6,868.2	7,085.0	7,333.4	1,327.4	22.1	100.0

Source: U. A. R. Central Agency for Public Mobilization and Statistics, Population Increase in the U. A. R. and Its Deterrents to Development (Cairo, 1966), p. 185, Table 81.

for 70 percent of the total employment increase. In comparison, the increase in service sectors of only 403,000 workers represented only 30 percent of the total employment increase in that broad sector.

The examination of the employment figures of each year of the five-year plan indicates that the big increase in the volume of employment took place in 1961-62 and 1962-63. No major changes took place in employment after 1962-63 until the end of the plan period. This sudden spurt in the volume of employment largely resulted, no doubt, from the 1961 Socialistic laws which enlarged the size of the public sector and enhanced the government's efforts to ease the unemployment of unskilled labor. Construction work provided a natural outlet for this category of workers.

When we examine the annual increments to employment by sector, a somewhat different pattern also emerges. For example, over 70 percent of the increases in the agricultural labor force took place in the first year of the plan (1960-61), and most of the remaining 30 percent took place in the last year, 1964-65. The three years in between recorded virtually no increases. In this regard, it is interesting to note that about 26 percent of the increase in the total labor force was recorded in the first year of the plan; most of the increase was due to the substantial increases in the agricultural labor force. It is not easy to explain such an uneven distribution of annual increments to employment in agriculture; nevertheless there is likely a relationship between the land reform laws of 1961 and the employment increases in that year.

Industry provides a somewhat different pattern: the annual increment to the industrial labor force increased sharply in the second year of the plan (1961-62), but rose much more slowly during the remaining years of the plan. Annual increments to the labor force employed in construction decreased in the second year but experienced a substantial increase in the third year; after that, it remained relatively stable. With regard to the services, there were no major fluctuations in the size of annual increments to the labor force in any subsector comparable to those observed in the commodity-producing sectors.

The differences between the planned and the actual employment expansion during the planning period become more apparent by considering the percentage distribution of additional employment.[21] It is interesting to note that the share of actual employment in agriculture and industry fell considerably short of the target, at the time the planned aggregate employment was virtually achieved. This of course is due to the unplanned expansion in other sectors, especially in construction. As will be seen later, this trend resulted in a further drop

TABLE 64

Sectoral Percentage Distribution of Planned and Actual
Additional Employment, 1965

	Planned	Actual
Agriculture	54. 1	40. 3
Idustry	21. 0	17. 2[a]
Construction	-1. 1	12. 1
Services	26. 0	30. 4
Total	100. 0	100. 0

[a]Industry and electricity.

Source: Computed by the author from Tables 61 and 62.

in the proportion of the agricultural labor force in the total labor
force (see Table 64). An important feature of the planning period,
however, is that employment in agriculture and industry, while
falling considerably below the target of 75 percent of total employment,
contributed more than 50 percent of all the new increases in employment (58 percent).

It is interesting to notice what a different configuration for employment growth was anticipated as of 1959 for the first planning
period. During the first stage, expansion of the services was expected to play a relatively moderate role in solving the employment
problem, while both agriculture and industry were expected to increase their rate of expansion. The planners may have felt that the
services sector as a whole was somewhat overextended in the base
year of the plan, with relatively modest expansion needed, [22] and
rapid employment expansion in the commodity producing sector was
their goal. However, the services continued to absorb a large part
of the increase in the labor force because of a rapid expansion of
employment in government and the nationalized, commercial, and
financial enterprises. Most of this expansion was designed to reduce
the plight of unemployment amoung university and high school graduates.

Employment in construction increased by more than 100 percent, largely because of higher investment activities undertaken under the plan. This suggests that construction rather than manufacturing may provide a short-run solution to employment problems.

The structural transformation of the labor force during the first stage of the planning period can best be ascertained by comparing sectoral percentage distribution at the beginning of the period and at the end of it (see Table 65). Admittedly, the period is too short to expect very noticeable changes; nevertheless, some tendencies can be observed. For example, the percentage distribution of the labor force between the two comprehensive categories, the goods-producing sectors and the services sectors, remained relatively unchanged during the first planning period. However, notable changes took place within the goods-producing sectors. The percentage of agricultural labor force in the total labor force declined from 54 percent in 1959-60 to 52 percent in 1964-65. The relative decline in the percentage of the agricultural labor force in the total labor force was compensated for by an increase in the percentage share of industry from 10 percent to 11 percent, and in construction from 3 percent to 5 percent. It is also interesting to note the relatively consistent percentage distribution of the subsectors in the services before and after the planning period. No really noteworthy changes occurred here during the 1959-60 to 1964-65 period.

In summary, during the first five years of the planning decade, the relative share of agriculture in the labor force continued to decline and the relative share of industry and construction showed an upward surge. The relative share of the services in the labor force remained unchanged. From an employment point of view the fact that fairly heavy investment in industry during the planning years did not increase its relative share in the labor force substantially constitutes a further indication that planned expansion in industrial employment alone will not solve Egypt's employment problems, at least not in the short run.

WAGES, PRODUCTIVITY, AND GOVERNMENT POLICY

Average wage and output per worker in the different sectors of the economy at the beginning and end of the first five planning years are shown in Table 66. As these data show, the percentage increase in average wages per worker was much higher than average output per worker in most sectors. For the aggregate, wages per worker increased by 31 percent in comparison to an 18 percent increase in output per worker. The lag of productivity increases behind wage increases was greater in the commodity-producing sectors than in the services, with the greatest discrepancies observed in agriculture and

TABLE 65

Structure of the Labor Force by Sector, 1959-60 and 1964-65

Sector	1959-60 Total (in Thousands)	Percent	1964-65 Total (in Thousands)	Percent
Agriculture	3,245.0	54.0	3,780.0	51.5
Industry	601.8	10.1	825.0	11.3
Electricity	11.9	0.2	18.0	0.3
Construction	185.0	3.1	345.2	4.7
Total goods- producing sectors	4,043.7	67.4	4,968.2	67.8
Transportation and communi- cation	218.7	3.6	277.7	3.8
Commerce and finance	635.7	10.6	729.7	10.0
Housing	16.0	0.27	21.0	0.29
General utilities	25.2	0.43	30.3	0.41
Other services	1,066.8	17.8	1,306.5	17.8
Total services	1,962.3	32.7	2,365.2	32.3
GRAND TOTAL	6,006.0	100.0	7,333.4	100.0

Source: Computed by the author from Table 63.

TABLE 66

Trends in Wages and Productivity per Worker
by Sector During the First
Five-Year Plan, 1960-65
(Current Prices)

| | | Average Wages and Productivity per Worker | | Percent Change |
		1959-60	1964-65	1959-60--1964-65
Agriculture	O	179.2	196.5	9.7
	W	30.2	44.1	46.7
Industry	O	1,805.7	1,968.0	9.0
	W	147.6	181.3	22.8
Electricity	O	1,546.2	2,172.2	40.5
	W	201.7	261.1	29.4
Construction	O	551.9	524.9	4.9
	W	161.6	155.6	3.7
Total Goods	O	442.4	520.6	17.7
	W	54.2	75.6	39.5
Transportation & communication	O	619.9	832.9	34.4
	W	179.8	218.6	21.6
Finance and commerce	O	260.0	317.8	22.2
	W	110.4	139.4	26.3
Housing	O	4,750.0	3,961.9	-16.6
	W	62.5	85.7	37.1
General utility	O	440.5	485.1	10.1
	W	214.3	254.1	18.6
Services	O	280.5	327.9	17.0
	W	167.1	211.4	26.5
Total service sectors	O	350.0	418.4	19.5
	W	149.9	189.5	26.4
Grand total	O	412.2	487.6	18.3
	W	85.5	112.3	31.3

O= Average output per worker (productivity measure).
W=Average wage per worker.

Source: U.A.R. Central Agency for Public Mobilization and
Statistics, Population Increase in the U.A.R. and Its Deterrents to
Development (Cairo, 1966), pp. 186-187, Table 82.

industry. Thus, in the former, average wage per worker increased by 47 percent in comparison to an increase of only 10 percent in average output per worker. The corresponding increases in industry were 22.8 percent for wages and only 9 percent for output. Among the services, the greatest difference characterized housing, where there was actually a decline in average per-worker output between 1959-60 and 1964-65. Only in electricity, construction and transportation, and communication did workers' productivity increase at a higher rate than wages.

A number of factors can be cited to explain the disproportionate increases in wages and productivity. First is the increase of the volume of employment. In addition, the 1961 employment drive, which continued during the plan period, was aimed at finding work primarily for two categories of the economically active: unskilled laborers and the educated portions of the manpower supply who were economically least productive. Skilled labor and professional and technical manpower, those segments of the labor force which are most productive, did not have any employment problem. While an increasing number of workers in these groups entered the labor force during the plan period, their relative proportion in the total labor force was on the decline. In spite of the fact that we have no detailed data on the distribution of the additions to the labor force by level of skills, some observations can be deduced from the data presented earlier in Table 63. More than 75 percent of employment during the 1960's was in agriculture, construction, and services. Normally, these sectors draw their sources from the pool of unskilled labor. The problem of the slow rate of productivity increase is no doubt tied to the problem of the scarcity of skilled and trained manpower emphasized earlier in the study.

Turning to a consideration of government policy, a major factor affecting employment was the nationalization of most industrial concerns in 1961. In Egypt, as elsewhere, it is usual to connect nationalization with Socialist ideology. However, as one observer commented, the beginning of nationalization in Egypt seems to have been an ad hoc step connected largely with international conflict. That is, the first nationalization acts connected with the Suez Canal were actually nationalistic rather than Socialistic.[23]

At least two important arguments in favor of nationalization of industry seem to be relevant to our discussion of labor and employment. First, it is argued that a large public sector is necessary to prevent exploitation of the working population by a limited number of private owners of big industries. Second, nationalization of industry is a necessary step toward effective mobilization of national saving by controlling the way in which it is invested in real capital. As far as exploitation of labor is concerned, most observers agree that the share of labor in industry in terms of wages in industrial value added had been declining since the late 1930's. For example, wages and salaries were estimated at 70 percent of industrial value added in 1939, at 40 percent in 1952, and at a little over 30 percent in 1960. [24] The development of money wage rates, industrial prices, and average labor productivity are factors responsible for the fall in the share of labor in relation to profit in industry. [25] Also, the increased capital intensity of industry (i.e., increase in the overall average investment per additional worker) may have been partially responsible. [26] However, the increased share of distributed profits in total industrial value added substantiated the tendency to accept the idea of the exploitation of the working population. [27]

Turning to the second reason, economists are divided in their appraisal of the nationalization of industry for the sake of mobilizing national saving for investment. Increasing national saving by simply increasing the taxes on profits has been suggested as an alternative to nationalization. [28] Others profess doubt that higher taxation on profit would have worked effectively as an alternative to the nationalization of industry. [29] Since the supply of new capital to industry is sensitive to the rate of distributed profits, the private supply of new capital might have declined more than the increase in public saving arising from increased taxation. What concerns us from this argument, more than anything else, is the allocation of national saving in the planning scheme. This brings us back to the highly controversial question of investment criteria discussed before under the choice of techniques in industrialization policy (see Chapter 2).

Almost all observers agree that in the planning years a growing part of investment has been directed by the government towards highly capital-intensive production. However, they differ greatly on the soundness of this policy in regard to the particular situation in Egypt. The investment policy of the planning years is considered irrational from an employment point of view, since it does not take into consideration the fact that Egypt is a country of surplus labor. [30] At the same time, the government's policy of allocating more investment to heavy industry is seen as the best possible alternative which will create permanent employment in the economy in the long run. [31] We need not go into the details of this highly analytical and theoretical argument except to suggest that priority of investment in certain industries was based on certain practical considerations. First, Egyptian planners seem to have given much attention to the immediate and the long-run impact of a given investment program on the balance of payments. Second, the government pursued this policy of capital-intensive production because it has favored such commodities as petroleum and steel, which require heavy investment in real capital. However, one cannot escape the impression that the government nationalization of industry (which was intended largely to control investment), coupled with the preference for capital-intensive production, was also designed to increase industry's share of invested profits and to produce a relatively lower share for labor. In other words, the government policy seeks to promote development by controlling the increases in the return of labor (in wages and salaries) at a moderate level while accelerating the increase in the return of capital. [32]

In light of this fact, one can understand the obvious inconsistency between governmental comments on the importance of increasing employment opportunities in rural and craft industries and the actual allocation of planned investment for this industry. The government is certainly aware of the advantages of this type of industry for employment and family income. Official statements describe this type of manufacturing as the kind that provides work which can be done by the fellahin in their homes, absorbs the energies of women and children, and plays an important part in the survival of the village by providing work for a large number of unemployed. [33] On the eve of the plan, rural and craft industries were estimated to have provided part- and full-time work for over 1 million persons. [34] One may then ask why these industries did not receive more than 3 percent of the investment? The answer probably lies in the fact that the products of rural industry account for only 3 percent of total industrial output. [35] The low share of investment in rural industries in the plan, in spite of its potential employment-creating effect, is due to the fact that rural industry is expected to make no direct favorable contribution to Egypt's balance of payment. It is also due to the fact that the portion of output going to profits (i. e., the reinvestment surplus) is among the lowest in manufacturing.

So far, we have noted that productivity increase lagged behind wage increase in most sectors of the economy during the first five-year plan. The nationalization of industry and the employment drive which started in 1961 were cited as being largely responsible for this trend. The question which arises from this fact is whether substantial increases in employment could be achieved without serious sacrifices in productivity, or whether they are two incompatible goals, especially in such developing nations as Egypt, where population pressure represents such a serious problem.

SOME MAJOR DEVELOPMENT PROJECTS

The implementation of a number of important projects prior to and during the planning period helped to create new employment opportunities during the 1960's. The following discussion is a brief assessment of the impact of the following major development projects: the High Dam, industrialization, land reclamation, agricultural cooperatives, education, and health and social welfare.

The construction of the first stage of the High Dam was completed in 1964. During this construction period it is estimated that employment opportunities were provided for 30,000 workers. The next two stages of the dam construction (the second ended in 1968 and the third terminated by the end of 1969) provided more opportunities for skilled and unskilled workers. The construction of the High Dam and the adjecent electric power stations was officially completed on January 15, 1971. The impact of the High Dam on employment has been great indeed. Nonetheless, the economic benefits expected from the projects are far more important to the economy than their role as a source of employment. The indirect effect of the construction of the dam on employment in the associated projects of land reclamation, electricity, and industry will no doubt be even more significant that the building of the dam itself. However, the construction phase served as good field training for the enhancement of the skills of a great number of professional technicians as well as skilled and semiskilled workers. Many other projects which form an integral part of the High Dam project were also implemented in the sectors of electricity, irrigation, transportation, public utilities, housing, health, and social development, all of which helped to attract many workers from rural areas and from other governorates to Aswan. Among the early projects that resulted from the high dam was the resettlement of approximately 50,000 Nubians from Nubia, which was to be flooded during the first stage of the High Dam construction.

The impact of industrialization on employment can be seen from the figures on industrial employment and wages between 1952 and 1965. In 1952 the number of industrial workers was approximately 500,000. The average annual wage of industrial workers was 47 Egyptian pounds. In 1960 the number of industrial workers had increased to about 750,000 and the average wage was 145 Egyptian pounds per year. By 1965 the number of industrial workers had risen to 840,000 and their average annual wage was estimated at 196 Egyptian pounds.

With the financial and technical assistance of the Soviet Union, Egypt embarked in the late 1960's on constructing a $1 billion industrial complex at Helwan. This project probably marks the beginning of a serious effect to establish heavy industry as an integral part of the Egyptian industrial structure. The project is another clear indication that the Egyptian government is definitely committed to highly intensive industry, at least at this stage of the country's development. It is no doubt that the iron and steel complex at Helwan will pave the way for the establishment of a series of heavy industries and lead to the establishment of consumer goods industries dependent on its products. Such a product would definitely mitigate the unemployment problem, especially among skilled and semiskilled workers. Whether it will have drastic effects on easing the unemployment situation is doubtful.

The efforts put forth for the decentralization of industry can be seen by the differential regional distribution of capital investment in relation to the share of employment in 1960. [36] To illustrate, Cairo and Alexandria, which employ 44 percent of the industrial labor force, received only 23 percent of total investment. The decentralization policy of the plan aimed at alleviating the problems of employment in the different regions of the centers.

Projects of land reclamation have added 536,000 feddans of reclaimed land to the cultivated areas during the first five-year plan at an annual rate of 107,000 feddans a year in comparison to an annual rate of only 12,000 prior to 1960. [37] A target was set to reclaim 636,000 feddans by 1970. These projects have generally been characterized by the ability to absorb a great number of skilled and nonskilled workers because they depend largely on manual work. It was expected that 20 percent of all new employment during the period from 1965 to 1970 will be absorbed by the land reclamation. In other words, out of 1.5 million workers expected to be employed in the second five-year plan, 300,000 were to be employed in different phases of land reclamation.

The cooperative movement was first introduced to Egypt in 1907. However, the movement did not gain momentum until after the promulgation of the Agrarian Reform Act in 1952 and its amendment in 1961. The cooperatives provided job opportunities for more than 15,000 workers during the first five-year plan. It is recognized that if farm mechanization is adopted vigorously on a large scale by the cooperatives, the result will be an enormous decrease of job opportunities in rural areas in the short run. Nonetheless, farm mechanization is recognized as a necessary policy for increasing production and raising the standard of living of the rural population. The government policy attempts to reconcile the two trends by encouraging farm mechanization at a reasonable pace. [38] Aside from providing direct employment for 15,000 workers, the impact of the combined unit on rural employment has been indirect and cannot be quantitatively measured. [39]

In recent years, elementary education has greatly expanded and was expected to reach all children between the ages of six and twelve by 1970. However, the impact of elementary education on rural employment is minimal. Most of the children who finished elementary school and did not have the chance to be enrolled in preparatory school or attend some vocational training course went back to the farm to perform the same work they would have performed, and as competently, without formal education. It was recommended, therefore, that the curricula of the rural elementary school be adjusted to meet the requirements and realities of life in rural areas, and that the compulsory period of education be extended to include the prepartory stage in the third five-year plan.

The turning point with regard to employment opportunities in rural areas is having the medium certificate from the preparatory level. Holders of this certificate have better chances to work as semiskilled workers in nonagricultural activities in the rural areas. On the other hand, the impact of secondary education in rural employment might be unfavorable, in spite of the employment of a number of rural students enrolled in secondary education since 1954. The employment opportunities created by the economic development projects in rural areas are neither qualitatively nor quantitatively sufficient to absorb secondary school graduates. Those high school graduates who do not go to college remain unemployed or migrate to urban areas to search for employment.

The impact of health and social projects on employment is difficult to measure quantitatively. This is so for a number of reasons: the impact of any improvement in health and social welfare on employment takes a long gestation period to be noticeable; improvements in health and social welfare are largely felt in changing work conditions and labor productivity; and it is not feasible to determine quantitatively or precisely how much improvement in manpower productivity resulted directly from improvement in health conditions. However, there is no doubt that the establishment of health units and social centers in the rural areas has improved living conditions and has helped to raise productive capacity of the rural population. Further, the staffing of these units has mitigated the pressure of unemployment among some semiprofessional occupations, especially nurses, health officers, social workers, and others.

In summary, then, it is clear that a wide variety of specific government programs have contributed, both directly and indirectly, to the growth of employment in Egypt in recent years.

NOTES

1. An excellent account of the transformation of the Egyptian economy from one phase to another can be found in Patrick O'Brien, The Revolution in Egypt's Economic System (New York: Oxford University Press, 1966).

2.   U. A. R. Budget Report, 1960-1961 (Cairo: Ministry of
Finance, 1960), p. 62.; U. A. R. Yearbook, 1960 (Cairo: Central
Agency for Public Mobilization and Statistics, 1960), pp. 336-37; and
General Frame of the Five-Year Plan for Economic and Social Devel-
opment, July, 1960, June, 1965 (U. A. R., Presidency of the Republic,
National Planning Committee: Cairo, 1960).

3.   C. Hsieh, "Planned Rates of Employment Increase in Development Plans," International Labour Review, LXXXXVII, 1
(January, 1968), 88, Appendix Table III.

4.   National Bank of Egypt, "The Next Ten Years," Economic
Bulletin, XI (1962), 8.

5.   For a general discussion of government policy on income
redistribution, see Ahmed El-Morshidy, Planning of Economic Development in the United Arab Republic (Cairo: Ministry of Planning,
December, 1962), pp. 39-40.

6.   The Central Bank of Egypt "Economic Planning in the
Southern Region," The Egyptian Economic and Political Review, VII,
7 (July, 1961), 13.

7.   Ibid., p. 14.

8.   The comparative figures were taken from Hsieh, op. cit.,
p. 67, Appendix Table 11.

9.   For a discussion of the measurement of the elasticity of
employment with respect to output, see Ibid., pp. 42-45.

10.   We followed closely the analysis provided in Ibid., especially
pp. 51-57.

11.   Ibid., p. 58.

12.   The guideline of investment in housing is financing low
cost housing projects with low rents either by the central and local
governments directly or by cooperative organizations. The construction of villas and luxury apartment houses has been restricted by
law. See El-Morshidy, op. cit., pp. 38-39.

13.   A fairly comprehensive account of investment in human
resources between 1927-1960 can be found in Magdi El-Kamash,
Economic Development and Planning in Egypt (New York: Frederick
A. Praeger, Publishers, 1968), pp. 112-14.

14.   Hsieh, pp. 57-62.

15.   Ibid., p. 60, Table V.

16.   Ibid., p. 64.

17.   In making this distinction we followed the ideas of Alfred Sauvy in his distinction between demographic investment and economic investment. See his "Investissements Demographiques et Investissements Economiques," International Population Conference, Vienna, 1959 (Vienna: International Union for the Scientific Study of Population, 1959), pp. 136-41.

18.   For a brief discussion and appraisal of these methods, see O'Brien, op. cit., especially pp. 156-164; M. Imam, "Models Used in Drafting the Plan (1962)," Institute of National Planning, Memos 255 and 238; and C. Hsieh, "Approaches to Fixing Employment Targets in Development Plans," International Labour Review, XCVII, 3 (March, 1968), 273-96.

19.   O'Brien, op. cit., p. 278.

20.   Ibid., Statistical Appendix, p. 326, Table 11.

21.   Additional employment here refers to additional workers.

22.   Donald C. Mead, Growth and Structural Change in the Egyptian Economy (Homewood, Ill.: Richard D. Irwin, Inc., 1967), p. 239.

23.   Bent Hansen and Girgis Marzouk, Development and Economic Policy of the U. A. R. (Amsterdam: North Holland Publishing Co., 1965), pp. 168-69.

24.   Ibid., pp. 136-37 and 160.

25.   Ibid., pp. 137-38.

26.   For a discussion of capital intensity and its effects on wages and salaries, see Robert Mabro, "Industrial Growth, Agricultural Under-employment and the Lewis Model; The Egyptian Case, 1937-1965," The Journal of Development Studies, III, 4 (1967), 333-46. Hansen and Marzouk, on the other hand, believe that the increased capital intensity may have influenced the distribution of income in industry, but according to them it is impossible to say a priori in which direction. See Hansen and Marzouk, op. cit., p. 163.

27.   See Hansen and Marzouk, op. cit., p. 169; and El-Kamash, op. cit., p. 170.

28.   K. Wheelock, Nasser's New Egypt, A Critical Analysis (New York: Frederick A. Praeger, 1960), p. 156.

29.   Hansen and Marzouk, op. cit., p. 170.

30.   This point has been stressed by several writers; probably the most outspoken critic of the policy is Patrick O'Brien. See his "Industrial Development and the Employment Problem in Egypt," Middle East Economic Papers (1962), 90-120, and his The Revolution in Egypt's Economic System, pp. 279-80.

31.   Hansen and Marzouk, op. cit., p. 298. They dismiss the critics of the employment policy of the five-year plan. In their opinion it is doubtful that Egypt is a country with labor surplus. Their argument is built solely on the notion of marginal productivity of labor in agriculture which is found to be higher than zero. However, their argument appears to this writer, among others, to be too weak. In fact, these authors acknowledged that the employment drive of 1961 was promoted mainly for social reasons, which implies awareness on their part of the existence of large part of unemployment and probably underemployment.

32.   Eva Garzouzi, Old Ills and New Remedies in Egypt (Cairo: Dar El-Maaref, 1958), p. 55.

33.   U.A.R. Central Agency for Public Mobilization and Statistics, op. cit., pp. 316-18.

34.   Ibid., p. 318.

35.   O'Brien, "Industrial Development and the Employment Problem in Egypt, 1945-1965," p. 106

36.   We followed closely the analysis provided by the Institute of National Planning, in Final Report on the Problem of Employment in Rural Areas U.A.R. (Cairo, 1968), especially pp. 59-76 in addition to other information from the U.A.R., Yearbook, different issues.

37.   Institute of National Planning, Ibid., p. 64.

38.   Ibid., p. 83.

39.   International Labour Office, Report to the Government of the U.A.R. on the Study of Rural Employment Problems (Geneva, 1966; ILO/OTA/UAR/R.8), p. 31.

As in most developing nations, the future pattern of population growth in Egypt is uncertain. The last official estimate put the population of Egypt at 34 million in July, 1970. This compares with a population of 26.1 million in 1960. The difficulty of forecasting precisely the likely course of population growth stems from a number of reasons: the relative social and economic factors which might affect the future trends of fertility are now in a state of flux; there is still great room for a decline to take place in mortality, especially among infants; and outmigration, which played only a negligible role in the population growth in Egypt until recently, might assume some significance in the coming decades.

POPULATION PROJECTIONS

The Central Statistical Committee has projected the future course of population growth at specific dates covering the period 1960 to 1985. For any date, five different series of projections were calculated on the basis of five different assumptions relative to fertility trends.[1] Table 67 presents a summary of the results obtained. Projection 1 assumes fertility rates will remain constant from 1960 to 1985 at the 1960 level of 190 per 1,000 females in the group covering ages fifteen through forty-nine; Projection 2 assumes fertility rates will decline 1 percent per year between 1960 and 1985, with a total decline of 25 percent; Projection 3 assumes fertility rates will remain at the 1960 level for 15 years and decline thereafter by 5 per cent each year for ten years; Projection 4 assumes fertility rates will decline by 50 percent between 1960 and 1985; and Projection 5 assumes fertility rates will decrease by 5 percent per year between 1960 and 1970 and remain constant thereafter. According to the highest projection (Projection 1), the population will be more than double

TABLE 67

Projected Size of Total Population of
the U.A.R., 1960-85

Projection	1960 Census	Population Estimates (in millions)				
		1965	1970	1975	1980	1985
1	26.1	29.9	34.5	39.7	45.7	52.5
2	26.1	29.8	34.0	38.5	43.3	48.3
3	26.1	29.9	34.5	39.7	44.7	48.3
4	26.1	29.7	33.4	37.1	40.6	48.6
5	26.1	29.2	31.7	33.8	36.2	38.8

Source: National Bank of Egypt, "Population and Manpower,"
Economic Bulletin, XVI (Cairo, 1963), 7, Table III.

its present size in 1985. On the other hand, the most conservative estimate shows that the population will have increased less than 50 per cent by the end of the period.

In light of the large differences between the minimum and the maximum projection estimates, it is extremely difficult to determine what is likely to be the most probable growth trend in the future. For example, Hansen and Marzouk believe that the most probable rate of growth for 1960-85 lies between 2.1 percent and 2.5 percent.[2] In their opinion, the high rate of growth during the 1960's, which reached nearly 3 percent, was influenced by a temporary upsurge of births after World War II. Therefore, they reason, continuation of the high fertility rate of the 1960 decade and the high growth rate of the 1947-60 period is unlikely. Further support for their position lies in the growing evidence of a fall in the level of fertility of the youngest women and the recent trend toward increase in the average age of marriage.[3] On the other hand, at least one observer feels that the growth rate will experience a steady rise: "If the current rate of increase is in the range of 2.5 to 3 percent per annum, perhaps a reasonable guess would be that by 1985 the growth rate would be in the range of 3 to 3.5 percent per annum."[4]

Since future population growth depends largely on the behavior of fertility, the latter merits further discussion. Such a discussion must focus on fertility in connection with two major elements: the new economic and social development and the subsequent rise in income, and the spread of family planning ideas and the dissemination of the various methods of birth control.

There is some evidence to suggest that fertility is not likely to be checked under any moderate increase in income which may result from the new economic development programs. In fact, any rise in per capita income of the poorer classes will probably result in an increase in the level of fertility, and a decrease in mortality.[5] Therefore, some observers argue that the demographic transition which Egypt is now experiencing corresponds neatly to Joseph Spengler's notion of population elasticity in relationship to the changes in income.[6] In Egypt, a society with an intermediate per capita income, income increases will probably affect natality more than mortality. Fertility tends to rise among income receivers who are situated at various levels and who are not disposed to increase their personal consumption as incomes rise.

Furthermore, as Spengler noted, economic change affects fertility through its impact upon the price structure, and the cost and utility of children.[7] In light of these factors, the future population trend in Egypt may be said to favor an increase in population. As far as the price structure is concerned, the Egyptian government, before and after the 1952 revolution, has operated largely with a policy designed to restrain the prices of necessities. In fact, the government has used price control as one method of redistributing income. In regard to the second factor, the utility of children is derived from the income they could produce and from the security they might supply their parents in old age, especially in agricultural communities.

In this respect, it must be kept in mind that in spite of the industrial development of Egypt, the agricultural sector remains, and will remain, a major sector, especially after the completion of the Aswan Dam. The fertility of the agricultural population in all probability will remain high until the time when the cost of raising children exceeds their utility. The time when the family no longer depends on the earnings of children and their work on the farms seems remote. This is especially so in light of the fact that Egyptian agricultural production depends on cotton and rice, two crops with large absorptive capacities for child labor. It is also reasonable to expect that within the new Socialist framework (i.e., the state is now responsible for the provision of such services as health and education free of charge), the decision to provide a higher standard of living and education for children will not operate effectively as a factor in reducing birth rates.

However, there are a number of factors which suggest the possibility that the level of fertility will ultimately be lowered in the process

of economic development. For example, the changing structure of production, with a decline in the importance of the family as a productive
unit, the growth of job bureaucratization, and the development of
economic roles for women outside of the home all tend to increase
the possibility of economic mobility that can better be achieved with
small families. At the same time, they tend to decrease the economic
advantages of large families. The fall in the fertility of the youngest
women in Egypt between 1947 and 1960 may point toward this direction
in the future. Also, there are some indications that the small family
ideal has started to emerge in the urban groups at the higher end of
the socioeconomic scale, and might spread to small cities and lower-
income groups.[8] This tendency brings us to the second point which
we would like to consider briefly in regard to the level of fertility in
the future: the acceptance of family planning ideals and the dissemination of birth control methods.

Prior to the 1952 revolution, the efforts made to increase public
awareness of the importance of family planning received no encouragement from the authorities. The first official recognition of the population problem in Egypt came in 1953 with the development of the
National Commission for Population Problems as an autonomous branch
of the permanent Council of Public Services. This committee was
composed of the ministers of Social Affairs, Health, Education, Agriculture, and Finance, and professors of related interests. In 1955,
after two years of indecision on the issue of family planning, government efforts in this area began on an experimental basis. In that year,
eight clinics were established in Cairo and Alexandria. In the ensuing
years, clinics were added in other areas, both rural and urban, so
that by 1964 there were 36 such clinics in operation. These clinics
operated as centers for data collection and experimentation and as
providers of birth control services.[9]

The probable impact of these birth control clinics is suggested
by the results (given in Table 68) of a sample survey taken in the
period 1956-58. This survey, which reached 6,067 women, revealed
that the use of birth control techniques has had fairly ready acceptance,
at least among the educated urban groups. More important, the returns
of the survey indicated that the practice of birth control is more widespread among younger wives than older ones (those who have completed
their family size).

Since 1962, the practice of birth control has spread further as
a result of a serious government compaign to educate and convince
the peasants of the importance of family planning.[10] In 1964, the
Charter of the Republic gave official recognition to the use of birth
control techniques as being healthy and necessary for providing a better
future for offspring. More recently, in February, 1966, a massive
family planning campaign was launched with a network of approximately

TABLE 68

Percentage of Wives Who Ever Practiced Family Limitation, by Education of Husband, 1956-58

Level of Education	Urban		Semiurban		Rural	
	Number of Wives Interviewed	Percent	Number of Wives Interviewed	Percent	Number of Wives Interviewed	Percent
Completed families:						
University and secondary	71	33.8	0	----	0	---
Primary and elementary	150	18.7	17	17.0	123	3.0
Illiterate	158	8.9	8	0.0	527	1.0
Total	379	17.4	25	12.0	650	1.5
Incomplete families:						
University and secondary	310	51.0	0	----	0	---
Primary and elementary	755	23.0	502	17.5	470	3.0
Illiterate	440	10.7	87	10.3	1,291	0.8
Total	1,505	25.2	589	16.4	1,761	1.0

Source: Hanna Rizk, "Fertility Patterns in Selected Areas in Egypt" (unpublished Ph.D. Dissertation, Princeton University, 1959), pp. 120-21.

250 centers covering almost all the country. A governmental budget of about $3.5 million was allocated to the program. In addition, a grant of approximately $500,000 was received from the Ford Foundation for staffing and training.[11] Also, a new council for family planning was formed under the direction of the prime minister to replace the National Commission for Population Problems, which became a nongovernmental organization under the name of the Egyptian Association for Population Studies.

Unfortunately, the lack of reliable data, due mainly to the recency of the program, precludes an adequate assessment of the effectiveness of family planning methods. It must be noted, however, that despite all of the efforts made since 1955, the rate of population growth (shown in Table 69) does not appear to have changed considerably. Since the latter is actually a result of a multitude of factors, the impact of birth control methods is not expected to be immediately visible. There is also the fact that the number of clinics available, at least until 1966, was relatively small in relationship to the size of the population. However, during the first quarter of 1963, it is estimated that between 150,000 and 200,000 women were receiving contraceptive pills regularly.[12] From the point of view of the birth rate of the country, this is a small but potentially significant amount. In any case, the practice

TABLE 69

The Number of New Cases Treated in the Urban Clinics for
Birth Control, Number of Clinics and the Annual
Rate of Population Growth, 1956-64

Year	Number of Cases	Number of Clinics	Annual Rate of Population Growth (percent)
1956	4,811	12	2.54
1957	5,929	12	2.07
1958	4,150	12	2.28
1959	3,421	13	2.67
1960	3,704	13	2.07
1961	3,506	14	2.82
1962	4,997	14	2.46
1963	4,880	20	2.40
1964	8,946a	24	2.47

a January-September
Source: Magdi M. E1 - Kamash, Economic Development and Planning in Egypt (New York: Frederick A. Praeger, Publishers, 1968), p. 143. Table 30.

of birth control seems to have gained some foothold among certain segments of the population in Egypt; and it is very likely that the fertility
of the well educated, high socioeconomic urban dwellers will show some
declines in the future. Also, the practice of birth control can be expected to spread slowly to other segments of the population. However,
given the agrarian structure of the economy, the conservative religious
beliefs of the laymen, the high illiteracy rate, and the generally fatalis-
tic outlook of the peasants, an effective birth control campaign requires
more than a positive emphasis on the value of family planning. It will
also require simultaneous negative attacks on those societal elements
that impede the adoption of birth control. These societal elements
have so far not received much attention.

In summary, it seems probable that any conceivable drop in fertility which might be brought about through the use of birth control in the
coming decade or two is likely to be offset by a slight increase in fertility
as a concomitant of a moderate increase in income, improvements in
health and nutrition, and, more important, as a consequence of the trend
toward a younger age structure of the population. It is our conclusion,
then, that the level of fertility will continue to fluctuate around its 1960
level for a decade or two. There is always the possibility that the
incipient declining trend might be accelerated by major structural
changes in the economy, increased education, and mobility of the population. However, in light of the preceding discussion, and considering
the fact that the annual rate of population growth during the 1960's fluctuated around 2.6 percent,[13] the most probable rate of growth for the
period 1960-85, in our judgment, will continue to fall between 2.5 and
2.8 percent per year.

Future fertility behavior has important implications not only for
estimates of annual rate of increase of the total population, but also
for its age distribution. Table 70 delimits the range of the potential
impact of fertility future on the age structure of the population. According to the highest estimates, younger people--fifteen and under--will
increase by approximately 10 to 11 million persons from 1960 to 1985.
If fertility declines by 50 percent during this period, their absolute
size will actually decline from 11.2 million in 1960 to only 10.7 million
in 1985. Given continuation of the 1960 fertility level, by 1985, the
Egyptian society will have to take care of twice as many young people
than it would if fertility declined to half of its 1960 level.

As expected, the projected size of the old age groups (sixty-five and
over) will be the same whether fertility declines or not. The absolute
size of the middle age groups (fifteen to sixty-five) will be larger by approximately 2.5 million, under the maximum estimates. All of these 2.5 million
additional persons will be in the age brackets between sixteen and twenty-
four.

TABLE 70

Projections of Population Estimates at Economically Signi-
cant Age Groups, 1960 –85
(in Millions)

Age Group	1960 M	1960 T	1965 M	1965 T	1970 M	1970 T	1975 M	1975 T	1980 M	1980 T	1985 M	1985 T
MAXIMUM												
Under 15	5.9	11.1	6.9	12.5	7.7	14.2	9.1	16.7	10.4	19.2	11.9	22.0
15-65	7.0	14.0	8.1	16.2	9.5	19.0	13.8	21.4	12.6	24.6	14.7	28.4
65+	0.4	0.9	0.5	1.2	0.6	1.3	0.7	1.6	0.8	1.9	0.9	2.2
Total	13.2	26.1	15.3	29.9	17.7	34.5	20.6	39.7	28.8	21.1	27.6	52.5
MINIMUM												
Under 15	5.9	11.1	6.3	11.9	6.2	11.4	5.9	10.8	5.6	10.3	5.9	10.7
15-65	6.9	14.0	8.1	16.1	9.5	19.0	10.8	21.4	12.3	24.0	13.3	25.9
65+	0.4	0.9	0.5	1.2	0.6	1.3	0.7	1.6	0.8	1.9	0.9	2.2
Total	13.2	26.1	14.9	29.2	16.3	31.7	17.4	33.8	18.7	36.2	20.1	38.8

Source: Computed from U.A.R. Central Agency for Public Mobilization and Statistics, Basic Statistics,
1964 (Cairo, 1965), pp. 34-35.

The significance of the potential changes in age composition can be seen by examining the dependency ratios that would characterize those alternative projections. Table 71 presents these dependency ratios (defined as the number of persons under fifteen and over sixty-five per 100 persons between fifteen and sixty-five). These figures clearly demonstrate that future fertility behavior is relevant not only to the rate of population growth, but also to its age structure. Under the minimum projection, the heavy dependency load which the population of the productive age groups suffered in 1960 will be greatly eased in 1985. However, if fertility remains at its 1960 level, the dependency ratio will probably show no major changes by 1985. The significance of fertility decline for dependency is most clearly revealed by the marked differences in youth dependency as opposed to aged dependency.

In summary, considering the fact that the official estimate has revealed that Egypt's population reached 34 million persons in 1970,[14] one is inclined to believe that the maximum population projection, built on the assumption of the continuation of the fertility level of 1960, is very plausible. As far as dependency is concerned, the data obtained from the highest estimates seem to be more consistent and most probable. It is highly unlikely that in such a short period of time Egypt will reach a dependency load equal to that of the most economically advanced countries of Europe and North America, of 40 or 50 dependents for every 100 persons between the ages of fifteen and sixty-five. Ironically enough, age structure is important not only because of its immediate economic and social consequences, but also because of its influence on the future trend of mortality, fertility, and the rate of natural increase. "So long as the birth rates are not changed, any

TABLE 71

Dependency Ratios: The Number of Persons
Under Fifteen and over Sixty-five,
per 100 Persons, Age
Fifteen to Sixty-five, 1960-85

Year	Maximum Projections			Minimum Projections		
	Young	Aged	Total	Young	Aged	Total
1960	79	7	86	79	7	86
1965	78	7	84	74	8	81
1970	75	7	82	60	7	67
1975	78	8	85	51	8	58
1980	78	8	86	43	8	51
1985	77	8	81	41	9	49

Source: Computed from Table 70.

addition to the adult population implies a proportionate increase in the number of births. If death rates fall while birth rates remain constant, the life of successive generations will be longer, but the average number of dependent children per adult will be practically unchanged."[15] That is precisely the situation which appears most likely to occur; the ratio of the age group fifteen years old and under to the fifteen-to-sixty-five age group in 1985 will remain close to its 1960 level of 79 young dependents for every 100 persons in the productive age groups.

LABOR FORCE PROJECTIONS

Two major planning agencies have made projections of future labor force trends in Egypt--the Central Agency for Public Mobilization and Statistics, and the Institute of National Planning. The following discussion presents a comparative assessment of these alternative projections.

The Central Agency for Public Mobilization and Statistics has prepared two sets of projections of the size of male and female labor force according to age at specific dates between 1965 and 1985.[16] While the first set of projections assumes constant fertility at the 1960 level, the second assumes an annual fertility decline of 2 percent of the 1966 level, starting in 1970. A comparison between projected figures in the two series shows no significant differences in the projected size of the aggregate labor force and of each age group above the age of fifteen. Any fertility decline will have very little effect on the size of the projected labor force, since such effect can only be seen in the size of the labor force in the age groups under the age of fifteen. This conclusion substantiates the fact that declines in the level of fertility will have no immediate impact on the size of the labor force. A period of at least 15 years or more is necessary in order to notice an appreciable decrease in the size of the labor force as a result of a change in fertility.

According to these projections, the male labor force will increase by approximately 82 percent between 1965 and 1985, from 8.3 million in 1965 to 15.1 million by 1985. As far as females are concerned, their absolute increase is projected from 717,000 in 1965 to about 1.2 million in 1985, an increase of only 69 percent. Thus, these figures indicate that by 1985 a slight drop in the share of females in the aggregate labor force will probably have taken place.[17] Such a drop in the share of women in the labor force, small as it might be, may appear contradictory to what has been said before concerning more female participation in economic activities in the process of social and economic development. However, large female entrance into the labor force might be a long-term trend rather than a short-term one. That female participation in economic activities may actually witness a

slight drop in the early years of social and economic development is
a consequence of more girls enrolling in schools, and consequently,
a reduction in female child labor. Most important will probably be
the speed of the structural transformation from a predominantly
agricultural economy (where women's participation in economic activities is relatively large) toward an industrial urban structure (where
women's participation in the work force is still relatively small).

TABLE 72

Projected Population, Labor Force, and
Participation Rates, 1960-85

Year	Population (in Millions)		Labor Force (in Millions)		Participation Rates	
	Total	Male	Total	Male	Total	Male
			Maximum			
1960	26.1	13.2	7.6	6.8	29.1	54.0
1965	29.9	15.3	9.2	8.3	30.8	54.5
1970	34.5	17.7	10.4	9.6	30.1	54.4
1975	39.7	20.6	12.7	11.2	32.0	54.2
1980	45.7	27.6	14.0	13.0	30.6	54.3
1985	52.5	27.6	16.1	15.1	30.7	54.7
			Minimum			
1960	26.1	13.2	7.6	6.8	29.1	54.0
1965	29.2	14.9	9.2	8.3	31.5	55.8
1970	31.7	16.3	10.4	9.6	32.8	58.9
1975	33.8	17.4	12.7	11.2	37.6	64.1
1980	36.2	18.7	14.0	13.0	38.7	69.0
1985	38.7	20.1	16.3	15.0	42.1	74.6

Source: Computed by the author. Population figures from Table
70. Labor force figures from U. A. R. Central Agency for Public
Mobilization and Statistics, Population Increase in the U. A. R.
and Its Deterrents to Development (Cairo, 1966), pp. 171 and 173,
Tables 73 and 75.

A simple way of seeing the relationship between the projected population and labor force is by computing a <u>participation rate</u> as the number in the labor force expressed as a percentage of the population. Table 72 presents, for the total population and for males, the projected size of population, labor force, and the participation rates at specific years between 1960 and 1985. Since the projected size of the labor force will remain virtually the same under maximum and minimum future population estimates, any fluctuations in the participation rates will be due mainly to differences in population size according to the two projections. Under the highest estimates, population is expected to double its size in the years between 1960 and 1985. The labor force will probably increase also by approximately 51 percent during the same period; therefore, the participation rate will remain around 30 percent, showing a very slight increase from 29.1 in 1960 to 30.7 in 1985. According to the minimum projections, however, population will increase by less than half between 1960 and 1985, while the labor force will more than double, thus influencing an increase in the participation rate from 29 per cent in 1960 to 42 per cent in 1985.

This latter trend seems to be quite unlikely for a number of reasons. In the first place, it will be contrary to all known experiences of the most developed or even the less developed countries. According to the previous experiences of other countries, the participation rate either will remain at its 1960 level or will show a declining trend. Further, in 1985, the participation rate of women in economic activities will fluctuate around the 1960 level. Therefore, it is not expected that women's participation rate will rise substantially to cause such an upsurge in the overall participation rate.

The remoteness of the minimum set of population projections becomes even clearer from examing the figures on the male population alone. From these figures, two major conclusions can be made. First, assuming fertility will remain at its 1960 level, the expected increase in the male population and the increase in the male labor force between 1965 and 1985 will be in the same proportion. The net effect is that the labor force participation rate will remain relatively unchanged at its 1965 level of 54 percent. Second, assuming minimum growth of the population in the future, the participation rate will presumably increase by 20 percent to reach an exceptionally high level of 75 percent in 1985. These figures on the projected male population and labor force raise more doubt on the likelihood that future population growth will coincide with that minimum estimate.

Changes in the age distribution of the labor force will result mainly from changes in the age composition of the population. Table 73 presents the age distribution of the labor force by sex in 1960

LABOR FORCE AND EMPLOYMENT IN EGYPT

TABLE 73

Future Age Distribution of the Labor Force,
1965 and 1985
(Percentages)

	Male (1965)		Male (1985)	
	Maximum	Minimum	Maximum	Minimum
-15	9.4	9.4	9.2	8.6
15-24	25.1	25.1	27.3	27.5
25-44	39.7	39.7	41.7	42.0
45-64	22.0	22.0	17.9	18.0
65+	3.9	3.9	3.9	3.9
	100.1	100.1	100.0	100.0
	Female (1965)		Female (1985)	
	Maximum	Minimum	Maximum	Minimum
-15	34.6	34.6	33.9	32.2
15-24	28.9	28.9	30.2	30.9
25-44	24.0	24.0	23.3	23.9
45-64	11.0	11.0	10.8	11.1
65+	1.5	1.5	1.8	1.9
	100.0	100.0	100.0	100.0

Source: Computed from U.A.R. Central Agency for Public
Mobilization and Statistics, Population Increase in the U.A.R. and Its
Deterrents to Development (Cairo, 1966), pp. 171 and 173, Tables
73 and 75.

and 1985. The figures for males show a possible increase in the
proportion of the middle age group (fifteen to forty-four) in the future.
According to these figures, the share of the old (sixty-five and over)
and the young (under fifteen) will remain relatively stable. The only
age groups which will show a noticeable decline are those between the
ages of forty-five and sixty-four. Since the age-specific participation
rate will likely remain constant, the most probable explanation for
these changes is the relative decline in the share of the population at
ages between forty-five and sixty-four in the total male population.
According to the maximum population projections discussed earlier,
this age group's share of the total population will decline from 13

percent in 1960 to only 10 percent in 1985. [18] Even if the unrealistic minimum projection were realized, its share would remain nearly constant.

The changes which might occur in the relative age distribution of the female labor force are also minor, and will not alter the general pattern observed in 1960. Thus, in 1985, females under fifteen will still constitute one-third of the aggregate. Under the minimum estimate of population growth, the age composition of the labor force will show very minor differences. The effect of declining fertility will be noticeable only in a slight decline of the share of ages fifteen and under.

To summarize, from the examination of the projected age structure of the labor force one can foresee a trend toward an increase in the relative share of the early middle age groups (twenty-four to forty-five) and a decline in the relative share of the late middle age groups (forty-five to sixty-five). Demographic changes in the age structure of the population will probably be the major factor responsible for any changes in the age distribution of the labor force.

The second set of projections which we would like to consider briefly (because of their different assumptions) are those prepared by the Institute of National Planning. [19] The labor force projections made by this group are confined to males only since the participating rates of females were too low according to the 1960 census to influence substantially any changes in patterns of labor force participation. The projections of the male labor force were based on the following assumptions: (1) age-specific fertility rates of 1960 would remain constant; (2) migration would play a very negligible role; (3) Egypt would continue to be an agricultural country until the year 1970; (4) from 1970 through the end of 1980, Egypt would be a semi-industrialized country; (5) Egypt would be a fully industrialized country starting by the end of 1980; and (6) the specific participation rates of males in Egypt in 1960 would continue without change until the end of the 1960's.

The United Nations model of age specific participation rates for economically active populations at the three stages of economic development (agricultural, semi-industrialized, and industrialized) was applied with a modified refinement. [20] The participation rate in 1970 through the end of 1980 was derived by multiplying the participation rates of 1960 by a ratio of the calculated United Nations participation rates of semi-industrialized and agricultural countries. The participation rate in 1985 was derived by multiplying the participation rates of 1960 by a ratio of the calculated United Nations rates of industrial and semi-industrialized countries.

Table 74 shows the estimated size of male labor force classified

TABLE 74

Estimated Male Labor Force Size by Age Groups, 1965, 1970, 1980, and 1985

Age	No. of Labor Force in 1960(000)	1965 Partici- pating Rates	1965 No. of L.F. (000)	1970 Partici- pating Rates	1970 No. of L.F. (000)	1980 Partici- pating Rates	1980 No. of L.F. (000)	1985 Partici- pating Rates	1985 No. of L.F. (000)
10-14	459	27.9	546	15.4	310	15.4	451	4.8	163
15-19	753	68.0	1,117	60.9	1,182	60.9	1,503	62.7	1,827
20-24	778	85.2	942	85.9	1,394	85.7	1,699	85.7	2,099
25-34	1,584	95.8	1,687	95.6	1,904	95.6	3,341	96.1	3,697
35-44	1,457	97.3	1,577	96.8	1,557	96.8	1,865	97.3	2,535
45-54	1,012	96.3	1,136	95.8	1,347	95.8	1,434	95.8	1,516
55-64	568	89.1	667	86.7	787	86.4	1,042	83.2	1,236
65+	257	62.1	321	54.8	309	54.0	443	33.4	314
Total	6,868	75.9	7,993	72.8	8,790	72.1	11,778	70.4	13,387

Source: Institute of National Planning, Final Report on the Employment Problem in Rural Areas, U.A.R. (Cairo, 1968), pp. 21 and 13.

224

according to the various age groups for selected dates between 1965
and 1985. According to these projections, the male labor force will
increase by 84 percent during the period from 1965 to 1985. In other
words, the male labor force, which amounted to a total of 6.8 million
in 1960 and increased to 8.7 million in 1965, is expected to reach
13.4 million by 1985.

According to this study, a declining trend in the participation
rates of the labor force in the male population similar to declines
that occurred in other countries who passed from being purely agricultural to semi-industrialized and fully industrialized economies
is contemplated. On the aggregate, the male participation rate is
expected to decline from 75.9 percent in 1965 to only 70.4 percent
in 1985. The participation rates of the very young (under fifteen)
and the very old (sixty-five and over) are expected to decline. The
decline expected is far greater for the economic activities of the
younger people (ten to fourteen) than for the older people. The decrease in the absolute number of working males at younger ages
from 459,000 in 1960 to only 163,000 in 1985, in spite of the expected
rise in the proportion of the younger population in the aggregate, is
consistent with an observed trend toward a decrease in child labor
in the past decade, especially among boys. However, a closer look
at the projected rates of participation for boys at ages ten through
fourteen leads one to suspect them. It is very doubtful that the participation rates of these age groups will drop from 27.9 in 1965 to
15.4 in 1970 (a drop of more than 40 percent in the five-year period)
to remain constant at the level of 15.4 percent for a period of ten
years, and then drop again from 15.4 to only 4.8 between 1980 and
1985 (a drop of more than 65 percent in five years). There is no reason
to believe that the structural transformation of the Egyptian society
which might work to reduce the participation rates of this age group
will be intensified between certain dates, and cease to work completely
between others. The assumption of a declining trend might be reasonable, but not one of such a pattern and magnitude. Similar observations could be made on the projected participation rates of the population aged sixty-five and over.

It is also important to point out that a slight decline in the participation rates of the age groups fifteen to nineteen and fifty-five to
sixty-four may be expected between 1960 and 1985. The participation
rate of the younger age group is expected to decline from 68.0 percent in 1960 to 62.7 percent in 1985, and that of the older age group
is expected to decline from 89.1 percent to 83.2 percent in the
respective years. Prolonged educational periods as well as larger
school enrollment are probably the major reasons behind the expected
decrease in the participation rates of males between the ages of fifteen
and nineteen. Earlier retirement and a trend toward an increasing
percentage of the labor force in industries and and services, where

retirement at younger age is more frequent than in agricultural sectors, could explain why the participation rates of males in the older age group are expected to decline. The participation rates of males aged twenty to forty-five are expected to remain fairly constant during the 25 years under study. This is because adult males at these ages are usually engaged in some type of economic activity to support a family.

So far, we have expressed some doubt concerning the projected labor force participation of both the young and old populations. Basic to this problem is the assumption that Egypt will be a fully industrialized country in 1985. This assumption, dubious as it appears, might prove to be correct. In 1985, Egypt might indeed be a fully industrialized country, but only in terms of the share of industry in national income, and not in terms of the share of industrial employment in the labor force. It is specifically on this point that the differences between the experience of the older industrialized and the newly industrializing countries lie. The newly industrializing countries might be able to promote industry without a large labor transformation from agriculture to industry. The borrowing of modern technology, especially capital-intensive machinery, will make the experience of the industrializing countries somewhat different from that of the countries who have already joined the ranks of industrialized societies.

TABLE 75

Projected Percentage Distribution of the Male Labor
Force According to Age Group, 1960-85

Age Group	1960	1965	1970	1980	1985
10-14	6.7	6.8	3.5	3.8	1.2
15-19	11.0	14.0	13.4	12.8	13.7
20-24	11.3	11.8	15.9	14.4	15.7
25-34	23.1	21.1	21.7	28.4	27.6
35-44	21.2	19.7	17.7	15.8	18.9
45-54	14.7	14.2	15.3	12.2	11.2
55-64	8.3	8.3	9.0	8.9	9.3
65+	3.7	4.0	3.5	3.8	1.6
	100.0	100.0	100.0	100.0	100.0

Source: Computed from Table 74.

The effects of the changes expected in the participation rates of the different groups in addition to the expected changes in the age and sex structure of the population on the age composition of the male labor force can be ascertained from Table 75. The expected changes in the age structure of the labor force between 1960 and 1985 reveal a plausible trend indicating a decline in the percentage at the very young ages of ten to fourteen, and also in the population aged sixty-five and over. Thus, the share of the age group between ten and fourteen, which constitutes 6.9 percent in 1960, will probably drop to 1.2 percent in 1985. The relative percentage of the older people in the labor force will drop from 3.7 percent in 1960 to 1.6 percent in 1985. Thus, it is very possible that while the population as a whole might be moving toward a younger age structure, the age structure of the labor force will be incorporating a larger percentage of middle age groups.

This analysis of the probable future age structure of the labor force brings out at least two facts which tend to counterbalance the unfavorable trend of the dependency load. The fall in the relative size of the age group under fifteen, caused by spreading education and training, tends eventually to raise the productivity of the workers. Furthermore, if the workers under fifteen and over sixty-five are the less productive, then the predicted decline in their relative share of the labor force should result in raising average productivity. Other demographic and manpower factors will also tend to increase labor productivity: among the developments that should have favorable effects are health improvement, the eradication of productivity-inhibiting diseases and most important, perhaps, the possible structural change in the future industrial and occupational composition of the labor force.

The question of which of these two sets of labor force projections would reflect future trends is quite difficult to answer. This is so because, first, all population and labor force projections constitute merely an educated guess, rather than an accurate prediction. Secondly, these two sets differ in their coverage of age and sex. However, considering the projections of male labor force only, we have seen that the two sets did not show any significant difference in their estimates of the size of the labor force in the middle age groups. The most noticeable difference is that while the Institute of National Planning projected a decline in the participation of young and old males in the labor force in the course of the coming decades, the Central Agency for Public Mobilization and Statistics ensures the continuation of the level of participation of that of 1965 during the coming two decades.

By estimating two alternative projections for the labor force

(under maximum and minimum fertility trends), the Central Agency
for Public Mobilization and Statistics seems to assume that changes
in the level of fertility, rather than changes in the participation rate,
will be the determining factor in shaping the age structure of the
labor force in the coming two decades. This assumption of probable
fertility changes stands in contrast to assuming a constant fertility
level in the projections prepared by the Institute of National Planning.
In the earlier discussion in this chapter we concluded that fertility
will probably remain at its 1960 level during the coming two decades.
We tend to view this assumption by the Institute of National Planning
as the most probable course for the near future. However, it is not
difficult to see the hypothetical patterns of the projected decline in
the participation rates of the younger and older population. In our
judgment, it is therefore reasonable to assume the continuation of
both levels of fertility and participation rates during the coming
two decades.

NOTES

1. For a detailed discussion of the methods of projection and
the assumptions of the different sets of projections, see U. A. R. Central Statistical Committee, Population Trends in the U. A. R. (Cairo,
1962).

2. Bent Hansen and Girgis Marzouk, Development and Economic Policy in the U. A. R. (Amsterdam: North Holland Publishing
Co. , 1965), pp. 28-29.

3. Ibid. , pp. 30-31.

4. Donald C. Mead, Growth and Structural Changes in the
Egyptian Economy (Homewood, Ill.: Richard D. Irwin, Inc., 1967),
p. 27.

5. Magdi El-Kamash, Economic Development and Planning
in Egypt (New York: Frederick A. Praeger, Publishers, 1968),
pp. 70-72 and 136-39.

6. Such an argument has been advanced by El-Kamash, Ibid. ,
p. 136; and by Joseph J. Spengler, "Population as a Factor in Economic Development," in Phillip M. Hauser, ed. , Population and World
Politics (Glencoe, Ill.: Free Press, 1958), p. 164.

7. Joseph J. Spengler, "The Economics of Population Growth, "
in Stuart Mudd, ed. , Population Crisis and the Use of World Resources (Bloomington: Indiana University Press, 1964), p. 89.

8. Hanna Rizk, "Fertility Patterns in Selected Areas in Egypt: Social and Psychological Factors Affecting Fertility in the U.A.R.," Marriage and Family Living, XXV (February, 1963), 69-73.

9. For an evaluation of the history and the development of family planning clinics, see Hasan M. Husein, " Evaluation of Progress in Fertility in the U.A.R.," U.N., Proceedings of the World Population Conference, 1965, IV, pp. 142-45; also Patrick Seal and Irene Beeson, "Babies Along the Nile," The New Republic, CLIV, 9 (May, 1966), pp. 10-11.

10. Mead, op. cit., p. 25.

11. Seal and Beeson, op. cit., 10-11.

12. Mead, op. cit., p. 25.

13. U.A.R. Central Agency for Public Mobilization and Statistics, Population Increase in the U.A.R. and Its Deterrents to Development (Cairo, 1966), p. 7.

14. Ibid., p. 8.

15. United Nations, The Determinants and Consequences of Population Trends (ST/SOA/Series A/17) (New York: United Nations, 1953).

16. U.A.R. Central Agency for Public Mobilization and Statistics, op. cit., pp. 171, Table 73, and 173, and Table 75.

17. Ibid., p. 173, Table 75. The number of females in the total labor force will increase from 808,000 in 1970 to 1,017,000 in 1985.

18. U.A.R. Central Agency for Public Mobilization and Statistics, Basic Statistics, 1964 (Cairo, 1965), pp. 34-35.

19. Institute of National Planning, Final Report on the Employment Problem in Rural Areas, U.A.R. (Cairo, April, 1968), p. 21.

20. United Nations, Demographic Aspects of Manpower, Sales No. 61, XIII, 4 (New York: U.N. Publication, 1962), pp. 10-12.

The purpose of this study was to present a demographic and socioeconomic analysis of the trends in population, labor supply, and employment in Egypt. Emphasis was placed mainly on the following issues: (1) demographic and nondemographic determinants of labor supply; (2) economic activities of the Egyptian population; (3) growth and structural changes in the Egyptian labor force; (4) associated structural changes in the Egyptian society; and (5) the extent of under-utilization of the supply of labor.

SUMMARY

Determinants of Labor Supply:
Socioeconomic Factors

In spite of the existence of a predominantly traditional society in Egypt, especially in rural areas, serious public as well as private efforts to improve the status of women have started to gain a strong foothold among the people. The biggest challenge to the older structure of male dominance stems from a rapid increase in female enrollment at the different levels of the educational system. Social legislation, especially that organizing divorce and family arrangements, is gradually helping women to improve their social standing. However, an absence of opportunities for women's employment outside the home remains a salient characteristic of Egyptian society. Major programs, such as rural and craft industry, which might have a favorable impact on future women's employment in rural areas, are either neglected or incorrectly administered. In addition, girls' educational training and the nature of their instructional programs do not consider the simple fact that their low rate of economic activity, especially in

230

urban areas, is due mainly to the high level of male unemployment and underemployment. In absolute terms, the employment of women in urban and industrial occupations continues to gain at a relatively moderate pace. The gradual erosion of the social and cultural blocks against the employment of females might ultimately speed up this prospect. At the present, Egypt has a large reservoir of potential labor supply in the female section of the country's population. A large percentage of this underutilized manpower is in the productive age groups.

Child labor has a long history in the rural agrarian structure of Egypt, largely because of the high level of fertility in the Egyptian family, and partially because of the country's dependency on cotton, a crop with a large absorptive need for children's work. In percentage terms, child labor was found to be gradually declining; however, because of a trend toward a younger age structure of the population, the number of children who are working was on the rise, at least up until 1960. Due to a number of factors, the bulk of child labor continues to be confined largely to the traditional sectors of the economy. Prominent among these are the following: In the agricultural sector, laws prohibiting child labor are not in effect: in fact, local authorities encourage putting boys and girls to work in certain field operations, especially in combatting cotton worms. The growing of cotton, rice, and other labor-absorbing crops explains the persistent need for child work in agriculture. The easy available input of child labor retards the use of modern machinery in performing certain field operations and, in turn, keeps the need for child labor constant. The prevalence of the small, family-farm type of land ownership puts economic limits on the use of farm machinery and in turn enhances the use of child labor. Finally, because of the low level of skills and training of young people, no alternative employment is open to them outside of agriculture and the domestic services.

The prevalence of child labor in rural areas more than in urban a r e a s was explained as reflecting basic differences in the type of economic activities, as well as differences in the levels of school enrollment between rural and urban areas. Employment of children in industry is regulated by strict legislations. However, a large part of the employment of young persons in industry is in the family craft enterprises as well as in the very small establishments.

Sex differences in child labor widened between 1937 and 1960. The relative share of girls in the aggregate figures of child labor showed a marked increase, from 11.4 percent in 1937 to 36.5 percent in 1960. Most probably, such differentials have been accentuated by differences among the sexes in school enrollment, especially in rural Egypt. Other factors include such things as the greater adaptability of young girls than boys for work in household services, as well as persistent elements of cultural bias in the make-up of the Egyptian family which favors boys over girls.

By Western standards, the health of the Egyptian population is poor. As far as labor productivity is concerned, the prevalence of debilitating diseases is generally recognized as the major health problem. Health conditions of the masses are affected by a poorly balanced diet characterized by a low consumption of animal protein. The malnutrition suffered by the poorest elements of the population is due not only to inadequate food production, but also to their low purchasing power. Recent efforts toward improving health and dietary conditions are apparent in the noticeable decline in death rates, especially infant mortality. However, the still relatively high infant mortality level in Egypt, even in comparison with other less developed countries, constitutes a serious economic and human loss.

The impact of health conditions and the level of nutrition on the supply of labor are largely qualitative in nature, especially in a country like Egypt, where there is a surplus of manpower. In this respect, malnutrition and the prevalence of debilitating diseases affect adversely the level of productivity of the Egyptian worker. Many cases of absent-teeism, dropout, and inability to handle heavy mental and physical work are reported as caused by ill health and poor nutrition. In addition to a number of health schemes, the government's efforts to improve health and dietary conditions focus on several policies for income redistribution, subsidizing prices of basic commodities, increasing production of certain food, and supplying the rural population with clean water.

Only a small elite of the industrial labor force received benefits from an elaborate body of labor legislation. In many instances, labor legislation which was intended to raise the quality of workers and work conditions put severe limits on the volume of employment, and subsequently limited the size of the labor force. For example, the effects of child labor laws, the provisions governing the employment of women with children, as well as the stipulations put forward for social security schemes for employees led employers to limit their hiring of laborers. In this respect, it is also relevant to note that the protective measures of the labor code, especially the restrictions on the right of management to fire unproductive labor, have caused managers to think twice before hiring workers.

Legislation which tied the hands of management in hiring and firing of workers was intended to prevent nepotism and favoritism; however, such legislation might have produced, indirectly, unfavorable effects on the productivity of workers. Thus, a number of laws were introduced to regulate the labor market and to balance the supply and demand of different skills. Provisions regulating labor inspection,

minimum wages, hiring procedures, hours of work, etc., introduced
an element of structure into the labor market. Labor market mobility
is, in principle, free in Egypt. There are no restrictions on the
movement of labor from one regional area to another, nor from one
sector of the economy to another. However, several governmental
policies were actually steps in the direction of a quasi-governmental
control of the labor market. Examples of such policies are regulating
the appointment of certain professional and skilled manpower, lowering
the differences in the wage structure of similar occupations, and limiting the practice of management of luring skilled workers from other
firms.

Trade unions were introduced in Egypt at a relatively early
date in this century. However, until recently, the labor movement
remained weak and isolated. The high level of illiteracy among workers,
an apathetic or ignorant public opinion, and a continually hostile and
suspicious attitude on the part of the prerevolution government kept
the labor movement relatively weak. The present government follows
a policy of encouraging and strengthening the movement while keeping
a firm hand on its activities.

The emphasis which the present regime has put on providing
education to all segments of the society is actually impressive. The
statistics on the growth of enrollment and the structural development
of Egypt's educational system are indicative of the change. Realizing
the extremely low level of literacy among the masses, the Egyptian
government put primary emphasis on combating illiteracy in both
rural and urban areas. The campaign against illiteracy has been
costly and slow because of the trends in the age composition of the
Egyptian population toward a younger age structure.

From an employment point of view, the impact of elemenatry
education on rural employment is minimal. A great percentage of
boys and girls who finish their periods of compulsory education return
to work in the fields or to idleness. Expansion in general secondary
education was relatively moderate in comparison with the expansion
which took place in compulsory education. However, even this relatively modest expansion created a serious unemployment problem
among high school graduates. The number of high school graduates
who are not admitted to universities is increasing. Inculcated in
a cultural perspective which disdains manual work, enforced by the
type of training and courses they received, they are actually thrown
into a highly competitive and limited market for white-collar jobs.
The rapid expansion in higher education which took place particularly
after the revolution reflects a concern on the part of the government
to increase enrollment in the sciences and the professions, as well as
a response to parental pressure desiring a university degree for their

sons and daughters. The expansion of enrollments in law, arts, and literature in the already overcrowded colleges is actually a response to these parental pressures.

The removal of financial barriers to higher education in terms of fees was another manifestation of government response to an increasing desire on the part of all socioeconomic segments of the Egyptian population for a university degree. This policy of minimum restrictions on enrollments in higher education started to produce an army of unemployed educated persons who were waiting to grab any job the authorities could provide. In the early 1960's, the government took on the task of providing jobs for large numbers of business, law, and liberal arts graduates. This drive toward the employment of university graduates was costly in terms of both money and productivity. Unemployment problems of the educated elite not only reflect the limited absorptive capacity of the Egyptian economy for further employment, but are also a manifestation of unrealistic enrollment policies in the educational system. The oversupply of graduates of certain liberal arts colleges has spread in recent years to other colleges of science, engineering, and agriculture. At present, Egypt's trainees in these professions are increasingly exceeding her capacity to employ them gainfully. An indication of this situation is the large number of graduates of engineering, agriculture and science colleges who apply for immigration visas to the United States, Canada, and other countries.

A major paradoxical feature recognized in the educational system in Egypt is the existence of a very high level of literacy at a time when the level of university enrollment in relation to total population is also relatively high.

Vocational schools were introduced relatively early in the Egyptian educational system. However, the inferior social and economic status accruing to the graduates kept their enrollment from expanding. This, in addition to the backwardness of the instruction in these schools, caused a serious shortage of technicians, supervisors, and foremen in many branches of industry and agriculture which, in turn, caused a great deal of the low productivity of the Egyptian workers.

It is generally recognized that by Western standards labor productivity is low in all economic sectors. Outside of the social factors of ill health, malnutrition, bad housing, and transportation, a number of other personal, managerial, and technical factor s are cited as causing low productivity of industrial workers. One study reported that regardless of the capital/labor ratio, the productivity of the Egyptian worker is lower than that of his Western counterpart. A number of other studies, however, have reported that the productivity of industrial workers increased with income increases and the

use of modern machinery. The lag of productivity behind wages,
which occurred in the first phase of the development plan in the 1960's,
in spite of heavy capital investment in industry, was accounted for
by the nationalization policies of the time, and changes in the structure of management, work hours, and other work arrangements.

The factors which affect labor productivity in agriculture are
many and are too interdependent to allow measurement of the relative effect of each. Among those factors peculiar to the agricultural
sector are the prevalence of small-size farms, the use of traditional
tools, and the concentration on growing crops which are labor intensive by nature. Perhaps the most important single factor affecting
the level of productivity per worker is the relatively high man/land
ration in Egypt. Most observers agree that the pressure of increasing population is behind the fall in the per capita output per man
which has taken place since the 1930's. The Malthusian law of
diminishing returns is seen as operating to cause a fall in productivity per working person. The increase which occurred in productivity per worker since the 1950's was attributed to two factors:
improvement in the methods of cultivation, irrigation, and drainage,
and more use of fertilizers; and stagnation of the size of the agricultural labor force in spite of a rise in the growth rate of the population as a whole. However, not all observers agree on the stagnation thesis of the agricultural labor force. To some of them, the
break in the trends which took place until the 1930's represents a
reduction in the rate of increase in the man/land ratio, rather than
a change in the direction of movement.

Estimates of labor productivity per worker in the services indicate a relative rise in the subsectors of commerce, construction,
and transportation, and a probable decline in the sectors of government and personal services. The rise in the productivity of workers
in the first three sectors was attributed to the introduction of modern
machinery, a fuller use of underemployed labor; and a decrease in
the relative share of those categories of workers who are least productive, especially women and children. Overstaffing in the government as well as in the services, which seems to have developed as a
result of overpopulation, is the major cause of the apparent decline
in the productivity per worker in these sectors.

Determinants of Labor Supply:
Demographic Factors

This study has revealed the effects of a number of demographic
determinants on the supply of labor. It was found that the burden of
dependency on the population at the productive age groups increased

sharply following the mortality decline after World War II. The impact of the younger age structure on the productive capacity of the economy is such that Egypt suffers from a serious financial expense: the younger population tends to consume far more than it produces. In addition, societal care for such a large percentage of the population in education, health care, etc., diverts funds from immediate economic investment. The fact that around 1960, more than 40 percent of the population was under 15 years of age, constitutes a limitation on the supply of labor, at least in principle. However, it is important to point out that in practice such a seeming "paradox" of overpopulation and undersupply of labor never really occurred in Egypt. The prevalence of child labor in the Egyptian society could partially be explained by its age structure which is skewed heavily toward the younger age groups.

The analysis of the financial status of the population in relation to sex and age indicated what is perhaps one of the most serious societal problems in Egypt. The fact that only 1.3 percent of females were classified as financially independent at the beginning of the 1960's requires a careful analysis of the sociological, as well as the economic, implications of females' total dependency to the structure of the Egyptian family, the level of fertility, and the prospects for future female employment

The available data do not permit a direct examination of the relationship between marital status and female rates of participation in the labor forces at different ages. However, an indirect test of this relationship was possible. Women were found to cease work after marriage. The magnitude of child labor among females participating in economic activities is well illustrated from the figures; the peak of female participation rates was found to occur around the ages of twelve to sixteen. Urbanization trends and increases in school enrollment caused the average age of marriage to rise and increased the proportion of women who are not married. These trends might ultimately help more females to participate in economic activities. However, urbanization and education effects on the rate of women's participation in economic activities will probably depend on the speed of the transformation of the Egyptian economic structure. In the short run, however, by shifting the population from a rural sector (where female participation rates are higher) to an urban sector (where female participation rates are low), the urbanization trends may actually cause a decrease in the rate of females working in the labor force. Also, prolonged educational periods and larger school enrollments will decrease child labor as well as delay the age of entry into the labor force, thus actually causing a drop in the overall rate of participation in economic activities.

The relationship between household size and the labor force participation rate was found to be as follows: in rural areas, household size increased with the increase in the percentage of the population in the labor force; in urban areas, the pattern was reversed. Most probably, this relationship reflects the nature of the traditional and modern sectors of the economy.   Thus the gradual transition of the economy toward a complex, modern structure will be associated with an increase in the number of households with fewer members who participate in the labor force. However, the rural-urban transition was found to have no direct effect on the size of the household as such. The effect of industrialization on household arrangements and in particular on the size of the household seems to be noticeable more than the mere rural-urban migration. This particular finding does not lend itself easily to generalization, since it was derived from a study of one industrial location. However, smaller house-hold size might be a correlate of industrialization, since work and living in an industrial location were found to have a noticeable effect on the age structure of the household as well as on the educational status of its members.

One of the main concerns of this study was to present a statis-tical analysis of the trends and differentials in the rate of economic activities. From the last three censuses, the observed overall pattern was a gradual decline in crude economic activities. Sex differences were quite apparent in the declining trend. The fall in the crude economic activity rate was relatively larger for females than for males. This long-term decrease in the rate of economic activities was primarily an outcome of demographic changes, es-pecially the trend toward a younger population structure. However, the returns of the labor force sample surveys for a shorter period (1957-60) showed a decline in the percentage of the labor force in the total population, at a time when the manpower portion was con-stant. These findings were explained as reflecting a stricter defini-tion of females working in agricultural activities, as well as enforc-ing legislations prohibiting the employment of children.

A general decline in the proportion of males working at the upper and lower levels of the age span was apparent. The proportion of males working at middle ages increased slightly. A general decline was observed in the proportion of total females working. The participation rates of younger girls (fifteen and under) increased between 1937 and 1960, whereas those of the middle ages showed a decline. Urbanization trends, at least in their early stages, where they were not accompanied by structural growth and differentiation in the labor force, seem to lower the participation rate of females, especially those of illiterate and unskilled women mostly in the middle ages. The increase in the rate of participation of younger girls could

either be apparent because of different timing of the census, or real
because of a tendency on the part of rural families to put girls to
work in the fields or as domestic servants while boys go to school.
Rural-urban differences in the rate of participation in economic
activities indicated higher rates of labor force participation in rural
areas than in urban areas for all ages, especially for the young and
the very old. The net effect of both trends, the changes in the age
structure of the population, and in age-specific rates of participation
in economic activities was a tendency in the age structure of the labor
force toward a predominantly middle age group. This took place at
a time when the age structure of the Egyptian population in general
was moving toward a juvenile age structure.

There was strong evidence to suggest that the dependency load
was compounded by a number of nondemographic trends, namely,
a prolonged educational period child labor prohibitions, social
security schemes, and various inducements for early retirement.

It was possible to ascertain developments after 1960 in the proportion of the labor force on the basis of recently published statistics.
The difficulty was that these new figures were not comparable with
the census data. In the first phase of the development plan (1960-65),
population and labor force seemed to grow at the same rate (2. 4 percent per year) thus keeping the rate of participation in economic
activities relatively unchanged.

Looking in perspective at the projected rates of economic activities between 1965 and 1985, the following trends seem probable: (1)
any substantial fertility decline in the coming decade or two will have
little or no effect on the projected size of the labor force; (2) considering the projected size of population, labor force, and participation rates during the period, one is led to expect that in all likelihood
population and labor force will continue to grow at the same rate,
thus causing the projected rate of participation in economic activities
to remain around its 30 percent level of 1960. A slight drop in the
relative share of females in the aggregate labor force is expected to
take place by 1985. This seemingly unexpected trend will be an
outcome of urbanization trends, increased girls' enrollment, and
prohibition of child labor.

Projections of future age composition of the labor force show a
continuation of the already observed trend toward an increase in the
proportion of the early middle age groups (fifteen to forty-four). The
share of the young and old age groups in the labor force will probably
remain constant or show a slight decline. The only age groups which
might show a relative decline are those between forty-five and sixty-
five. This will be largely attributable to a projected decline in the

share of the male population aged forty-five to sixty-four. Probably
in the coming decade or two, the relative age distribution of female
labor force will not be altered from the general pattern observed
in 1960.

Growth and Structural Changes
in the Labor Force

According to the adjustment figures of the census, the labor
force expanded by approximately 1. 1 million between 1937 and 1947
and by 800, 000 from 1947 to 1960. This represents a total increase
of 1. 9 million, or 32. 5 percent between 1937 and 1960. The population increase during this same period was about 10. 2 million, or
64 per cent. In other words, population growth far outstripped increases in the size of the labor force. An interesting feature of this
trend is that between 1947 and 1960, labor force increased at a
much slower rate (less than 1 percent per year) than the total population (2. 5 percent per annum). The enforcement of compulsory
education and a change in the age structure of the population are
largely responsible for this phenomenon. Also, it might reflect
a certain inability of the economic system to provide employment
for a larger portion of the manpower.

Until 1947, agriculture continued to be the sector with the
largest absorptive capacity for additional workers, in spite of the
fact that between 1927 and 1947 the rate of employment expansion
in agriculture decreased from 60. 3 to 46. 7 percent. Between 1947
and 1960, the services expanded much more than in previous periods,
and more than both agriculture and industry. Between 1947 and 1960,
the services absorbed more than one-third of all additions to the
labor force, agriculture absorbed one-fifth, and industry absorbed
only 15 percent. However, labor transfer mechanisms were operating from rural to urban areas, where most of the industries were
located. In the large governorates, a pool of unemployed, unskilled
workers became permanently available to the industrial sector.

With the population growth in view, and the failure of the
industrial sector to grow rapidly, the agricultural sector did not
witness a reduction in the absolute number engaged in agricultural
activities, and the services continued to increase in order to absorb
the release out of agriculture. Thus, a transference of underemployment between these last two sectors might have taken place.

Population increased by 40 percent at a time, the average cultivated area per active individual increased by 3 percent, and the
crop area per active individual rose 16. 3 percent. We have noted

a disagreement on assessment of the actual trend in the size of agricultural employment between 1937 and 1960. The controversy over
whether employment in agriculture experienced a stagnation or a
slack period between 1937 and 1960 does not constitute a serious
problem, since it stems largely from different interpretations of the
statistics. All observers, however, agree that the rate of growth
in the agricultural sector slowed down considerably during this
period.

Between 1937 and 1960, while population increased by 64 percent, the economically active population increased by 33 per cent,
and economic activity in industry increased by 75 percent. In spite
of an absolute increase in the number of workers in industry between
1937 and 1960, the share of industry in the labor force increased very
little (around 10 percent). From an employment point of view, there
was no evidence to support the belief about a stagnation period in
small scale industry. Employment in this part of industry continued
to grow at a rate equal to that of the aggregate.

The structure of employment in Egyptian industry reveals a
larger share of both large-scale and small-scale firms, and a moderate
share of middle-sized firms. Monopolistic tendencies, the preference given for capital intensive industries, and the concentration of
industry in urban areas account for the biggest share of large firms
in industrial employment.

The pre-1960 years witnessed a large increase, relative as well
as absolute, in employment in the services. Such increase was more
pronounced in the period from 1947-1960. During this last period,
increase in government employment alone accounted for 40 percent
of all new jobs in the economy. Most of the subsectors of the services recorded some increase in employment between 1937 and 1960,
but employment in government and personal services accounted for
nearly 75 per cent of all increases.

The analysis of the labor force according to the international
standard of occupational classification indicated that in 1960, half
of the labor force was employed in agricultural occupations, 16 per
cent as craftsmen. White collar occupations constituted 15 percent
of the labor force. Half of the white-collar occupations were classified as professional, managerial, and clerical occupations. The
rural character of the labor force in Egypt is indicated by the very
low percentage of white-collar workers (15 percent), a figure which
we believe to be inflated.

An important aspect of any labor force analysis is its breakdown according to employment status. The most obvious change in

the working status of the Egyptian population, recorded by the census between 1937 and 1960, is a decrease in the number of employers, and self-employed. Such a trend was congruent with the increase which took place in the employment in government and public organizations. Other manifestations of this trend were a noticeable increase in the category of employees and the unemployed. The increase in the first category reflects the bureaucratic trend in which the state is increasingly assuming the role of the employer. The absolute rise in the category of unemployed reflects serious population pressures and an inability of the economy to provide jobs for all of its manpower, leading to a transference of a good deal of disguised unemployment from agriculture to open unemployment in urban areas.

Analysis of labor force statistics of the first phase of the plan (1960-65) indicated a further drop in the relative share of the agricultural labor force. The relative share of employment in industry showed no substantial increase, in spite of heavy investment in this sector. The share of both agriculture and industry, the commodity producing sectors, in additional employment during the planning years was very substantial, around 70 percent. However, the services continued to provide employment for a large portion of the increment to the labor force in spite of an original attempt to reduce their rate of growth, at least in the first phase of the plan.

In the second phase of the plan (1965-70), the labor force was projected to increase at a greater rate than in the first five-year plan (7.3 percent per year in comparison to 2.1 percent). Such an expectation was reasonable due to the fact that a sizable proportion of the young population would be joining the labor force in the second half of the plan. Employment was projected to increase at a rate approximately twice the increase that was expected in the labor force. This was probably too optimistic an estimate in view of the results obtained from the first five-year plan and considering the fact that investment will not increase substantially between the two phases of the plan to affect such a large increase in employment.

Statistics on employment targets by economic sector projected a marked decline in the planned percentage contribution of agriculture to additional employment, from 54.1 to 34.1 between the two stages of the plan. As envisaged, the major outlet for employment in the first five-year plan lies in the production sector, and in the services in the second phase.

Further analysis of future growth and structural changes in the labor force in Egypt after the year 1970 was seen as hazardous for a number of reasons: (1) no actual statistical data have been released on the implementation phase of the second five-year plan to help make

any assessment of future trends possible; (2) the present circumstances in Egypt are quite unusual due to the hostilities in the Middle
East (in this context, manpower movement as well as the concern over
planning targets have been definitely affected); and (3) since employment objectives depend on the volume of investment, and since no
available figures on investment targets for the 1970's are planned,
further analysis becomes quite impossible.

Structural Changes in the Society

The importance of the trends in size and structural distribution
of a labor force becomes more relevant to larger societal changes,
once their relationship becomes apparent. In this study, such relationships as those between urbanization trends, directions and streams
of internal migration, structure of industry, industrialization policies,
and agrarian reform laws on one side and the supply of labor and
employment from the other were analyzed.

A number of <u>migration</u> streams were identified. Most were
found to be associated with the movement of labor between different
geographical areas, as well as between different sectors of the
economy. These migration streams include the following: rural-
metropolitan movement, mainly to Cairo and Alexandria, but also
to other large metropolitan centers; rural-urban movement of a large
number of students and workers from villages to towns and big cities;
rural-industrial movement, from villages to major industrial centers
in Aswan, Giza, Beheira, Gharbia, and others; rural-rural resettle-
ment--a movement from the heavily populated provinces of upper and
lower Egypt to newly developed rural settlements in the newly reclaimed land (this is a relatively new stream of migration which will
probably grow in significance following the reclamation of an additional
2 million feddans from the High Dam area in the near future); a
traditional movement from upper to lower Egypt, especially from
Aswan to Cairo and Alexandria, mainly by Nubians who seek work as
domestics and as services personnel in the two large metropolitan
centers; a very recent movement from lower to upper Egypt (especially to Aswan, where a large number of industrial complexes and
projects besides that of the High Dam required workers); and a beginning stream of migrants from the valley to the desert, to work in
mining, quarrying and the oil/gas industry, and to settle the new valley
of the western desert. A great deal of rural-urban migration seems
to be of the family type rather than of the individual type. However,
sex differentials in rural-urban migration exist, especially male
preponderance among the young and the early middle ages.

A unique pattern of the traditional migration stream is that of

the Nubians who leave ample employment opportunities in their home
governorate, Aswan, to be filled by other immigrants from neighboring governorates, in order to seek special domestic and service jobs
in Cairo and Alexandria. This pattern seems to constitute a deviant
case to the principle of "intervening opportunities."

Population movement and labor mobility, which started at the
turn of the century, were accelerated in the period between 1927 and
1960. During the war period, expansion in employment with the Allied
forces instigated the rapid trend, which continued after the war until
the end of the economic boom which followed the Korean War. The
recess which occurred in the economy during the 1950's slowed the
rate of population movement from rural to urban areas.

According to the 1966 sample census, the population classified
as urban reached 40 percent of the total. Part of the recorded increase
in urban population was due to a mere numerical growth in the size of
some villages, and part from annexation of small farms neighboring
the big urban centers. The large portion of this trend, however, was
an outcome of the rural-urban movement. The rapid rate of growth of
the major metropolitan cities, especially of Cairo and Alexandria, in
comparison with other urban and rural areas, makes it possible to
refer to them as "primate cities." No doubt the concentration of
industry and other economic and business activities in these two large
centers has kept the economic and technological basis of other urban
areas at a relatively low level. Outside of several industrial centers
in textile, food industry, and fertilizers, the occupational structures
in other urban areas are not large or differentiated enough in relation
to their population size. Thus, in some parts of Egypt, largely in
major metropolitan centers, trends of industrialization and urbanization seem to be concomitant factors. In most other urban areas,
manifestations of urbanization trends, as far as the structure and
differentiation of labor force and employment are concerned, seem
to be either missing altogether or apparent only in a very elementary
and crude form. In yet other areas, industrialization exists without
any accompanying urbanization trends of size, complexity of housing,
transportation, and other structural features of urban life. This
last pattern exists only in areas where many industrial complexes of
textiles, food processing, and other branches of industry are located.

Large-scale industrialization trends, which started in the 1920's,
continued to grow throughout the 1930's and 1940's. A peak of demand
for industrial and manufactured products was reached around the time
of World War II. The recession in the economy which took place
following the boom of the Korean War caused a slack in industrial
production, a slack which continued through the 1950's and into the
early 1960's. Certain characteristics of the structure of industry in

Egypt were seen to be relevant to labor force and employment. First
is the concentration of most industrial concerns in large cities, which
is a major cause of attracting migrants from outside areas and an
indirect cause of this phenomenal numerical growth. Second is the
prevalence of large-scale and small-scale firms, and the relative
absence of middle-size firms. This is mainly a reflection of the
predominance of capital-intensive types of industry, as well as of
rural crafts and small-scale enterprises.

A major element of the industrialization policy which remained
so controversial among observers of the Egyptian economy is the
tendency toward more use of capital intensive techniques of production.
Critics of this policy point to Egypt's most abundant factor of production, namely labor, and point to the inconsistency of this policy with
the country's factor endowment. However, supporters of the techniques
of capital-intensive production refer to it as the best alternative which
will create permanent productive employment, at least in the long run.

A number of labor problems which arise from industrialization
were outlined and discussed. These were grouped into the following
three sets of problems: those pertaining to the industrial worker,
those pertaining to the human organization of industry, and those
pertaining to the labor market. The agrarian character of the industrial worker, the gradual decline of artisans and artisanship in the
face of modern industry, and the relative inefficiency of financial
incentives in raising both mobility and productivity have been cited
as representative factors in the relative backwardness of the industrial worker in Egypt as compared to his counterpart in the Western
countries.

A major set of problems relates to the labor market. In the
modern urban-industrial areas of Egypt, some definite features of
a labor market exist, such as the prevalence of training and retrain-
ing as well as the development of complex and differentiated occupations. In most rural areas, however, the labor market in this sense
does not exist. In fact, because labor is abundant in nearly all localities, an effective mechanism of supply and demand is not operating.
For example, industrial recruitment, in many cases, does not come
from the labor market (the unemployed industrial and urban workers),
but rather from the undifferentiated rural surplus. Government intervention into the labor market, which started gradually after the revolution, had a number of objectives. The stipulations in labor legislation
concerning hiring, firing, and training and insurance schemes, aim
largely at improving qualitative aspects of manpower and labor force,
and at giving some structure to the market. Most of the government's
efforts in this respect benefit an elite of industrial and urban workers.
Until very recently, the agricultural sector remained relatively untouched.

Legislative provisions concerning conditions of employment, wages, and hours of work were not enforced, either because attempts to enforce them failed or because the authorities did not press hard to enforce them.

Until 1961, government efforts to improve money wages were negligible. Since 1961, the guiding policy of government activities in this respect has been to keep the prices of elementary consumer goods low instead of attempting to improve real wages by raising money wages. The nationalization of big industries and enterprises put the direct responsibility for the development of money wages on the government. Whether this would mean that the factors of supply and demand would cease to work in affecting industrial wages depends on the future development of the private sector.

The Egyptian schemes of land and agrarian reforms have been considered from an employment perspective. No doubt there are many provisions in the laws of agrarian reform which qualify them to be basically labor policies. Because of population pressure on the land, agrarian reform laws have not been effective in reducing the unemployment problems, or ensuring full employment for the underemployed in agriculture. In fact, the implementation of the laws produced negative results on the employment situation. Some estimates put unemployment created from the first law as high as 8 to 10 percent. Most of the unemployment problems created from land reform schemes were prevalent among the category of hard-core paid laborers, who have not benefited from land distribution. A further indication that agrarian reform laws did not work effectively in solving the employment problem is the persistent low level of wages in agriculture, which continued until 1962 in spite of certain promises stipulating minimum wages in the first land reform law of 1952. In fact, the slow but steady rise in wages in agriculture which took place in the early 1960's was instigated from other developments outside the agriculture sector.

Cooperative movements which were enlarged and reorganized in agriculture during the late 1950's and early 1960's had their favorable and unfavorable effects on employment. The staffing of a large number of units with professional, managerial, clerical, skilled, and unskilled workers was no doubt an outlet for employing a large number of persons. Cooperatives also helped to increase investment in the agricultural sector either directly or indirectly through credit. Subsequently, such investment produced its favorable effects on employment. However, by encouraging the use of modern machinery, and through their success in organizing agricultural rotation and land consolidations, cooperatives moved both agricultural techniques and technology toward more laborsaving methods.

The reduction which took place in employment as a result of land reforms was somewhat mitigated by an expansion in land reclamation schemes which are usually labor-absorbing projects. In spite of the fact that land reform laws were less successful in solving the employment problem in the agricultural sector, their effects have been noticeable in raising the standard of living for those who owned the distributed land. Their success was even more noticeable in raising the level of productivity per acre.

Utilization of Labor Supply

One of the primary concerns of this study was an evaluation of past and recent discussions and measurements of both the existence and extent of unemployment and underemployment. We have seen that Egypt has always been cited as a classic agricultural, overpopulated economy where underemployment constituted a serious form of underutilization of labor supply. This opinion, prevailing among most observers of the Egyptian economy, was challenged recently by Hansen and Marzouk. Their empirical evidence was largely based on the fact that the ongoing rate of wages in agriculture is less than the marginal productivity of workers--an indication that the marginal productivity of workers is not zero or even close to it. Others, especially Mead, who examined more closely a number of different indexes of underemployment, remained unconvinced that underemployment is no more a serious problem in the agricultural sector of Egypt. Our critical analysis of the two sides of the argument showed that this disagreement stems largely from different conceptual analysis, as well as from inclusion or exclusion of different categories in the agricultural labor force. A study conducted in 1964-65 by the Institute of National Planning in collaboration with the International Labor Organization left no doubt that both disguised and seasonal underemployment are substantial in agriculture. Underutilization of labor supply is apparent both in terms of the amount of work hours, and in terms of duration of employment. In this respect, variations among governorates was apparent because of differences in the man/land ratio as well as differences in cropping patterns. An overall age and sex estimate of rural underemployment in the governorates where the survey was conducted was 12.5 percent for men, 25.4 percent for women, and 64.7 percent for children. An estimate of unemployment of 4 percent in rural areas was reported in the study referred to. In our discussion of the figures on unemployment, we believe it to be greatly underestimated for a number of reasons, but mostly because of the exclusion of certain categories which could be discribed as "discouraged groups."

According to the plan, employment objectives were higher than the projected growth rate of the labor force in the 1960's, in the hope of employing all increments of the labor force, as well as a large part of the then already unemployed or underemployed. Judging from the absolute figures of the first phase of the plan, up to 1965, unemployment objectives were achieved. However, the mere fact that about 75 percent of all employment in the first phase of the plan took place in agriculturel and services--two sectors with a relatively high degree of underemployment--means that employment figures in these sectors included a large portion of persons who are not fully employed.

CONCLUSIONS

Systematic analysis of the complex relationship between trends in population size, distribution, and composition on the one hand, and the size and structure of labor supply and employment on the other, has been grossly neglected by demographers as well as economists in Egypt. Much more attention has been given to other demographic problems, such as the effects of rapid population growth on food supply.

At the present, there are some encouraging signs concerning the relationship between population growth and food supply in Egypt. Available figures indicate an increase in total food production of 3. 5 percent per year in comparison with an increase in population of only 2. 8 percent between 1952-56 and 1960-64. [1]   There is nothing wrong with the fact that most of such improvement in food supply came largely from an increase in importing food stuffs. Egypt's specialization in the production of other agricultural products in which she has relative advantages follows a rational policy, especially in an age when complete self-suffiency is becoming an economically unattainable goal.

The problems of labor force and employment are coming to the forefront now that the population explosion of the 1950's is swelling the labor force. Therefore, it is time to put this problem in a better perspective. In this respect, an adequate knowledge of the determinants of the supply of labor, both demographic and nondemographic, is a prerequisite for any systematic analysis of the growth and structural changes in the labor force, as well as in understanding employment problems.

In Egypt, the problems of employment have two aspects: the problem of adapting the labor force to changes in the economic structure; and the problem of how to use the labor force to bring about the changes in economic structure that are needed if the level of living is to improve. In some respects, then, employment problems are products

of such socioeconomic changes. As we see it in present day Egypt,
the first set of problems--i.e., the effective use of human resources--
is by far its more serious employment aspect.

Having stated these general conclusions, we will proceed toward
more specific ones concerning the substantive issues considered
throughout this study.

Determinants of Labor Supply:
Socioeconomic Factors

The likely success of the present efforts to improve women's
status socially will be greatly hampered by an absence of similar
successful efforts to enhance employment opportunities for them outside the home. Massive female entry into the labor market, as it
occurred in the West, remains a remote possibility, especially in
the present context of a large surplus of male unemployment as well
as underemployment. From an employment point of view, such a
large female entry into the labor market will be a serious issue for
Egyptian planners to contend with. However, having such a large
portion of the country's potential productive manpower so idle
constitutes a serious social and economic paradox of the Egyptian
setting. For a long time to come, Egypt will probably continue to
have a large reservoir of labor supply in the female section of the
population. This will be the case even if a state of full employment
were to be achieved among the country's male population.

Child labor seems to be heading toward a further decline.
Increased school enrollment and child labor legislation will continue
to enhance this trend. Probably more than any changes in values or
government intervention, the adoption of technological inventions will
be a decisive factor in eradicating child labor. Mechanization of
certain agricultural operations (pest control and cotton picking), as
well as introducing modern technology into household activities, will
ultimately do the job. How fast this trend will develop depends in
turn on the availability of cheap child labor. Probably for some time
to come, child labor will remain a sizable yet unofficially recognized
part of the labor force in Egypt.

Most of Egypt's elaborate schemes of labor legislation are
intended to improve the qualitative aspects of the labor force. From
an employment point of view, the prohibition of child labor, the various
inducements for early retirement, and the provisions governing the
employment of married women might enhance the employment prospects of males in the productive age groups (the real backbone of the
labor force). Labor legislation has produced, so far, beneficial

qualitative effects for a very small circle of industrial laborers. The large bulk of the labor force in agriculture and the services have received relatively few benefits. It is very unlikely that the government can extend schemes such as social security, workmen's compensation, disability benefits, etc., to the bulk of the agricultural labor force. Government intervention into the labor market in one form or another is assuming a growing role. The growing trend toward a Socialistic economy, the weakening of private concerns, and the assuming by the state of the role of the main employer, are factors leading toward a quasi-governmental control of the labor market.

The continuous efforts on the part of the Egyptian government to keep the labor code up to date, according to the standard of the International Labor Organization, leads one to pose the following questions: Is Egypt adopting-- at least in principle--much of an advanced scheme of labor legislation, in terms of the country's present economic and social structure? And would it be more beneficial if the efforts were geared to increase employment opportunities rather than to the imposing of qualitative restrictions?

There is really no other socioeconomic factor which has more direct bearing on both the quantity and the quality of manpower and labor force than education. The relationship between educational training and policy, as these are related to developments in manpower and labor force, revealed a number of problems which need to be resolved. Strangely enough, despite the adoption of rigorous economic planning, educational policy has failed to follow any guiding principles of manpower planning. Sensible policies of manpower planning have always given way to a policy of appeasement and accommodation in public pressure. The impacts of education on the supply of labor and employment are actually two: favorable and unfavorable. Among the favorable impacts of education on the development of manpower and employment are the following: (1) enrollment in the different levels of education absorbs, temporarily, a large portion of Egypt's manpower and delays its entry into the labor force; (2) education channels a large percentage of Egypt's manpower from agricultural pursuits to industrial and white-collar occupations; (3) education increases the percentage of females in the economically active population, especially in urban areas; and (4) the staffing of schools, universities, institutes, and other learning organizations is an important avenue for employment of certain professions and white-collar jobs. The unfavorable effects of education include the following: (1) heavy investment in education puts some burden on the economy, which subsequently limits investment in industry and other economical activities; (2) training of a large number in liberal arts, literature, and other nontechnical professions, has created and probably will continue to augment an army of unemployed intellectuals; (3)

compulsory elementary education, by itself, does not enhance the employment prospects in rural areas; and (4) educational training has so far failed to provide the economy with the much-needed categories of foremen, supervisors, and technicians.

The discussion of <u>labor</u> <u>efficiency</u> <u>and</u> <u>general</u> <u>productivity</u> leads us to conclude the following:

(1) There is nothing peculiar in the personality of the Egyptian worker that keeps his level of efficiency substantially lower than that of his European counterpart. The factors responsible for his present low level are known, and could be summarized under three major causes: first, socioeconomic factors outside of the work environment-- largely the low level of health and nutrition, the bad housing and transportation system, and the low standard of living; second, factors associated with work environment, including such things as managerial problems and the low level of supervisory qualities; and third, low capital/labor ratio in most industrial concerns in Egypt in comparison to that of the Western countries.

(2) In the present context of large population pressure, especially in the agricultural sector, it is obsolete to speak mainly in terms of productivity per worker. At the present, emphasis should be placed on improving productivity per acre, at least until the agricultural labor force shows some signs of decrease in absolute, rather than relative, size.

(3) The slow rate of increase in productivity per worker in comparison to the rate of increase in wages and the heavy investment in the industrial sector during the first five-year plan is not as terribly disappointing as it might seem. First, industrial wages were low to begin with, and any moderate increase in them would appear substantial. Second, a period of gestation has to lapse before a wage rise affects worker's productivity. Finally, there was actually a noticeable increase in worker productivity in all subsectors of industry in spite of the dislocations that occurred in management and hours of work and other features of work as a consequence of the nationalization of most industrial complexes.

(4) Perhaps the most disappointing case of worker productivity is to be found in the services, especially in the government, where employment and wage increases were not matched by productivity increases. In the government, overstaffing constitutes the real problem.

The experience of Egypt during the planning years in respect to future increases in employment, wages, and productivity of workers seems to indicate the following: the productivity of additional new workers in all economic sectors will often be very low; in light of this fact, some sacrifice in economic growth might be expected in order to provide more employment quickly; moreover, quick employment is economically desirable, as far as it is positive at all, since; with its present oversupply of labor, Egypt can neither afford nor administer extensive social security plans or other schemes for the redistribution to income as alternative to providing all able persons a chance to work for a decent wage.

Determinants of Labor Supply: Demographic Factors

This study has shown that the growth of the Egyptian population at a rapid rate is perhaps the most significant factor affecting changes in the supply of labor. Another demographic factor which might be of equal significance is the trend toward a younger age structure. The trend toward a predominance of younger ages in the population of Egypt caused the following: a heavy load of dependency on the productive age groups; an imbalance between the production and consumption capacity of the economy; a sudden swell in the labor force in the mid-1960's; and a subsequent aggravation of the problems of unemployment.

However, in spite of the existence of an unfavorable dependency load, the supply of manpower far exceeds the economic opportunities in all sectors. In this respect, our major conclusion is that changes in the size and age structure of the population will put pressure on the Egyptian economy to provide jobs and work for an increasing number of persons in the coming decades. It is highly doubtful that the Egyptian economy in its present capacity can meet such demands. Yet, if such pressure will be met to avoid social and political repercussions, it is expected to be met in ways which are not terribly beneficial to the economy as a whole. Providing economically productive employment for a growing army of job seekers in the coming decade or two will be a major task for Egyptian planners to consider.

Two major conclusions could be arrived at from the reduction in mortality and the noticeable increase in life expectancy in Egypt in so far as they affect the supply of labor. The first considers the trend as an advantage to the economy, since an increase in life expectancy means, in general, an increase in the opportunity to make productive contributions. This is so, especially when employment is high and there is little or no disguised underemployment. This is not the case in Egypt, however, and an increase in the length of life could mean an increase in average working life, and subsequently a reduction in the rate of separation from the labor force. Such a phenomenon can be effected in only three ways: expansion in employment which is primarily an economic factor; decrease in fertility, which is primarily a demographic factor; or an inducement for early retirement, which is basically sociological in nature. Thus, the solution depends on the Egyptian position and requires solution on all fronts.

The relevance of demographic characteristics to the supply of the labor was pertinent also in understanding variations in proportions of workers within various age-sex groups of the population. Child labor was partially an outcome of relatively young age structure. Marital status was found to be related to the rate of female participation in economic activities. The observed pattern was a cessation from work after marriage. The noticeable trend toward a rise in the average age of marriage might increase female participation. The relationship and association between household size and the number of people working in the household was ascertained; both household size and the number of workers in the household were found to be functions of the type of household--rural vs. industrial urban. Effects of urbanization on the size and characteristics of the household were found to be less pronounced than those of industrialization. Urbanization trends have been shown to reduce the female labor force. This is so because of the following: in Egypt, women contribute a large share of the labor force in agriculture but a relatively small share in urban occupations; urbanization tends to increase girls' enrollment in school and subsequently cuts down on the extent of child labor, which constitutes a sizable portion of female labor force; and because of the separation of work from the household, gainful employment for city women tends to conflict with their long-established role as homemakers and mothers.

In the final analysis of the relevant effects of the demographic and nondemographic determinants of labor supply, we conclude that the large increase in the overall supply of labor is mainly an outcome of demographic trends, caused especially by the rate of population growth, and by the trend toward a younger age structure. Most of the socioeconomic factors discussed operate as factors limiting the size of the supply of labor. Thus, the traditional ban against women's work, the prohibition of child labor, the increase in the enrollment of a good portion of manpower in the different levels of education, as well as the restrictive conditions of hiring certain categories of manpower as stipulated by the labor code limit the size of labor supply.

A distinction between short-term and long-term implications of the effects of socioeconomic factors might be worthwhile. At the

present stage of Egypt's economic transformation from a basically
rural-agrarian economy to an urban-industrial one, the overall
effect of factors such as urbanization, education, and industrialization might be a reduction in the size of the labor force. The long-
term impact of these factors might actually be the reverse. Ultimately, the long-term societal trends will enhance the prospects
of employment, especially outside the agricultural sector.

This study shows us that at this stage of Egypt's modernization,
the burden of economic activities is entrusted largely to males at
their productive age. At its early stage, modernization trends reduce
the overall participation ratio by curtailing child labor, by reducing
female participation in economic activities, and by keeping a large
portion of manpower outside the labor market through prolonged
periods of education and training. In later stages of Egypt's modernization, females will probably join the labor force more than at the
present, due to the high level of education and training they will
possess in the future. This expansion might be enhanced with a
possible enlargement in white-collar jobs most suitable for women's
employment.

Another manifestation of the later phase of modernization might
be a trend toward early retirements because of various inducements.
The overall ratio of the economically active population to the total
population, therefore, will probably remain relatively stable for some
time to come. It is highly unlikely that a declining trend in the
economically active in the total population, similar to trends noticeable in the highly industrialized countries, will take place in Egypt
in the coming decades. We based such explanation on at least two
reasons: first, there will always be a pressure to increase employment for social reasons in the coming decades; second, a larger
portion of the population is reaching the age of joining the labor
force, and this situation will remain so as long as fertility continues
its currently high level.

Examination of age patterns of the economically active indicates
a gradual increase of the relative share of workers at middle ages;
this trend, which will eventually help to raise the overall level of
productivity, will probably be enhanced further by an increase in the
relative share of males in the early middle age groups in the total
labor force in the coming decades. The productive capacity of the
labor force will be affected upwardly by this trend, since in Egypt as
in most underdeveloped areas, the productive capacity of workers at
this middle age (twenty to forty-five) is relatively higher than those
in later middle age groups (forty-five to sixty-five).

Growth and Structural Changes
in the Labor Force

Population and labor force will probably grow at the same rate in the coming two decades. However, because of the larger share of people at the working age groups in the population, it is expected that more people will be working at the same time that the number of those unemployed will also increase.

In spite of a noticeable rise in the nonagricultural sectors in terms of employment, agricultural workers still constitute a large majority of workers. In agriculture, the structure of family farms prevalent in Egypt exhibits a tendency to retain people beyond the limit of relative advantage against other industries. At the same time, because of population pressure, a tendency exists for the rural surplus population (largely paid workers) to be squeezed out of farming because of lack of sufficient employment under prevailing conditions.

Declines in the relative share of the agricultural population took place during the period under study, although absolute numbers continued to increase. Moreover, due to a combination of high rate of population increase with a low rate of industrialization in terms of employment, there is no reason to expect a reduction of absolute numbers of the agricultural population within the near future. Continued increase of the agricultural population must be expected for quite a long time to come, especially after the construction of the Aswan Dam and the possibility of putting more than 1 million feddans into cultivation. If this trend were to take place, it would be definitely in a much later stage of the country's economic development. Also, it would depend upon a much lower rate of population growth, as well as on a greater rate of expansion of nonagricultural employment.

The process of industrialization has failed, so far, to absorb all annual increments to the labor force, let alone to reduce the existing surplus in agriculture. Thus, migration to towns and cities and expansion in other largely tertiary occupations is not necessarily a sign of change in the productive structure of the labor force, at least not to the extent that the data might suggest. Modern technology and a modern planned economy might be able to build an industrial structure which in a relatively short period of time could be of a great asset to the country's economic growth, yet might fail completely to solve the unemployment problems. This seems to be the case in Egypt.

Industrialization in itself is less likely to provide a solution to the problem of general employment. However, the rise in national income which might result from a successful expansion of industry could increase employment in secondary and tertiary activities, but there is no way to estimate such a rise in advance. Probably more than any other thing, the expansion of labor-intensive public works, such as the building of dams, irrigation projects, roads, and housing is more likely to alleviate the problems of unemployment in the near future. Encouragement of rural and cottage industry constitutes another possibility which needs relatively little diversion of investment funds. In brief, employment in construction, rural industry, and possibly new employment in tertiary activities might constitute future avenues for additional employment.

Structural Changes in the Society

We have seen throughout this study how modernization trends are closely related to growth of and structural changes in the labor force. In some cases, social trends precipitated certain trends in the labor force, in others, changes in employment as well as in the structure of the labor force have caused certain adjustment in the larger social and economic structure. We have attempted, as much as the research design permitted, to outline the direction of the relationship among trends in labor force and employment from one side and urbanization, internal migration, industrialization labor market structure, and laws of agrarian reform from the other.

In terms of size and number of streams, population mobility in Egypt, especially since the late 1930's, is relatively advanced in relationship to the labor market situation in terms of differentiation and structural features. Population pressure seems to be a major factor in keeping rural-urban migration at a relatively high level after World War II. Rural-urban migration has contributed greatly to urbanization, a phenomenon which seems to be quite distinct from industrialization in many parts of urban Egypt. Urbanization, defined as the percentage of population living in urban centers of 20,000 and over, seems to be relatively more advanced than industrialization, defined as the relative share of employment in industry. Urbanization trends and industrialization trends are not necessarily concomitant factors in urban Egypt.

In Egypt, industrialization did not follow an evolutionary trend from craft industry toward the use of complex modern technology. The weakness of the middle range of industrial enterprises explains how Egypt was able to embark on industrialization schemes by borrowing the relatively advanced, larger-scale machinery from the highly industrialized countries. Egyptian industry will probably continue to grow in terms of its contribution to the national economy, and this might help indirectly in opening more employment opportunities in tertiary activities. Yet, by itself industrialization will not be the panacea by which all the employment problems will be solved. Experimentation with some forms of intermediate technology suitable to the Egyptian supply of labor and raw materials might be effective in alleviating some of the unemployment problems in a relatively short period of time. The closeness of the industrial worker to his rural roots gives the labor force an agrarian character. Yet, Egypt seems to be building up gradually an industrial tradition among her labor force. The republican government has tried vigorously to organize the labor market: the hiring and firing practices have become regulated, and vocational and technical training are controlled by law in many cases. The organization of the supply and demand of certain scarce professional personnel, such as physicians and engineers, is also regulated by government decisions. Another manifestation of government control is the manipulation of the wage structure in order to minimize income inequality.

Gradual government control over the labor market is beginning to weaken the initiative of the private sector in terms of its ability to attract certain professional and technical skills. Legislation which structures the employment aspects in the state-controlled establishments is normally adopted by other private enterprises. The general trend is moving toward more government control over the public sector, and to more dominance by the public sector over the private sector. The government is gradually assuming the responsibility of creating employment, and such a responsibility will definitely put greater pressure on the government to provide employment for a rapidly growing labor force in order to avoid social and political unrest.

Land reform laws were successful in changing land ownership and raising productivity per feddan. The social and political implications of such legislation were far greater than the laws' economic results. Land reform changed the institutional structure of power of the aristocracy. Land reforms had limited success in solving the core problem of the chronic relationships between population and land. Looking at the laws as basically labor laws concerning employment, we noticed how partially successful they were in promoting a better level of income for those new landowners. At the same time, the reform laws have adversely affected a large segment of the overall labor force, mainly paid workers. The extent of unemployment resulting from land distribution was probably underestimated. The fact that the land reform laws of the early 1960's coincided with expansion of employment in industry and other nonagricultural activities helped to improve the wage level of paid agricultural workers which remained relatively unchanged during the 1950's in spite of provisions regulating minimum levels.

The major conclusion in this respect is that land reform laws cannot solve the problem of employment in an overpopulated country like Egypt. The pressure of population will always be felt to put further ceiling on land ownership and to distribute more land. The authorities in the U. A. R. seem to be yielding to such pressure. In 1969, President Nasser limited further land ownership to 50 feddans only, half of the ownership permitted by the 1961 law and distributed the expropriated land among the peasants. As a temporary relief such measures could be effective, but not as long-term solutions.

Utilization of Labor Supply

Admittedly, the extent of the utilization of labor supply in Egypt was and will probably remain a matter of controversy for some time to come. It was beyond the scope of this study to ascertain precisely the waste of labor supply. What we attempted to do was to examine the various evidences and indexes of employment, as well as the pro and con arguments concerning its limits in rural Egypt. Our initial analysis of the subject led us to conclude that overt underemployment constitutes a very substantial portion of the supply of labor (probably between one-fourth and one-third). The problem, however, is that visible underemployment is no more than the tip of a massive underemployment which exists in both agricultural and nonagricultural activities.[2] Underemployment remained the major form of underutilization of labor in Egypt. Along with labor reallocation between sectors, a transfer of underemployment induced by population growth from one sector of the economy to another seems to have taken place. With the rise in the relative share of nonagricultural sectors of the labor force, open unemployment is also increasing.

IMPLICATIONS

Theoretical Implications

A major task of this study was to present a descriptive analysis of trends in population and labor force in Egypt. Another objective was to ascertain the relationship between labor force trends and other socioeconomic changes. Therefore, a great deal of the discussion has been descriptive, comparative, and analytical in nature. Nevertheless, a number of theoretical issues have been discussed throughout the study, most of which was devoted to various demographic as well as economic models widely associated with the experiences of developing countries. In this respect, the experience of Egypt as it conforms or deviates from a number of these models is summarized in the following paragraph.

This study has shown us some evidence that future population growth is not likely to be checked under the socioeconomic development and a consequent moderate increase in income. The demographic behavior of fertility is closer to the Malthusian prediction at the present stage of Egypt's economic development than to the model of demographic transition (see below). However, we have also noted other factors which support the theory of demographic transition as far as the emergence of differential fertility and the ultimate decrease of birth rate are concerned. A different aspect of the Malthusian model considered in this study is the productivity per worker in the agricultural sector. In this respect we tend to agree that behind the fall in production per man prior to the early 1930's lay the pressure of increasing population, which led to a rapid rise in the number of workers per acre. The law of diminishing returns was probably responsible for the fall of production per working person. Developments in the late 1930's in irrigation and drainage, as well as the wide use of fertilizers, account for the gradual increase in productivity since then. Today some observers even argue that "we are far away moved from the Malthusian nightmares usually associated with the agricultural situation in underdeveloped countries."[3]

The data presented in this study as well as in others indicate that the demographic structure of urban and rural areas in Egypt do not conform to generalizations about urban-rural demographic differences that have been developed from the experience of industrialized countries. Abu-Lughod's observations concerning effects of differentials in fertility (notably the rate of natural increase, age composition, sex ratios, and marriage and divorce rates) are similar to our findings on these points. The data on size of the household and rate of women's participation in economic activities showed not only that the expected rural-urban differences failed to materialize but that in some cases reverse differentials have been observed. The attempt to explain most of the deviation of the Egyptian case as a function of the temporal sequence of the demographic transition from a preindustrial to a postindustrial equilibrium ignores structural as well as qualitative differences between developed and developing countries.[4] In spite of the emergence of differential fertility in urban areas, Egypt is not so close to terminating her period of explosive population growth.

A popular model in the literature of economic development which has been developed with Egypt in perspective is that of Lewis, "development with unlimited supply." The examination of the Lewis model was not the main goal of this study. We were concerned only with the labor reallocation process in its relation to economic growth. In this respect Lewis assumes disguised unemployment in the agriculture sector, which implies that the supply curve of unskilled labor to industry is perfectly elastic. The operation of the model can best be summarized in the following quotation: "As long as the individual real wage remains constant and provided that profits are reinvested, the share of profits in national income will increase. And since profits mean larger investment, capital formation will also grow relatively to national income. The development of the industrial sector will draw more and more labor from agriculture. Where the model operates it achieves simultaneously economic growth and labor absorption."[5] Two of the leading empirical tests of Lewis's model to Egyptian data presented completely different conclusions.[6] First, Hansen has rejected the a priori assumption about the existence of a large volume of disguised unemployment in Egyptian agriculture, since the assumption of a constant subsistence wage is not supported by fact. Second, Mabro concluded that the Egyptian situation conforms remarkably well to certain fundamental assumptions of the Lewis model, but as far as employment is concerned the result is negative. In his view, the most important challenge to the Lewis model is that it underestimates population growth. Mabro correctly observed how population pressure dominates the labor allocation process, adding to the pools of underemployment at a rate that may exceed for a long time the rate of absorption into industry.

In an earlier part of this book (Chapter 6), Colin Clark's sectoral distribution model as it applies to Egypt was discussed. Simply stated, Clark's scheme assumes that the movement of the working population from agriculture to manufacturing and from manufacturing to tertiary areas is the most important concomitant of economic growth. Our findings indicate only partial confirmation of this thesis. Our data indicate that labor reallocation takes place directly from agriculture to the services of Egypt. It also shows that the share of industry in labor remained relatively constant over the last four decades at a time noticeable economic growth took place. The deviation of the Egyptian case from this sectoral model is partially due to the following: First, in Egypt, as in most developing economies, capital is scarce and unskilled labor is abundant. This results in the mass use of unskilled labor instead of capital in the performance of the task of distribution of goods (tertiary activities). Second, Clark's argument rests mainly on the idea that industrialization and urbanization are concomitant developments in the course of modernization and that industrialization will precede urbanization in most cases. This assumption proved not to be the case in most developing countries in general and Egypt in particular; the two trends are not necessarily simultaneously developed. Third, Clark's reference rests also on the idea that industry develops in an evolutionary fashion from crafts to small-scale enterprises to the use of the highly technological equipment of modern countries. In most cases, large-scale industrialization in the newly developing countries is due to the adoption of the latest technological developments of the highly industrial countries, most of which are labor-saving devices designed to meet the requirement of the labor market in the advanced countries.

In line with these findings, we tend to view these models as not being comprehensive explanatory devices of the development experiences of Egypt, and probably not for most developing countries as well. Their incompleteness as explanatory devices renders them more inadequate as predictive models of the course of development as well as of the temporal process the development will take. Further, most of these economic-demographic models suffer from the following: each of them puts great emphasis on the role of certain trends in the economy at a time they minimize or ignore others; most of them assume a static relationship between factors of the society; even the most dynamic of these models does not account for the possibility of introducing exogenous factors to the equilibrium; and most models do not consider the possibility that the onset of different trends at different times of development may lead toward completely different configurations than the ones originally expected. Finally, the models developed from the experiences of advanced countries do not provide an accurate description of today's developing countries.

Methodological Implications

We have approached this study with a preconceived set of basic concepts derived from traditional labor force analysis of developed economies. However, we soon became aware of the real problem of whether making fuller use of human resources in developing countries can be precisely approached and analyzed in terms of categories developed from the experiences of more developed countries.[7] Therefore we believe that most of our statements, especially those on the extent of labor utilization, should be interpreted as suggestive of trends rather than being their precise measurement.

This study has shown us how it is most difficult to measure a number of conventional labor force categories, such as economically active women, child labor, and family workers. Statistics on women's contribution to economic activities seem to underestimate their real contribution to the economic life of Egypt. The same could also be said about child labor. The groups classified as family workers are recognized as a separate category only for statistical purposes. The responsibility in making and applying a definition of family workers is left to the enumerators to decide for themselves. The lack of blueprints to go by in collecting statistics on this category is perhaps a major cause of the relatively low ratio of family workers in Egypt in comparison to other developing countries. This is so because of the low level of females who share in this group, which is deflating the ratio of economically active females as well as the overall ratio of economically active population to total population.

This study also made us aware of a number of flaws in ascertaining labor force and employment trends. First, there is the inconsistency of the phenomenon which certain concepts are presumably measuring. For example, we have omitted the groups classified as salary and wage earners from our analysis, in spite of the fact that such omission robs the discussion of a good indicator of trends toward labor force **bureaucratization.** Yet such an omission stems from the fact that those classified as salary earners engage in economic activities some of the time, but for how much of the time and with what degree of efficiency is hard to tell. Second is the inconsistency in the use of certain concepts, a serious problem in the analysis of employment in "industrial establishments." Third is an abrupt cessation of data collection concerning certain trends in assuming that phenomena to be measured will cease to exist on a legal or administrative order. The lack of statistical data on trends in child labor following the 1960 census is an example. Legal prohibition of child labor under age twelve does not necessarily mean that it would cease to exist and that collection of statistical data therefore is worthless.

In addition to the difficulty of measuring certain labor force categories, there are a number of other problems related to the applicability of certain theoretical concepts to the situation of labor force and employment in newly developed countries. First we believed that Colin Clark's widely accepted classification of the structure of the economy comprising primary, secondary, and tertiary activities is less applicable to developing areas of today than it was for the more developed countries. If these categories are taken to mean roughly agriculture, industry, and services, such a conceptual approach needs some modification probably along the following lines: agriculture, agrarian, industrial, and urban sectors of the economy. The fact that about 20 to 30 percent of the agricultural labor force was classified as engaged in nonagricultural activities explains the need for an agrarian category to designate those engaged in nonagricultural activities of the rural labor force. This percentage of nonagricultural activities in rural Egypt will probably continue to increase in the coming decades. Therefore, we see these categories to be more helpful in allowing precise statements concerning the following: (1) the extent of labor reallocation among sectors; (2) the degree that labor reallocation between sectors corresponds to larger societal changes; (3) the extent of employment and underemployment in agricultural activities proper; (4) the extent that industrialization is helping directly in solving the unemployment problem; and (5) a better assessment of the effects of employment in the construction sector. Because of the growing role which the construction sector assumes in providing temporary employment for a large portion of unskilled manpower, there is a growing problem of assessing the long-range implication of different kinds of construction work on the prospect of employment. The proposed four-type classification of economic sectors might help in making a clearer distinction between employment in construction activities which will ultimately lead toward an increase in the productive capacity of the economy, and employment in construction which will ultimately enhance the social-overhead capital such as schools, hospitals, roads, and housing.

A major problem of labor force statistics in Egypt is that of measuring underemployment in both agriculture and nonagriculture sectors. Economic analysis of underemployment usually centers on the idea of the marginal productivity of labor approaching zero. This approach might help in understanding underemployment, but it does not lend itself readily to direct measurement. Therefore, underemployment is usually discussed through the use of a number of indirect methods as well as the use of alternative concepts and measurements. In this regard, statistics on underemployment in agriculture have been the subject of certain development. First, Egypt has experimented with labor force sample surveys from which data on some aspects of underemployment can be obtained for limited purposes. Also available statistics on man/land ratios depict to some extent trends concerning underemployment. Seasonal variations in the employment of agricultural labor can be also ascertained from available statistics. In addition, the marginal productivity of labor in Egyptian agriculture has been quantitatively measured. But, due to incompatible conclusions obtained from these measurements, Egyptian planners resorted to "labor record surveys" as a way of ascertaining underemployment as well as seasonal unemployment in agriculture. However, most of these indices are measures of visible underemployment, and there is ample evidence that in Egypt visible underemployment usually makes up only a fraction of the total labor time unit that would become available for extra work if there were ample employment opportunities and other things remained unchanged. The prevalence of hidden underemployment as a distinctive category from visible underemployment is largely attributed to the wide prevalence of "work spread," or working at a low intensity, mainly by these groups classified as self-employed or family workers. However, an attempt to adjust the work spread to be meaningfully susceptible to measurement would involve assumptions regarding "norms" of labor (time) units required for a given operation or output. In this regard, what Egypt needs is a measurement of underemployment similar to the one adopted by Yugoslavia, known as "the labor force reserve" approach. [8]

Since Egyptian agriculture is growing under visible organizational and technological changes, two types of labor force reserve estimates should be made. One is to measure the current reserve under existing conditions, and the second is to measure future reserve based on assumptions regarding improvements in organization and technology. Assessment of underemployment in nonagrarian activities of the economy should be given serious attention, now that underemployment seems to have spread out from agriculture to the services and probably to industry. In this respect, Egyptian planners might take cognizance of the ways underemployment in the nonagricultural industries was measured in a number of developing countries. The design of the Panama manpower sample survey might be applicable to Egypt with little modification. [9]

In conclusion, the many kinds of problems which arise from the use of the conventional conceptual approach lead one to question the efforts currently set forth by the United Nations and its affiliate, the International Labor Organization, toward standardizing concepts and procedures as well as the timing of data collections among nations. These efforts might be useful for allowing comparative analysis of available data, yet they should be used with careful knowledge of their limitations.

Policy Implications

Given the objectives of improving the level of living of the population, one finds two distinct and in part conflicting employment needs in developing countries. The first is to ensure an available labor force with the skill and characteristics needed to contribute to a rapid and substantial increase in national output. The other is to ensure, through full employment, an acceptable distribution of this increased output in the form of earned income. These needs are not necessarily incompatible but quite often they are conflicting needs, especially in developing countries which suffer from population pressure. The conflict stems from the fact that to ensure skilled labor may result in an efficient, well-organized, well-paid, but relatively small work force in the highly capitalized modern sector of economy, while in the traditional sector of the economy, low earnings and a large volume of unemployment and underemployment may continue. On the other hand, efforts to speed up the distribution of income through rapid employment could result in a break in industrialization and efficiency, thereby reducing the rate of output. In any case, it is now evident that the ideal of full employment is unattainable in the short run in developing countries with a rapidly growing population. Egypt is a typical case of such a situation.

Three alternatives are open to cope with this situation: enforce rapid employment; ensure redistribution of national output through a number of social and economic measures which might amount to utilizing the welfare state approach; and encourage alternative productive activities among persons unable to find employment in the modern sector of the labor force. In our assessment, the case of Egypt requires solution on all fronts. The problem, however, is how far the authorities can go on with each of these alternatives. More and rapid employment should be planned but not at any cost or regardless of any economic consequences. Employment should be enlarged by all means as far as its net effect on the economy is positive at all. This should especially be the course outside industry. Egyptian industry has followed a process of development which favors capital intensive techniques. It would be beyond the limits of reason to advocate a reversal of this policy and/or overstaffing of the present industrial complex over its absorptive limits in such a way to be detrimental to industrial output. The absorptive capacity of the industrial sector of the economy could be enhanced without adverse effects on growth if an imaginative exploration is given to small-scale, more decentralized, and more labor-intensive forms or organization. This should include the development of an intermediate technology adapted to the possibilities of ''unlimited supplies'' of labor, as well as less encouragement to monopolies together with an efficient system of taxation to force saving.

Egypt is slowly moving toward a ''welfare state'' with Socialistic leanings. A large number of social, medical, and labor legislations are designed to enhance income redistribution and to grant minimum income for certain segments of the population. As we have stated earlier, it is not feasible economically or administratively for a country like Egypt in such an early stage of development to adopt a rigorous model of the welfare state. In fact, experience in this direction might be detrimental to work motives and to productivity in general. Yet to grant some distribution and equality of income, in the absence of full employment, the government has to enforce some form of welfare measures. Publicity should be given also to the third approach. Alternative productive activities among persons unable to find employment in the modern sector of the labor force should be encouraged. This could be done by raising the age of leaving schools, increasing school attendance and postschool training, and by encouraging useful community services outside regular paid employment.

As long-term measures, sincere efforts should be given to reduce the rate of natural increase by sponsoring family planning programs. In addition, efforts could be made to encourage migration, though the danger of losing persons with essential but scarce manpower skills and experience is a real one.

THE FUTURE

The major focus of this study has been on the process of growth and the changing structure of the labor force in relationship to economic development and social change in Egypt. Actually the comprehensive conclusions we arrived at could be subjected to further detailed tests. Specialized studies exploring the causal relationships between certain population and labor force trends and other societal trends are badly needed to provide further insights on the problem. For example, the causal relationships between population pressure on land and the degree of agricultural mechanization remains a matter of conjecture rather than an empirically tested proposition. Explorations of appropriate forms of intermediate technology for Egypt's manpower supply and natural resources are very much desired. Also, an over-all appraisal of the country's present educational policy in light of its employment capacity of professional and technical manpower is badly needed. In brief, there is a great deal to be added to the present knowledge on the important problem of the role of "labor force and employment" in the modernization of Egypt.

While this study was being undertaken, hostilities erupted in the Middle East. The U. A. R. was at the center of this conflict. The out-come of the present circumstances is difficult to forecast, especially where elements of political, cultural, military, and foreign interest are involved. As things stand now (early 1971), no doubt the continua-tion of a state of war will have some implications on the present and potential manpower allocation and labor force mobilization. If the present conflict moves toward a total war, where Egypt stands a great chance of a big loss in manpower, the shape of events to come will be greatly affected. Probably the best lesson we have from the present circumstances is to accord the uniqueness of each individual developing country.

With the sudden death of President Nasser, Egypt became the focus of world attention. For many years, the world had seen Egypt as "Nasser's Egypt." The orderly transference of power which followed the president's death was remarkable indeed. However, the indivisibility that characterized the leader and his nation in a critical period of Egypt's modern history makes it difficult to visualize Egypt without him.

The new president, Anwar El-Sadat, and the prime minister, Dr. Mahmoud Fawzi, stated on several occasions that there would be no change, and that the policies of the late president would guide their actions. However, one cannot fail to see a change, at least in style if not in policy. [10] The new regime which has emerged under

President Sadat does not project "charismatic" quality as much as it presents pragmatic ability.

It is too early to assess the effect of new developments on the course of events in Egypt; however, some trends can be gleaned from the official statements of the new leaders. In an address to the National Assembly on December 18, 1970, Dr. Fawzi announced that steps will be taken to prepare a new four-year plan for economic and social development to terminate in the fiscal year 1974-75. This plan would be financed largely from private and public savings. [11] There is nothing definite as to the frame of the plan, but at least one thing is clear--Egypt is committed to the development of heavy industry. President Sadat outlined his government's goals as follows: (1) the completion of the iron and steel complexes in Helwan (350 million Egyptian pounds); (2) the establishment of petrochemical complexes (100 million Egyptian pounds), phosphoric complexes (45 million Egyptian pounds), and aluminum complexes (40 million Egyptian pounds); and (3) the construction of an oil pipeline from the Red Sea to Alexandria. [12] The ambitious planning for industries, which has been under way for 15 years, has a chance of succeeding now that the power grid is ready. [13] It is counted on to help ease the population problem by moving the growth rate of the country's economy up above the present 2.8 percent population growth rate.

It is interesting to note that the first action of the cabinet was intended to seek solutions to the problems of seasonal and migratory laborers. A state committee was formed from several cabinet members, representatives of the National Assembly and the Arab Socialist Union, to study the problem. [14] Also among the immediate concerns of the new government is the problem of craftsmen and craft industry. The intent is to ease the plight of craft workers, who are troubled by the crushing forces of large scale industry.

Dr. Fawzi emphasized the need to reexamine Egypt's educational system. He called for a reform in education which would put emphasis on science and technology. The prime minister's first public statement on taking office in November echoed this need: "We are menaced by ignorance in a world where there is no dignity or power without scientific development--and no false pretenses of pride should close our eyes to this fact." [15]

Internal affairs are not the only factors affecting Egypt's destiny. Egypt's relationship with the rest of the Arab world and with the world at large is of great significance. On November 8, 1970, the leaders of the United Arab Republic, Libya, and the Sudan announced in Cairo their agreement to work toward an eventual federation of their countries. The three countries have been linked in an economic, military, political

and cultural alliance since December, 1969, under an agreement
reached at a meeting in Tripoli, Libya. The death of President
Nasser loomed largely behind the decision to move toward a federation.
During his life, the late president stressed the need for proceeding
carefully toward any new federation because of the experience of the
1958 union of Egypt and Syria, which was dissolved three years later.
In October, 1970, the new regime in Syria announced its intent to join
the confederation. It is too early to guess the prospects for success
or failure of the new proposed link, or the shape of the new state
which has to emerge. If it does materialize, the new state would be
more self-sufficient, with each of the component states complementing
the other economically. Egypt has the surplus population and trained
professional and skilled manpower that Libya and the Sudan lack;
Libya has the oil revenue which provides capital for industrial development; and both Sudan and Syria could provide their partners with food
stuffs from their surplus agricultural land.

However, whether a successful federation could be a grass-roots
solution for Egypt's critical labor supply and employment situation is
questionable. Such a federation could provide only a temporary outlet
for the employment problem of professional and trained manpower.
The very slow and cautious steps the leaders of the four states have
taken so far makes it harder to envisage a movement of 3 or 4 million
Egyptians to settle and work in any of the three other states. Large-
scale migration of this kind is a long-range prospect.

Overshadowing all these efforts and all future hopes is the long-
standing Arab-Israeli conflict. In economic terms alone the war is
diverting millions of pounds and much manpower from the task of
building the economy.

Finally, looking on the problem in retrospect, "ancient Egypt's
crucial innovation in the course of human evolution pertained to manpower organization, the mobilization of her services for large collective
enterprises."[16] Egypt's success in these endeavors will ultimately
decide the future.

NOTES

1. K. C. Abercrombie, "Population Growth and Agricultural
Development," Monthly Bulletin of Agricultural Economics and
Statistics, XVIII, 4 (April, 1969), 3, Table 2.

2. Visible underemployment involves persons involuntarily
working part-time or for shorter than normal periods of work. Invisible employment exists when a person's working time is not abnormally

reduced but when his employment is inadequate in such other respects as: (1) when his job does not permit full use of his highest skill or capacity; (2) when his earnings from employment are abnormally low; and (3) when he is employed in an establishment or economic unit whose productivity is abnormally low. See, for example, Donald J. Bogue, Principles of Demography (New York: John Wiley and Sons, 1969), pp. 222-23.

3. B. Hansen and G. Marzouk, Development and Economic Policy in the U.A.R. (Amsterdam: North Holland Publishing Co., 1965), p. 77.

4. Janet Abu-Lughod, "Urbanization in Egypt: Present State and Future Prospects," Economic Development and Cultural Change, XIII, 3 (April, 1965), 313-43.

5. W.A. Lewis, "Economic Development With Unlimited Supply of Labor," The Manchester School (May, 1954). Reprinted in A. Agarwala and S. Singh, The Economics of Underdevelopment (New York: Oxford University Press, 1963), pp. 400-49.

6. Hansen and Marzouk, op. cit., p. 64; and Robert Mabro, "Industrial Growth, Agricultural Underemployment and the Lewis Model: The Egyptian Case, 1937-1965," The Journal of Development Studies, III, 4 (1967), 322-51.

7. An exception to the conventional approach is Gunnar Myrdal, Asian Drama: An Inquiry Into the Poverty of Nations, A Twentieth Century Study (3 Vols; New York: Pantheon, 1968). His analysis of factors affecting the degree of utilization of the labor potential of South Asian countries is conducted in terms of these ratios: the population of working members (i.e., people who do some work) in the population of working age; the average number of hours of work per working member; and average output per hour. It is too early to try to estimate the impact of this study on the methodology of others working in this field.

8. C. Kailas, "Recent Progress in Underemployment Statistics and Analysis," Proceedings of the World Population Conference, 1965, IV (New York: United Nations, 1967), pp. 351-52.

9. A. J. Jaffee and L. E. Quesada, "Assessment of Under-employment in Non-Agricultural Industries of the Less Developed Countries," Proceedings of the World Population Conference, 1965, IV (New York: United Nations, 1967), pp. 359-63.

10. Nasser's long-time confidant and the influential editor of

Al-Ahram called for a change in the style of the government after Nasser's death. See especially his article "Nasser Was Not a Story, " Al-Ahram (Cairo), November 6, 1970.

11. Al-Ahram, December 18, 1970.

12. Al-Ahram, (Cairo), November 6, 1970.

13. A goal of the present government is to introduce electricity to all rural areas in Egypt in the next ten years. See Al-Ahram, December 18, 1970.

14. Ibid.

15. Al-Ahram, November 9, 1970.

16. Talcott Parsons, Societies: Evolutionary and Comparative Perspectives (Englewood Cliffs, N.J.: Prentice-Hall, 1966), p. 56.

SELECTED BIBLIOGRAPHY

BOOKS

Baer, Gabriel. Population and Society in the Arab East. New York: Frederick A. Praeger, Publishers, 1964.

Berger, Morroe. Bureaucracy and Society in Modern Egypt. Princeton, N.J.: Princeton University Press, 1957.

Cho, Yong Sam. Disguised Unemployment in Underdeveloped Areas With Special Reference to South Korean Agriculture. Berkeley, Calif.: University of California Press, 1963.

Clark, Colin. The Conditions of Economic Progress. London: Macmillan Co., 1940.

_____. Population Growth and Land Use. London: Macmillan Co., 1967.

Cleland, Wendell. The Population Problem in Egypt. Lancaster, Pa.: Pennsylvania Printing Corp., 1936.

Coale, Ansley J., and Hoover, Edgar M. Population Growth and Economic Development in Low Income Countries: A Case Study of India's Prospects. Princeton, N.J.: Princeton University Press, 1958.

El-Gritly, Ali. Population and Economic Resources in the U.A.R. Cairo: Dar El-Maaref, 1960.

_____. Population and Economic Pressures in Egypt. Cairo: Misr Press, 1962.

El-Kamash, Magdi. Economic Development and Planning in Egypt. New York: Frederick A. Praeger, Publishers, 1968.

Gadella, Saad. Land Reform in Relation to Social Development in Egypt. Columbia: University of Missouri Press, 1962.

Garzouzi, Eva. Old Ills and New Remedies in Egypt. Cairo: Dar El-Maaref, 1958.

Grunwald, Kurt, and Ranall, Joachim. Industrialization in the Middle East. New York: Council for Middle Eastern Affairs Press, 1960.

Hansen, Bent, and Marzouk, Girgis. Development and Economic

273

Policy in the U.A.R. (Egypt). Amsterdam: North Holland Publishing Co., 1965.

Harbison, Frederick, and Ibrahim, Abdel Kader Ibrahim. Human Resources for Egyptian Enterprise. New York: McGraw-Hill, Inc., 1958.

Harbison, Frederick, and Myers, Charles A. Education, Manpower, and Economic Growth. New York: McGraw-Hill Book Co., 1964.

Hoselitz, Bert F., and Moore, Wilbert E., eds. Industrialization and Society. Mouton: UNESCO, 1963.

Issawi, Charles. Egypt at Mid-Century. New York: Oxford University Press, 1954.

_____. Egypt in Revolution: An Economic Analysis. New York: Oxford University Press, 1963.

Kotb, Yusef Salah El-Din. Science and Science Education in Egyptian Society. New York: Bureau of Publications, Teachers College, Columbia University, 1951.

Lacouture, Jean, and Lacouture, Simonne. Egypt in Transition. London: Macmillan Co., 1958.

Lewis, W. Arthur. Economic Development with Unlimited Supplies of Labor: Readings in Economic Development. Belmont, Calif., 1963.

_____. The Theory of Economic Growth. Homewood, Ill.: Richard D. Irwin, Inc., 1955.

Mansfield, Peter. Nasser's Egypt. Baltimore: Penguin Books, 1965.

Marei, Said. Agrarian Reform in Egypt. Cairo: S.O.P. Press, 1957.

Mead, Donald C. Growth and Structural Change in the Egyptian Economy. Homewood, Ill.: Richard D. Irwin, Inc., 1967.

Moore, Wilbert E., and Feldman, Arnold L., eds. Labor Commitment and Social Change in Developing Areas. New York: Social Science Research Council, 1960.

Mountjoy, Alan B. Industrialization and Underdeveloped Countries. Chicago: Aldine Publishing Company, 1963.

Myrdal, Gunnar. Asian Drama: An Inquiry Into the Poverty of
    Nations, A Twentieth Century Study. 3 vols. New York: Pantheon,
    1968.

Namiq, Salahidel-din. Treatises on Population. Cairo: An-Nahdahal-
    Misriyyah Press, 1959.

O'Brien, Patrick. The Revolution in Egypt's Economic System.
    New York: Oxford University Press, 1966.

Parsons, Talcott. Societies: Evolutionary and Comparative Perspec-
    tives. Englewood Cliffs, N.J.: Printice-Hall, Inc., 1966.

Quabain, Fahim I. Education and Science in the Arab World. Balti-
    more: The Johns Hopkins Press, 1966.

Raj, K. N. Employment Aspects of Planning in Underdeveloped
    Economies. ("National Bank of Egypt Fiftieth Anniversary
    Commemoration Lectures.") Cairo: N.B.E. Printing Press,
    1957.

Ross, Arthur M., ed. Industrial Relations and Economic Development.
    International Institute for Labor Studies, London: Macmillan Co.,
    1966.

Saab, Gabriel S. The Egyptian Agrarian Reform, 1952-1962. London:
    Oxford University Press, 1967.

Warriner, Doreen. Agrarian Reform and Community Development
    in the U.A.R. Cairo: Dar El-Taawan Publishing and Printing
    House, 1961.

_____. Land and Poverty in the Middle East. New York: Royal
    Institute of International Affairs, 1948.

_____. Land Reform and Development in the Middle East. London:
    Oxford University Press, 1962.

Wheelock, Keith. Nasser's New Egypt: A Critical Analysis. New
    York: Frederick A. Praeger, Publishers, 1960.

ESSAYS IN COLLECTIONS

Cleland, Wendell. "A Population Plan for Egypt." Demographic
    Studies of Selected Areas of Rapid Growth. Edited by Clyde V.
    Kiser. New York: The Milbank Memorial Fund, 1944.

El-Badry, M. A., and Rizk, Hanna. "Regional Family Differences among Arab Countries of the Middle East: A Survey of Present Information." Proceedings of the World Population Conference, 1965. Vol II. New York: United Nations Publication, 1967.

Ezzat, M. A. W. "The Land Tenure System in Egypt." Land Tenure. Edited by Kenneth H. Parsons, et al. Madison: University of Wisconsin Press, 1956.

Harbison, Frederick. "Egypt." Land and Economic Development. Edited by William Galensen. New York: John Wiley and Sons, 1959.

Husein, Hassan M. "Evaluation of Progress in Fertility in the U. A. R." Proceedings of the World Population Conference, 1965. Vol IV. New York: United Nations Publication, 1967.

Ibrahim, Abdel Kader Ibrahim. "Socio-Economic Changes in Egypt (1952-64)." Industrial Relations and Economic Development. Edited by Arthur M. Ross. London: Macmillan Co., 1966.

Jaffee, A. J., and Quesada, L. E. "Assessment of Underemployment in Non-Agricultural Industries of the Less Developed Countries." Proceedings of the World Population Conference, 1965. Vol. IV. New York: United Nations Publication, 1967.

Kerr, Malcolm H. "Patterns and Problems of Educational Underdevelopment, Egypt." Education and Political Development. Edited by James S. Coleman. Princeton, N.J.: Princeton University Press, 1965.

Marcura, Milos. "Relation Between Demographic Projections and Formulation of a Development Program." Proceedings of the World Population Conference, 1965. Vol. IV. New York: United Nations Publication, 1967.

Martin, Cyril J. "Demographic Aspects of Capital Formation in Economies With Large Subsistence Sectors (Africa)." Proceedings of the World Population Conference, 1965. Vol. IV. New York: United Nations Publication, 1967.

_____. "The Relationship of the Labor Force in East Africa to Economic Development." Proceedings of International Population Conference. New York: United Nations Publications, 1961.

Penniment, K. J. "The Influence of Cultural and Socio-Economic Factors on Labor Force Participation Rates." Proceedings of the World Population Conference, 1965. Vol. IV. New York: United Nations Publication, 1967.

Rizk, Hanna. "Population Growth and Its Effects on Economic and Social Goals in the U.A.R." Population Crisis and Use of World Resources. Edited by Stuart Mudd. Bloomington: Indiana University Press, 1967.

Sarhan, A. E. "Mortality Trends in the United Arab Republic." Proceedings of the World Population Conference, 1967. Vol. II. New York: United Nations Publication, 1967.

Sinha, J. N. "Dynamics of Female Participation in Economic Activity in a Developing Economy." Proceedings of the World Population Conference, 1965. Vol. IV. New York: United Nations Publication, 1967.

Spengler, Joseph J. "Population as a Factor in Economic Development." Population and World Politics. Edited by Phillip M. Hauser. Glencoe, Ill.: Free Press, 1958.

Stanev, Stefan. "Socio-Economic Characteristics of the Economically Active Population." Proceedings of the World Population Conference, 1965. Vol. IV. New York: United Nations Publication, 1967.

Stewart, C. M. "Degree of Urbanization and Patterns of Labor Force Participation." Proceedings of the World Population Conference, 1965. Vol. IV. New York: United Nations Publication, 1967.

Stougger, Thomas B. "The Industrial Worker." Social Forces in the Middle East. Edited by S. Fisher. New York: Cornell University Press, 1955.

United Nations. "Demographic Aspects of Labor Supply and Employment." Proceedings of the World Population Confernece, 1965. Vol. IV. New York: United Nations Publication, 1967.

Zikry, Abdel-Khalik M. "Fertility Differential of the U.A.R. Women." Proceedings of the World Population Conference, 1965. Vol. II. New York: United Nations Publication, 1967.

ARTICLES AND PERIODICALS

Abdel-Aty, S. H. "Life-Table Functions for Egypt Based on Model Life Tables and Quasi-Stable Population Theory," The Milbank

Memorial Fund Quarterly, XXXIX, 2 (April, 1961), 350-77.

Abdu-Rahmen, Ali Badri. "Internal Migration in the U.A.R.,"
L'Egypte Contemporaine, No. 319 (January, 1965), 31-44.

Abercrombie, K. C. "Population Growth and Agricultural Development," Monthly Bulletin of Agricultural Economics and Statistics,
XVIII, 4 (April, 1969), 1-9.

Abu-Lughod, Janet. "The Emergence of Differential Fertility in
Urban Egypt," The Milbank Memorial Fund Quarterly, XLIII,
2 (April, 1965), 235-53.

_____. "Migrant Adjustments to City Life: The Egyptian Case,"
American Journal of Sociology, LXVII (July, 1961), 22-32.

_____. "Urbanization in Egypt: Present State and Future Pros-
pects," Economic Development and Cultural Change, XIII, 3
(April, 1965), 313-43.

_____. "Urban-Rural Differences as a Function of the Demographic
Transition," American Journal of Sociology, LXIX (March, 1964),
476-90.

Al-Arabi, M. "A Modern Apprenticeship School in the U.A.R.,"
International Labour Review, LXXXIV (December, 1961), 478-98.

_____. "Experience of Apprentice Training in the United Arab
Republic," International Labour Review, XCII, 6 (December,
1965), 490-505.

Audsley, M. T. "Labor and Social Affairs in Egypt Middle East
Affairs," St. Antony's Papers, No. 4 (1958), 102-109.

Bashier, Abdel Mawla. "Price Policy for Agricultural Products,"
L'Egypte Contemporaine, No. 334 (October, 1968), 911-14.

Bauer, P. R., and Yamey, B. S. "Economic Progress and Occupational Distribution," Economic Journal, LXI (December, 1951),
741-45.

_____. "Economic Progress, Occupational Distribution and
Institutional Wage Rigidities; A Comment," Review of Economics
and Statistics, XXXII (November, 1954), 461-62.

Coale, Ansley J. "Population and Economic Development," Economic
Development and Cultural Change, V, 1 (October, 1956), 50-68.

Cook, Robert C. "Egypt's Population Explodes," Population Bulletin,
    XII (July, 1956), 57-69.

Dodd, Peter C. "Youth and Women's Emancipation in the U. A. R. , "
    The Middle East Journal, XXII (Spring, 1968), 159-61.

El-Atar, A. Fawazi, and El-Molahi, Elidisoki A. "Analytical Study
    of the Problems of Labor Resources in a Combined Center Area, "
    L'Egypte Contemporaine, CCCXXXIII (July, 1968), 619-21.

El-Badry, M. A. "Some Aspects of Fertility in Egypt," The Milbank
    Memorial Fund Quarterly, XXXIV (January, 1956), 22-43.

_____. "Some Demographic Measurement for Egypt Based on the
    Stability of Census Age Distribution," The Milbank Memorial
    Fund Quarterly, XXXIII, 3 (July, 1955), 268-305.

_____. "Trends in the Components of Population Growth in the
    Arab Countries of the Middle East: A Survey of Present Informa-
    tion," Demography, II (1965), 140-85.

El-Daly, Abdel Hamid. "The Birth Rate and Fertility Trends in
    Egypt," L'Egypte Contemporaine, XLIV (October, 1953), 1-12.

El-Gritly, Ali A. "The Structure of Modern Industry in Egypt, "
    L'Egypte Contemporaine, Nos. 241-42 (November-December,
    1947), 534-54.

El-Shafei, A. M. N. "The Current Labor Force Sample Survey in
    Egypt," International Labour Review, LXXXII, 5 (November,
    1960), 209-69.

El-Shanawany, M. R. "The First National Life Table of Egypt, "
    L'Egypte Contemporaine, No. 62 (March, 1956), 209-69.

El-Tonbary, A. A. "Measures of Efficiency in the Organization
    and Use of Farm Labor," L'Egypte Contemporaine, XLVII
    (April, 1957), 64-76.

Franklin, N. N. "Employment and Unemployment, 1919-1969, "
    International Labour Review, XCIX, 3 (March, 1969), 293-314.

Handley, W. J. "The Labor Movement in Egypt," Middle East
    Journal, III, 3 (July, 1949), 277-92.

Harbison, Frederick, and Ibrahim, Abdel Kader Ibrahim. "Some
    Labor Problems of Industrialization in Egypt," Annals of

American Academy of Political Review, CCCV (May, 1956), 114-24.

Hsieh, C. "Approaches to Fixing Employment Targets in Developing Plans," International Labour Review, XCVII, 3 (March, 1968), 33-72.

_____. "Planned Rates of Employment Increase in Development Plans," International Labour Review, XCVII, 1 (January, 1968), 33-72.

International Labour Office, "Dismissal Procedures--U.A.R.," International Labour Review, LXX (November, 1959), 452-57.

_____. "Recent Development in Social Insurance in U.A.R.," International Labour Review, LXXV (May, 1962), 522-27.

Issawi, Charles. "Egypt Since 1800: A Study in Lopsided Development," Journal of Economic History, XXI, 1 (March, 1961), 1-26.

_____. "Population and Wealth in Egypt," The Milbank Memorial Fund Quarterly, XXVII (January, 1949), 98-113.

Jaffee, A. J., and Azumi, K. "The Birth Rate and Cottage Industries in Underdeveloped Countries," Economic Development and Cultural Change, IX, 1-2 (1960), 52-63.

Kabl, Subhi. "Industrial Human Capital In the U.A.R.," As-Sinai, III (September, 1964), 9-17.

Kiser, Clyde V. "The Demographic Position of Egypt," The Milbank Memorial Fund Quarterly, XXII, 4 (October, 1944), 383-408.

Lyyla, Majid. "Upgrading Training of Skilled Workers in the U.A.R.," International Labour Review, XC (July, 1965), 35-44.

Mabro, Robert. "Industrial Growth, Agricultural Underemployment and the Lewis Model: The Egyptian Case, 1937-1965," The Journal of Development Studies, III-IV (1967), 322-51.

Marzouk, Girgis Abdu. "Fertility of the Urban and Rural Population in Egypt," L'Egypte Contemporaine, XLVIII (January, 1957), 27-34.

McClelland, David C. "Does Education Accelerate Economic Growth?" Economic Development and Cultural Change, XIV, 3 (April, 1966), 257-78.

Mehta, Surinder K. "Some Demographic and Economic Correlates of Primate Cities: A Case for Reevaluation," Demography, I, 1 (1964), 136-47.

Moore, Wilbert E. "The Exportability of the Labor Force Concept," American Sociology Review, XVIII, 1 (February, 1953), 68-72.

Murad, Muhammed Hilmy. "Modern Trends in the U.A.R. Labor Legislation," L'Egypte Contemporaine, LII (October, 1962), 5-18.

Mutawalli, Sami. "Nutrition Standard in the U.A.R.," Majallat Ghurfat Tijarat H. Al-Qahirah, Nos. 7-8 (1965), 10-14.

Nakaoka, S. "A Note on the Evaluation Work of the Agrarian Reform in the U.A.R. (Egypt)," The Developing Economics, I, 1 (January-June, 1963).

Nassif, E. L. "L'Egypte Est Elle Surpuplée," Population, 5:3 (July-September, 1959), 513-32

National Bank of Egypt. "The Census of Establishment," Economic Bulletin, XXI, 3 (1968), 239-47.

_____. "Economic Planning in the Southern Region," The Egyptian Economic and Political Review, VII, 7 (July, 1961), 9-15.

_____. "The Next Ten Years," Economic Bulletin, XI (1962), 5-10.

_____. "Observations on the Urbanization and Distribution of Agricultural Population in Egypt," Economic Bulletin, VIII (1955), 171-81.

_____. "Population and Manpower," Economic Bulletin, XVI, 1-2 (1963), 5-16.

_____. "Statistics of Labor Force in the Southern Region," Economic Bulletin, XIII (1960), 86-93.

O'Brien, Patrick. "Inudstrial Development and the Employment Problem in Egypt, 1945-1965," Middle East Economic Papers (1962), 90-120.

Parsons, Kenneth H. "Land Reforms in the U.A.R.," Land Economics, XXV, 4 (November, 1959), 319-26.

Rizk, Hanna. "Fertility Patterns in Selected Areas of Egypt; Social and Psychological Factors Affecting Fertility in the U.A.R.," Marriage and Family Living, XXV (February, 1963), 69-73.

Said, Gamal Eldin. "Productivity of Labor in Egyptian Industry," L'Egypte Contemporaine, 259-260 (May-June, 1959), 504f.

Sayigh, Yusif P. "Management-Labor Relations in Selected Arab Countries: Major Aspects and Determinants," International Labour Review, LXXVII (June, 1958), 519-37.

Seal, Patrick and Beeson, Irene. "Babies Along the Nile," The New Republic, CLIV, 9 (May 7, 1966), 10-11.

Sekelani, M. "Population Active et Economique de L'Egypte," Population, 3 (July-September, 1962), 465-90.

Weir, J. M., et al. "An Evaluation of Health and Sanitation in Egyptian Villages," Journal of the Egyptian Public Health Association, XXVII, 3 (1952), 90-91.

Zikry, Abdel-Khalik M. "Urbanization and Its Effect on the Level of Fertility of U.A.R. Women," L'Egypte Contemporaine, No. 318 (October, 1964), 27-42.

EGYPTIAN PUBLICATIONS, OFFICIAL AND SERIAL

Note: Official government publications are generally printed either by the Government Printing Office (more recently, General Organization for Government Printing Offices), by the Societé Orientale de Publicité (S.O.P.) Press, or by Dar Memphis Press. Almost invariably, however, they are not available from the publisher, but may be procured either from the Central Documents Office (Opera Square, Cairo) or from the ministry or office responsible for producing them.

El-Dine, H. Kheir. The Cotton Production-Function in the U.A.R. and Its Relation to Technical Progress and to Disguised Unemployment. U.A.R., Institute of National Planning Memo. No. 370. Cairo, 1936.

El-Imam, M. M. A Production Function for Egyptian Agriculture 1913-1955. U.A.R., Institute of National Planning Memo. No. 259. Cairo, October, 1962.

El-Tomy, M., and Hansen, Bent. The Seasonal Employment Profile in Egyptian Agriculture. U.A.R., Institute of National Planning Memo. No. 501. Cairo, October, 1964.

Hamza, Mukhtar, et al. Final Report on Employment Problems in Rural Areas, U.A.R. U.A.R., Institute of National Planning. Cairo, April, 1968.

National Planning Committee. Report of the Committee on the Mechanization of Agriculture. Memo. No. 253. Cairo, 1959.

Republic of Egypt. Permanent Council of the Public Services. The Population Problem of Egypt. Cairo, 1955.

Trade Union Federation. Legal Department. Labor Legislation Past and Present in U.A.R. Cairo, 1963.

U.A.R. Central Agency for Public Mobilization and Statistics. Population Increase in the U.A.R. and Its Deterrents to Development. Cairo, 1966.

U.A.R. Central Statistical Committee. The Labor Force Sample Survey in the Egyptian Region of the U.A.R. Cairo, 1959.

_____. Population Trends in the U.A.R. Cairo, 1962.

U.A.R. Department of Statistics and Census. Population Census, 1960. Cairo, 1963.

U.A.R. Ministry of Labor. Public Relations Department. Egyptian Labor: New Horizons. Cairo, 1963.

U.A.R. Presidency of the Republic. National Planning Committee. General Frame of the Five-Year Plan for Economic and Social Development, July, 1960-June, 1965. Cairo, 1960.

OTHER OFFICIAL PUBLICATIONS

Correa, Hector. Technology, Employment and Economic Growth. Geneva: International Institute for Labour Studies, Conference on Problems of Employment in Economic Development, 1963.

International Labour Office. Employment Objectives and Policies. Report No. 1. Geneva, 1963.

_____. Report to the Government of the U.A.R. on the Study of Rural Employment Problems. I.L.O./O.T.A./U.A.R./R8. Geneva, 1966.

International Labour Organization. Employment and Economic Growth.

Studies and Reports. New Series No. 67. Geneva, 1964.

_____. Employment Objectives in Economic Development. Studies and Reports. New Series No. 62. Geneva, 1962.

_____. International Standards of Labour Statistics, Geneva, 1959. Report of the Meeting of Experts on the Measure of Underemployment. Document M. EMU/B4. Geneva, 1963.

_____. Measurement of Underemployment. Report of the Meeting of Experts on the Measure of Underemployment. Document No. 21. Geneva, 1963.

_____. Selected Recent National Surveys on Labour Force, Unemployment and Underemployment. Document M. E. M. U. /D. 2. Geneva, 1963.

_____. Why Labour Leaves the Land: A Comparative Study of the Movement of Labour Out of Agriculture. Studies and Reports. New Series No. 59. Geneva, 1960.

Nugent, Daniel F. Jr., Land, S. Lewis, and Colar, Carl S. Development of Manpower Resources for Egyptian Industrialization. U. S. Agency for International Development Memo. Cairo, December, 1962.

United Nations. Demographic Aspects of Manpower. Sales No. 61, XIII. 4. New York: United Nations Publication, 1962.

_____. The Determinants and Consequences of Population Trends. ST/SOA/Series A. 17. New York: United Nations Publication, 1953.

_____. The Development of Manufacturing Industry in Egypt, Israel and Turkey. New York: United Nations Publication, 1958.

_____. Inquiry Among Governments on Problems Resulting From Interaction of Economic Development and Population Changes. United Nations Document E/3895. New York: United Nations Publication, 1964.

_____. Proceedings of the World Population Conference, 1965. 4 Vols. New York: United Nations Publication, 1967.

United Nations. Economic Commission in Africa. Industrial Growth in Africa: A Survey and Outlook. United Nations Document E/CN. 14/INR/1. New York: United Nations Publication, October 15, 1962.

United Nations. Food and Agriculture Organization, and International Labor Office. Progress in Land Reform, Third Report. New York: United Nations Publication, 1962.

U.S. Department of Labor. Bureau of Labor Statistics. Labor, Law and Practice in the U.A.R. Washington, D.C.: Government Printing Office, 1965.

U.S. Department of Labor. Survey of the Labor Situation in Egypt. Washington, D.C.: Government Printing Office, 1955.

UNPUBLISHED MATERIAL

Amin, G. "The Food Problem and Economic Development in Egypt." Unpublished Ph.D. dissertation, London University, 1964.

El-Shafie, Mohamme Ahmed. "Population Pressure on Land and the Problem of Capital Accumulation in Egypt." Unpublished Ph.D. dissertation, University of Wisconsin, 1951.

Farrag, Abdelmegid Mostafa. "Demographic Developments in Egypt During the Present Century." Unpublished Ph.D. dissertation, London School of Economics and Political Science, 1957.

Kenadjian, Berdj. "Disguised Unemployment in Underdeveloped Countries." Unpublished Ph.D. dissertation, Harvard University, 1957.

Mohiedien, A. "Agriculture Investment and Employment in Egypt Since 1935." Unpublished Ph.D. dissertation, London University, 1966.

Rizk, Hanna. "Fertility Patterns in Selected Areas in Egypt." Unpublished Ph.D. dissertation, Princeton University, 1959.

Ruprecht, Theodore. "The Demographic Factor in Egyptian Economic Progress." Unpublished Ph.D. dissertation, University of California, 1961.

Mostafa H. Nagi is a demographer and sociologist, now serving as Assistant Professor of Sociology at Bowling Green State University, Bowling Green, Ohio. He has had a first-hand knowledge of the different aspects of the population problems of Egypt while he was serving with the U.A.R. Government. For a number of years he occupied several positions on the National Council of Public Services and in the Ministry of Agriculture in Egypt and Syria.

His professional experience in the United States centers largely on research and teaching in demography and sociology. He also participated in and served in an advisory capacity on a number of national and statewide conferences and committees on population, environment, and social gerontology. He is the author and coauthor of a number of research papers and reports on different aspects of population trends.

Dr. Nagi is a graduate of Cairo University and received his Ph.D. from the University of Connecticut.